The Roman Province of Gallia Narbonensis

After graduating in European history from the University of East Anglia, Philip Kay-Bujak spent ten years in the Royal Anglian Regiment as a TA officer and twenty-three years teaching history and classics in the independent sector. He was a housemaster at Langley School, in Norfolk and Headmaster of Stover School, in Devon. An Associate of the Royal Historical Society, he is now retired and is a full-time writer. His previous works include *Undefeated* (2008), *The Bravest Man in The British Army* (2018), *The Life of Cicero* (2023) and *Gallia Narbonensis*, which details the Roman invasion and occupation of what is now southern France. He lives in East Sussex.

Other books by Philip Kay-Bujak

Norfolk & Suffolk in the Great War

Attleborough: the evolution of a town

Undefeated

Around the World in 100 Years

The Bravest Man in the British Army: The Extraordinary Life and Death of John Sherwood Kelly VC

My Heart is in the Highlands: The Life and Work of Archibald Kay

The Life of Cicero: Lessons for Today from the Greatest Orator of the Roman Republic

Empire Javelin, D-Day Assault Ship: The British vessel that landed the US 116th Infantry on Omaha Beach

The Roman Province of Gallia Narbonensis

The Occupation and Governance of Southern France, 118 BCE to 235 CE

Philip Kay-Bujak

PEN & SWORD
HISTORY

First published in Great Britain in 2024 by
Pen & Sword History
An imprint of Pen & Sword Books Limited
Yorkshire – Philadelphia

ISBN 978 1 39903 230 8

A CIP catalogue record for this book is
available from the British Library

Typeset by Mac Style
Printed in the UK by CPI Group (UK) Ltd, Croydon, CR0 4YY.

MIX
Paper | Supporting
responsible forestry
FSC® C013604

Pen & Sword Books Limited incorporates the imprints of After
the Battle, Atlas, Archaeology, Aviation, Discovery, Family History,
Fiction, History, Maritime, Military, Military Classics, Politics,
Select, Transport, True Crime, Air World, Frontline Publishing, Leo
Cooper, Remember When, Seaforth Publishing, The Praetorian Press,
Wharncliffe Local History, Wharncliffe Transport, Wharncliffe True
Crime and White Owl.

For a complete list of Pen & Sword titles please contact

PEN & SWORD BOOKS LIMITED
47 Church Street, Barnsley, South Yorkshire, S70 2AS, England
E-mail: enquiries@pen-and-sword.co.uk
Website: www.pen-and-sword.co.uk
or
PEN AND SWORD BOOKS
1950 Lawrence Rd, Havertown, PA 19083, USA
E-mail: uspen-and-sword@casematepublishers.com
Website: www.penandswordbooks.com

Contents

Acknowledgements

The eternal city of Rome poses eternal questions and none so important than what drove it onwards to create the largest, and probably the most successful, empire that human history has ever experienced. Part of the answer lies in the provinces of Rome – those places sucked into the orbit of a city whose dominion grew to overwhelm most of the known world at that time. By a process of reverse engineering, we can see a little more clearly as to what it was that Rome wanted and what their order of priorities was as they maintained an empire not just for a few years but for four centuries.

The province of *Gallia Narbonensis* is unusual in that, in very many ways, it was, and still is, simply an extension of Italy itself. Many Romans lived in the Greek, Gallic and Celtish settlements of Narbonensis for hundreds of years prior to the annexation of Narbonne in 118 BCE. Such was the Roman presence that we could argue with some justification that there was no need to conquer Narbonensis at all – it was already just an extension, a holiday resort for some, of the homeland itself. Southern France has always shared a similar identity with Italy. In language, customs, attitude to life, geography, cuisine and wine and history, it is only a few tunnels through the rocks and passes that separate them politically. For the Romans, the acquisition of southern France was, for the most part, a soft colonisation, a steadily increasing application of pressure, a creeping awareness that this was not a place to be conquered but rather one to be admired.

This book relies heavily on the scholarly work of many researchers whose articles appear all over the world and take on aspects of colonisation that we generally do not consider, so to all of those whose work is referenced in this book, I am hugely grateful. There is so much more that could have been accessed but I hope that I have brought together a wide field of research that demonstrates how the Romans went about exploiting this particular province.

It is to the writers of antiquity that I also tip my hat in appreciation and admiration. It was their foresight to record and try to interpret what they heard and saw that has left humanity with an endless resource for our own interpretations and knowledge of exactly how and why events unfolded as they did.

My thanks go to Dr Noel Chamois, Helen Pritchard and Graham Cohen for their help in accessing records and images in the numerous French record centres and archaeological museums. The staff of the various museums in southern France that I have contacted were never less than superbly positive and helpful, but special mention must go to the Musée de la Romanité in Nîmes, the Narbo Via in Narbonne, and Musée Départemental Arles Antique in Arles. Also, I am indebted to Mr Brian Elliot MA Cantab, whose editorial advice and interest has certainly helped create a more accurate book. Any remaining errors are to be laid at my door.

The '*Following Hadrian*' blog, created and maintained by Carole Raddato, has remained a constant companion as I have sought a closer understanding of an imperial journey through the provinces and I recommend this to any student of the emperor Hadrian and thank Carole for her assistance and advice.

Researching and writing the ancient history of a large geographical area in a foreign country is a challenge and I can only hope I have done justice to such a beautiful part of the world and the people that live there. I have been fortunate enough to visit many of the locations in the book and as such I am eternally grateful to my wife and children for their patience and support, even when they had heard enough about ancient Rome to last a lifetime, and for the many hours lost to writing when the family dinner was on the table.

As one of my university tutors used to implore her students to think – there is no right or wrong in history, just varying levels of competence in putting together a convincing argument. In that vein I hope that this attempt at capturing how and why the Romans acquired their provinces and how they administered them is a positive contribution to the eternal story.

Preface

The anniversary of the foundation of the city of Rome is approaching its third millennium. With some 300 years of historical and archaeological research still to take place before we, hopefully, reach this milestone in human history, what prospect is there that we will have finally come to conclusions about the growth of the Roman Empire? The fact that many of the fundamental notions regarding the causes and nature of Roman imperialism remain in doubt may come as a surprise to many readers but, as matters currently stand, historians are divided over exactly what it was that energised Roman expansion, whether there was an imperial plan at all and what was the true nature of Roman rule over its provinces. These are all matters that still provide fertile ground for new research, inspired revisions and reactions to new evidence and reinterpretations of existing resources.

As people of the twenty-first century, we have the benefit of being able to look back and review nearly 3,000 years of human history in Europe. The rich variety of political, social and economic events and imperial designs that have come, gone and been repeated however not only create opportunities to be measured against the great ages of Roman expansion but in parallel serve to muddy the waters or darken the glass through which we view the past. Additionally, the twenty-first century has provided us the technology to dig far deeper into our past that our predecessors could not even have imagined. We are able to instantly share new discoveries around the world at the touch of a button and view the accumulating and enlarging field of research in ways which even we could not have foreseen. The increasing number of academic institutions funding the research and debate regarding the true nature of Rome, its people and policies also creates large numbers of new university departments, each with their own agenda of research and desire to report new findings.

It is against this plethora of new research and discoveries and thousands of articles and books on the dynamics of Roman imperialism that this book attempts to look at one province in particular to understand how History happened – how Rome acquired one of the greatest (in terms of impact on future history) empires the world has known and how she governed what lay inside its boundaries.

To Skye and Cameron, who began this journey with me in La Turbie
and finished it in Biscarrosse.

'Conversation enriches the understanding, but solitude is the school of genius.'

Edward Gibbon
The History of the Decline and Fall of the Roman Empire

Part I

How was the Roman Empire Created?

Chapter 1

The Background to Roman Imperialism

'Rome engaged in military and diplomatic expansionistic state behaviour, which we now describe as "imperialism", since well before the appearance of ancient sources describing this activity.... How and why they did this is a perennial source of scholarly controversy.'

Paul J. Burton

Geographical Advantage

It was never going to be in doubt that, once the Romans had defeated their local tribal enemies within the peninsula, they would start to move northward across the Alps, to the south in the direction of Sicily and the Mediterranean, and towards the east over the Adriatic into what they called Asia and what we now term the Middle East.

The physical geography that surrounded the settlement that became Rome was, as always, the pivotal element in the evolution of a community and had many advantages for the city state of Rome as it emerged in the sixth century BCE. The central position of Rome on the western coast of the Italian peninsula coupled with a well-chosen location traversing the banks of the Tiber River, gave the people known as the Latins many advantages over their local competitors. Facing westwards into the Mediterranean made the Latins a seafaring people – an oft forgotten fact amongst the glories of their future success on land. Access to the sea created a trading people, giving them a perspective on the wider world and, very importantly, a spirit of adventure.

From the earliest times, the Romans had a strong sense of being both masters of land and sea and they were not afraid of either. Roman naval architects were talented and relied on building techniques that shared the best of ancient Phoenician and Greek technology with their own innovative additions. From what they considered ancient times, their ports had been meeting points for the exchange of ideas, events, gossip and directions of travel since before records began and Rome was a multi-cultural city from the start. The Romans were also very self-aware of their geographical position and what the horizons held for them both in Italy and across the seas. Trade provided information, and both had been flourishing for centuries as the regular discovery of new wrecks from the ancient period further reinforces our understanding of the widespread and busy trading routes that extended far into Europe, Asia and Africa.

Despite their awareness of what lay around them, and their growing economic and military power, there is little evidence of desire to expand what they already had. Indeed, early texts tend to underscore quite the reverse, suggesting a desire to grow their own city-state rather than come into conflict with others, dealing with their own challenges rather than taking on fresh ones and avoiding risk. The Latins of Roma were a people comfortable with their own position, militaristic yes but warlike no, traders yes but monopolistic no, aware of the power and prestige of other empires but desirous of working with them rather than competing with them. These then are the people that form the backdrop to this book.

Climate and Geopolitics

As far as the other city states were concerned, the position of Rome was one to be envied. Central Italy, made up of the areas today of Tuscany, Umbria, Lazio and Marche provided large scale natural resources without which no embryonic ambitious domestic, let alone imperial, power could have flourished. The Italian peninsula has always acted as a physical path between southern Europe and north Africa and, according to the Köppen climate classification, the various climatic zones contained within this extended land bridge are impressive.[1] From warm Mediterranean in the far south, through to temperate Mediterranean in the Apennine Mountain range, onto a warm oceanic climate on the eastern coasts, humid continental climates in the north east and even tundra, as in the north Italy joins the southern reaches of the Alps and stretches across more climate regions than any other country in Europe. It was a country where the people who travelled the longest distances, such as the army, needed to plan their journey – different clothes for many different climatic regions and a peninsula of great variety north to south and east to west over the Apennine chain.

Geopolitically, the Italian peninsula falls down the centre of the Mediterranean Sea and cuts it into two parts – in the west the Tyrrhenian Sea and to the east the Adriatic and Ionian Seas. The Tyrrhenian Sea was the ancient trading basin of Rome, linking to Sardinia and Corsica, and then joining the coastal waters of southern France via the Ligurian Sea which was to the north. Although smaller areas than the great oceans, by ancient standards these different coastal waters of the western Mediterranean were the equivalent of the Atlantic and were treated with respect. These trading routes were already widely in use even before the foundation of Rome in the eighth century BCE and the beginning of the Republic in 509 BCE. Today, if one flies from London or Paris to Valetta in Malta for example, the blue seas are striking as they appear south but were it possible to take the same flight Indiana Jones style in the third century BCE, these sea routes would be full of wooden sailing ships and oared galleys. The Romans may have discovered new lands and conquered tribes and whole races – but it was not to the south that they did this, but the north and east in Europe. That was where the largely unknown still lay ahead.

Closer to home, Rome was blessed with fields for farming with alluvial soils rich in nutrients, a sunny and warm Mediterranean climate that was a joy with rains when they were needed and sunshine throughout the year, protection from frosts and navigable passes in between. Rivers encouraged internal trade and the mountain regions of Italy were not so dramatic as to stifle expansion or living space once Rome became pre-eminent. Some areas of the peninsula were without doubt attractive to Rome – the Etruscan lands to the north were richer in farmlands and the great wheat fields of Sicilia to the south must have seemed, to some in the Roman senate, another area of great value to any city state able to unify Italy.

Looking further, beyond Italy, once through the often-snowbound northern passes to the north that defend modern day France, Switzerland, Austria and Slovenia, the Romans knew that there were fertile lands similar to that of their homelands – they were especially knowledgeable because economic imperialism had already been developing for hundreds of years even before the mid-eighth century BCE foundation of Rome. As they walked and rode further south than Sicilia, Roman merchants felt the increasing sunshine and warmth of the winds of the Mediterranean where they would encounter a strong enemy, the Carthaginian successors to the Phoenicians. They knew this because a form of military imperialism had also been evident as far back as anyone could remember, with frequent conflicts with their key trading competitor in North Africa. Gazing eastwards, perhaps over the walls of the key port of Brundisium, the Romans recognised that their aesthetic and intellectual superiors drew them onwards like a magnet towards Athens where the Greeks had experienced a Roman cultural imperialism – a never-ending tide of Roman interest, exploitation and imitation. Further east there were the vast unknown deserts and spaces of Asia where only Alexander the Great had so far travelled and rumours of a land full of spices were tales of legend. They knew this through a form of social imperialism, where Romans explored, trade deals were struck, and exploratory missions travelled and disappeared never to return from the edge of the world. On many levels therefore, there would seem to be no question that the Romans were bound to become an imperial power and they were already engaged in three differing forms of imperial activity – military, economic and social – and it was inevitable that state policy in the form of political imperialism would one day turn attention to the horizons.

The Debate on Roman Imperialism

Media history, that of the misinformed and popularist providing for the consumer, sees the Roman Empire as a paradigm of imperial policy and expansion, a model to be imitated, an empire to be matched or exceeded – a measure of a nation's prowess and their range of power. For centuries, potential emperors selected what they viewed as the best features of Roman Imperialism as the blueprint for convincing their supporters that this was the model to be followed and that they too could replicate and enjoy the fruits of imperial power.

However, political leaders are often narrowly educated individuals and rarely trained historians able to view past events from the angles of often uncomfortable truths. Thus, it is rare – if not completely absent – for political decisions involving national expansion or imperial policy to be based on reference to anything verging on historical fact. Selecting abstract events and separating them from their context, shrouding them in lies is a commonly-used tool by the unscrupulous politician as well as for the foolish. A little knowledge is a dangerous thing and ignorance is bliss are not idle sayings – they are born of many examples in human history of catastrophic levels of ignorance amongst political leaders whose gifts do not extend to recreating history but only reinterpreting history. The exact causes of Roman expansion both during the Republic and the period begun by Augustus are far from clear. The origins, directions and speed of Roman imperialism remain under debate and, however tempting it may be to feel that we can see what happened, we remain in a state of ignorance.

The discussions on the causes and dynamics surrounding Roman Imperialism are complex and contentious – but we do have the advantage of current events. Decisions made in Beijing, Washington, Paris or Tehran reveal as much about Roman history as about our own age in that the motivations for imperial power have similar origins. How and why Rome expanded also reveals much about how Roman society changed, how the senate regarded growth and how Roman government adjusted to cope with new territorial acquisitions – successfully or otherwise. The focus of this book is to assess the addition of just one province of the many that Rome acquired to try to see more clearly how and why events moved as they did, what the impact was, and how Rome coped with adding further territory to her enlarging imperial possessions.

Chapter 2

The Historical Debate on Imperialism

Imperialism means different things to different people. Only a century ago it was regarded as a positive force, an engine of civilizational change and the inevitable consequence of progress. Today in the early years of the twenty-first century, imperialism is seen as contemptuous, evil and a force for cultural and civilizational oppression. Uncomfortable as it may be, the truth is somewhere in the middle.

We still have generations in our world for whom imperialism means maps coloured in red displaying an empire upon which the sun never set, the flags of the great European nations blended into modern day flags of independent nations, slavery, exploitation, missionaries, great battles of white men putting down indigenous black tribes and heraldic eagles on columns with majestic European buildings set in far eastern hillsides. The same is true for how simple mental constructs of Rome dominate our understanding of history. For nearly two millennia, since the collapse of what we think of as a single entity of the Roman world in 476 CE, the most commonly-held image of Rome is the map of an empire stretching all around the Mediterranean, dominated by metal-clad legionaries and led by a white toga-clad class of opulent Romans and, yes, the inevitable eagles. The parallel reflections of eagle standards, roads, SPQR, glorious victories in hard fought battles, inevitably slain enemies and stability between the ancient world and that of the nineteenth century have not occurred by chance. This simple construct is how Rome has been envisioned since its demise by societies around the world and it is also how many dictators have preferred to see the history of Rome – one where ruthless, all-powerful emperors with plans to build their empire ever larger hold power over their territorial acquisitions – exploiting what they have taken by force and installing eagles everywhere to mark the extent of their new territories. As incorrect as these images are, they nevertheless represent misconceptions that have represented Roman imagery in the public consciousness for over 1,500 years, despite being nothing even remotely like the truth as we now understand it. Indeed, the Romans did not even have an equivalent word for 'imperialism' – their nearest similarity was *imperium* and this is where the modern version is derived from, but *imperium* means 'command' and the geographical area where that command was the law, it did not denote the extension of control over lands.

Our understanding of Roman imperialism has been seen, and continues to be seen, through the prism of our own ages – that is to say that, with imperialism alive and well in the twenty-first century, we have to be acutely aware of our own misconceptions about the dynamics surrounding national policies of expansion and control. Equally, in Europe it was only within the last 100 years that some of the largest imperial possessions in world history came to an end and they have left a legacy of misleading interpretations and post-colonial reactions that are very much still being debated. The word 'imperialism', though lifted from the Roman *imperium*, did not surface in common usage until the second half of the nineteenth century and even then, only in relation to the great powers of Europe as they gradually become engaged in the Scramble for Africa and the race to create large empires across the globe. It may have seemed to the various governments of France, Germany, Austro-Hungary and Great Britain that what they were doing was simply mirroring what the Romans had done but this was a complete misconception. The Roman Empire was not created in any race to grow lest another power seized it – there were few powers other than Egypt and Carthage able to rival Rome, ergo there was no need to race to do anything.

If we are to accurately understand how and why the Roman Empire was established and, equally importantly, how it was administered, then it is important to be aware of our own prejudices and preconceptions regarding modern imperialism and even what early political theory says about imperialism. Laying these aside, the expansion of Rome can be viewed as a unique phenomenon and not something that could be replicated. This is how we must view Roman imperialism – as a major cornerstone of the development of European history that has never been repeated, whose causes were unique and whose evolution was singular and not a model for future history. This book cannot be but a guide and overview to the causes of Roman imperialism and cannot claim to have a definitive set of answers – there are other books that attempt to do that. Before we grasp our own opinions of the causes of imperialism we should first be aware of how historians and social commentators of the past have viewed the same question.

J.A. Hobson and V.I. Lenin

Two of the most read of the twentieth-century debates on imperialism came in the shape of J.A. Hobson and V. Lenin.[2] They viewed the eras in which they lived as part of the inevitable post-industrial thirst for new raw materials and markets – driven inexorably by capitalist greed. This socialist view of the late-nineteenth and early-twentieth century imperial power struggles was a logical extension of the impact of the industrialisation of western nations and economies. It conveniently explained why the great powers clashed with each other before and in 1914, invested vast sums of money into arms races to extend their control and dominions, and led to a world war. But straight away we can see a major difference between modern imperialism and the expansion of Rome – there was no exhausted or exploited industrialised economy at the end of the Roman republic. Rome and what became its empire, was a largely agricultural pre-capitalist society and, while there may have been a demand for raw materials such as silver and gold in various times, these were not drivers on their own and not essential to the survival of the state. Even when economic ruin was a possibility, there was never any scramble based on international competition for resources. It was Hobson who pointed out that it was nationalistic pride that drove European nations into conflict for imperial domains along with capitalist oligarchies – what he called the 'taproot' of imperialism. Rome certainly was ruled by oligarchs and, although for centuries they were forbidden to engage in work or commerce, this did not stop them amassing considerable fortunes. Whether we can lay the cause of Roman imperialism purely at their feet however, requires care.

J.A. Schumpeter and K.H. Marx

In his book published in 2004, *Roman Imperialism – Readings and Sources*, Craige Champion counters these ideas by pointing to J.A. Schumpeter.[3] As a German living in the post Imperial Weimar Republic and as a Czech with roots in a nation only just created out of imperial collapse, he was perhaps well suited to make observations on what caused imperial policies that had affected his life. He was at one time the Minister of Finance under the early Republic and then a banker who became bankrupt himself. Schumpeter moved into an academic life and eventually landed at Harvard in 1932 where he lectured and wrote on economics until his death in 1950.

For Schumpeter, it was evolutionary economics that was the central cause of change and destruction – capitalism being an evolutionary process of continuous change and ultimately 'creative destruction'. We live in the age of AI – could artificial intelligence be the final phase in Schumpeter's theory that capitalism through endless creativity will ultimately create its own destruction? Whether or not this turns out to be the case only the future will tell, but for our purposes, Schumpeter opposed the ideas of Marx in so far as he felt that it would not be a proletarian revolution – for him, capitalism would wear itself out and collapse internally. Equally, for Schumpeter there was no grand plan of racing to acquire raw materials, instead just a warlike social class of capitalist-backed political leaders whose aim was 'the objectless disposition on the part of a state to unlimited forcible expansion'. Schumpeter cited occasions in history where war and conquest were the only central policies of certain leaders. Energised by warlike instincts, the history of some nations was simply dominated by a desire for conquest for the sake of maintaining a warlike nation, with no limits, no plan and ultimately untenable. Now it could be and it is very likely that it was the impact of the First World War that dramatically affected Schumpeter's philosophy. As we have already been warned, it is vital that we extract from our analysis all of our own prejudices, experiences or preconceptions when we evaluate the past.

For countless historians, the events leading up to and including the horror of The Great War were so immense and so inexplicable that they searched for a logic to understand events where the facts were still very unclear. In any event, Schumpeter was correct in that Rome always contained a warlike class – the martial element of Roman manhood – and the prowess of the Army and the essential nature of military experience in any sort of political career all pointed to his ideas of continual military conflict, but this is simply not true. As Champion and many other scholars of Roman history will agree, there were long periods of time where the Army was very small and inactive. Indeed, it was not until the Marian reforms very late in the history of the Republic in 107 BCE that a standing army of expensive-to-maintain legions, based on a new efficient system of recruitment, retention and training, that the Roman Army as we understand it came into existence – hardly the basis for a previous five hundred years of supposed warlike ambition. However, the contrary could also be true, that with the Augustan reforms, where the army became a standing force, so the corollary was true – that there had to be a standing need for their continued existence – guarding an empire.

J.R. Seeley

'We seem, as it were, to have conquered and peopled half the world in a fit of absence of mind'. This is how the British historian John Robert Seeley saw the expansion of British rule around the world in his book *The Expansion of England* in 1883.[4] To Seeley, it was primarily the demand for trade stemming from industrialisation that was the main driver for British imperialism – there was no policy to begin with, but later and with threats to this trade in the late-eighteenth century, the British East India Company was forced to defend itself and this morphed into a political policy largely under Conservative and Tory administrations. However, Seeley was precise in his desire to point out that national amnesia accompanied this development – there was no particular government or popular groundswell for an Empire until much later. Exploiting a territory and defending it in order to maintain this exploitation is one thing, but taking on responsibility for the people and their welfare is quite another and this is a quite pivotal distinction – at what point does a territory one trades with and subsequently defends become a province or colony? Seeley was far more than just the creator of one idiosyncratic quotation, he stimulated thought about what it was to become responsible for a whole sub-continent such as India, or indeed an entire continent as in the case of Africa. What this meant in practice was the creation of a whole new political mindset with the administrative, economic, military and spiritual resources to undertake such massive responsibility – often to the point where the obligations of Empire began to outweigh the initial economic advantages.

The Moral Dimension

Lurking in the background of any discussion on the causes of imperialism or what type of imperial expansion was pursued by the Roman state are the moral issues. Until the late-twentieth and early twenty-first centuries, the morality of imperialism was not commonly conceived or covered. Today we are far more acutely aware of what comes with the dominance of one country over another. The Victorians had a convenient way of dealing with this by preferring to feel that they were civilised as a society (which of course in very many ways they were not, compared to our own age) and bringing progress and civilisation to the dark continent of Africa, the deserts of Australia or the islands of the South Pacific. This may have soothed the conscience of missionaries and sensitive souls but the reality of political and military subjugation was and is of course very different.

Today the word imperialism has so many negative connotations that it is hard to see any benefit at all – cultural appropriation, enforced religion, racism, social restructuring, ruthless commercial practice overpowering innocent and unworldly local inhabitants, not to mention a view of legality and legal judgement that almost always favoured the invader rather than the invaded, all combine to undermine any regard for imperialism as a good thing. Thus, when we look at Roman imperialism, it is again important not to assume that their approach brought the same attitudes of mind. Roman expansion was individual and unique and while it may share some similarities with modern imperialism in terms of causation – that of the nineteenth, twentieth and twenty-first centuries – it was not a model followed in the modern period – despite the ignorance or deliberate perversions of modern rulers.

Chapter 3

The Current Debate on Roman Imperialism – Three Theories

'Imperialism was born when the ruling class in capitalist production came up against national limits to its economic expansion.'

Hannah Arendt

Mindful of the past debate on the causes and effects of imperialism as a process, we can now focus solely on Rome to try to determine a substantive and cogent understanding of why and how this city came to dominate the known world in its time. Along the way, it is possible that we can identify a symmetry with the more modern forms of imperialism – or far better, treat Rome as a totally individual case bearing no relation to what came 1,500 years later.

T. Mommsen, G. De Sanctis and William Harris – the Metrocentric view

In essence there are three main modern theories on Roman expansion. The first, which can be referred to as metrocentric, stems, as the name suggests, from the metropolitan area of Rome itself and has at its core the theory put forward by Theodor Mommsen, the noted nineteenth-century scholar of Roman history, which argued that Rome adopted a defensive imperialism where the city of Rome, mostly during the Republican era, reacted to outside threats and thereby acquired territories for strategic protection rather than as part of some wilful acts of aggression and aggrandisement. For Mommsen it was all about the city and the small number of powerful metropolitan political classes that made these decisions.[5] During the early-twentieth century, and as Craige Champion points out, this metrocentric theory was strongly opposed by an Italian historian named Gaetano De Sanctis, who was in no doubt that, in tandem with Schumpeter, it was the militarism of Rome with its constant emphasis on military glory to underpin political leadership that was the key dynamic, and that it was a class constantly looking for war that created the empire of Rome. These views of both Schumpeter and De Sanctis have more recently been buttressed by a masterly series of arguments from William Harris – until 2017 Professor of History at

Columbia University. Amongst his wide-ranging scholarly achievements, Harris published his *War and Imperialism in Republican Rome 327–70 BC* in 1979, and this together with his article *On War and Greed in the Second Century BC* provides the reader and researcher with convincing arguments that the main dynamics for Roman expansion originate within the city, within the minds, opinions and body of a few, and within Roman culture.[6] The main impact of these two works was to 'tread on the toes' of the established wisdom about the causes of Roman imperialism.

For Harris, it is important not to ignore the economic need and greed of the decision makers. While commercial and mercantile interests obviously played their part, there is not enough evidence to suggest that these alone provided anywhere near enough impetus to raise armies and take on long campaigns with the concomitant longer-term commitments of victory. The real economic dynamics came from other sources and changed over time. Harris reminds us that we are now in an area of constant speculation. The men who made the key decisions, certainly during the long years of the Republic and more specifically the second and first centuries BCE of the Republic, held their discussions in private and no records exist, and those debates that were held openly in the senate and were recorded no longer survive. It is largely thanks to Atticus and Cicero that we have any speeches and letters at all that guide us through some of the decision-making processes but these apply to a narrow period of time and cannot with any justification be applied more widely – even when Cicero does refer to past events in the long distant history of the city of Rome.

Much later, in the second century CE and in Book 53 of the eighty books he wrote on the history of Rome, L. Cassius Dio (c.165-235 CE) further reminds us of how difficult it was then, and is now, to assess decisions in the Empire because of the main decisions were made behind closed doors:

> *'In this way the government was changed at that time for the better and in the interest of greater security; for it was no doubt quite impossible for the people to be saved under a republic. Nevertheless, the events occurring after this time cannot be recorded in the same manner as those of previous times. Formerly, as we know, all matters were reported to the senate and to the people, even if they happened at a distance; hence all learned of them, no matter to what extent fear or favour, friendship or enmity coloured the reports of certain writers, was always to a certain extent to be found in the works of other writers who wrote of the same events and in the public records. But after this time most things that happened began to be kept secret and concealed, even though some things are perchance made public, they are distrusted just because they cannot be verified;*

for it is suspected that everything is said and done with reference to the wishes of the men in power at the time and of their associates.'

Cassius Dio[7]

From this short passage we can peer clearly into the new, secretive world of the senate as manipulated by Caesar. Even in almost contemporary sources, so much was discussed and agreed behind closed doors that it is impossible to be accurate about the true motives behind imperial expansion and acquisition in the period of the Empire. Dio also warns us that, even during the earlier Republic, writers often corrupted the truth to put their own slant on the speeches and reports to the people in the forum, so again we must tread carefully when assessing what was true and what had been perverted for public consumption. Cicero would often use his glorious rhetorical skills to favour one course of action over another whether or not it carried merit and his own personal political objectives. A good case in question is his speech in support of Pompey's command against Mithridates where, in 66 BCE, a huge Roman crowd in the forum were treated to *De Imperio* – a series of disastrous economic scenarios should Mithridates be allowed to succeed on the eastern borders of the then empire. The picture painted for the crowd in Cicero's beautifully crafted and multi-layered view of why Rome needed to launch a further war of conquest – it was not a policy nor a collective decision of government that was needed, but a commitment from the people of Rome:

'Every day, letters arrive from Asia for my good friends the Roman knights who are concerned for the great sums they have invested in the farming of your revenues: and on the strength of my close connexion with that order they have represented to me the position of the public interests and the danger of their private fortunes.'[8]

Moving from the economic threat that Mithridates posed both to the tax farmers but also to the pockets of the Roman tax payer, Cicero then emphasised the duty that Romans had to the past – and here we have a better glimpse of what Roman imperial policy, if there was a policy, was based upon in previous centuries:

'Whenever, in the past, Roman traders or ship owners had been treated somewhat high-handedly, our ancestors often went to war for their protection. With this in mind I have to ask you to reflect how you yourselves ought to react when, at one and the same time and on one man's single order, thousands upon thousands of Roman citizens have been slaughtered. Because their emissaries had been rather insolently addressed, your forefathers ordained that Corinth, the shining light

of all Greece, must suffer annihilation. Surely you therefore, will not let off the king who compelled a Roman general of consular rank to endure imprisonment, beating, every kind of torture and finally death. Your ancestors refused to tolerate the slightest restriction upon the liberty of Roman citizens. Will you on the other hand remain indifferent when their very lives are taken away from them?'[9]

As if Cicero had not already given a fine history lesson on just how fearsome and quick to react Romans had been in previous centuries. Cicero also opens a window – even if it is one exaggerated by his mind legally-trained in the art of manipulating truth – that shows how quick to war and conquest his fellow Romans had been. It was in Roman DNA to not only protect her borders but take any opportunity to expand them should an offence to their prestige arise. This is not defensive imperialism so much as offensive when offence has been taken.

Cicero ends this part of his speech with another telling reminder to the assembled crowd. This time he tells them, and therefore reveals to us, just how important the obligation of protecting the empire was to each and every generation:

'Your ancestors won themselves glory by the magnificent empire they handed down to you. See to it that you do not earn a corresponding load of shame by failing to protect and safeguard the heritage you have received as their gift.'

This approach to needing to protect the heritage of empire was echoed 150 years later by Dio, so we can be certain that Romans saw their responsibility to the empire as one of obligation to the legacy of past achievements. The effect of this was that decisions on policy or war were made by the senate or emperor with this in mind – that they should maintain the legacy they had inherited, and it was perhaps not until the reign of Hadrian that this changed and partial withdrawals from some of the more distant parts of empire were ordered. In other words, if there was an imperial policy, it was not driven by a need to enhance empire but to take advantage when circumstances arose – coupled with a desire to protect what had been gained as some sort of duty to the heroes of the past.

At the end of the day, we must accept that there were few Ciceros with either his ability or desire to record and broadcast their thoughts to a wide public. Equally distressing is that it is only his speeches and letters that have survived in such abundance, while those of equally talented orators have not. Thus, decisions on going to war and acquiring territory are far more difficult to determine when we assess Roman Imperialism when compared with more recent times, but even so Cicero and Dio have left us enough to be able to interpret the lines of thought coming from the metrocentric centre of power on imperialism during the Republic.

The Pericentric Approach – Wallerstein

Given the expanding borders of the early Republic it is easy to understand how new pressures created new policies to deal with the strategic and political issues that stemmed from relations with neighbouring tribes or states. The pericentric approach argues the case for a permissive approach – not a policy driven from the senate at the heart of Rome, but a flexible stance depending on how events unfolded, and energised by events on the periphery. This can be seen to be an especially convincing argument in the second and third centuries BCE when the majority of the large-scale acquisitions of territory took place and Rome was constantly having to readjust to increasing competition in trade around the Mediterranean.

In the east, where the Greek states were almost constantly at war, Rome needed to respond to the problems on the edges of her territories when smaller Greek states sent emissaries to plead for support from the Roman military machine in their struggles against Philip V of Macedon and again with Antiochus III of Syria. These were requests for Roman protection and involvement in overseas territories, and not part of some centrist expansionist policy or the musings of a dictatorship – or, as Plutarch commented in his *Cato*, 'empire by invitation'. The pericentric explanation is quite a convincing argument when one considers how little accurate information was available to the decision makers and perhaps a 'better to be safe than sorry' approach was followed in diplomatic decisions on foreign policy. The work of Immanuel Wallerstein links into these ideas and his 'world-systems theory' in that Rome grew into an ancient world hegemony which was both 'rare and unstable'. This growth in effect weakened the Roman empire to such an extent that it was unable to sustain the size and power it needed and ultimately divided and collapsed as the 'waves' of economic power around it changed and other hegemons developed. The Marxist response was that this theory did not give enough weight to class and their view that it was the class system that created social and therefore political tension.[10]

What About the Systemic Theory?

The third and last of these three propositions suggests that it was the system of international relations – or lack of them – that existed at the time that allowed for wars and territorial aggrandisement to have a free hand. In the absence of international organisations or treaties that were uniformly observed, it was a matter of the laws of survival that applied and nations simply had to look after their own self-interests and this was the driver behind international conflict and the accumulation of newly-won lands – Champion refers to this era as a 'self-help' system. In this case then we can see Rome not reacting to events but proactively doing what she needed to do in order to survive within a given set of circumstances – not driven by a metrocentric plan or group of individuals acting in unison, nor the actions of a dictator with megalomanic ambitions, nor being invited into a state to offer the protection of *Pax Romana.*

Throughout the ancient world there was a state of almost constant conflict. There was no ancient equivalent of the United Nations nor was there was any codification of what constituted morally right and proper conflict such as we have in the Geneva Conventions. Human Rights were unheard of and there was no international court by which 'war criminals' as we see them could be prosecuted for their actions in war. Instead, the Mediterranean world in which Rome became pre-eminent, was a militarised region where conflicts were, in the normal course of events, solved by war and quite often whole states eliminated and erased from history. In the world of the sixth to the second century BCE, Rome evolved into the supreme, but not the only, militarised state where internal social, religious and cultural norms were founded on the bedrock of a military caste system. The Roman state revolved around an acceptance that the army, and to a lesser extent the Roman navy, underpinned political control, advancement and social behaviour. Naturally, to service this desire for militaristic success there had to be conflict and where there was conflict the Roman military machine was often able to emerge victorious, and thus enemies and territories were subjugated – again this was not a policy but the result of chance opportunities.

Chapter 4

How do Carthage and The Punic Wars Add to the Analysis of Roman Imperialism in the Third and Second Century BCE?

The classic case often referred to in respect of eradication of a defeated enemy is that of the fate of Carthage. In one of his excellent chapters in an outstanding book on the dynamics of Roman Imperialism, Neville Morley examines a number of established themes but he specifically references the history of the Punic Wars fought between Rome and Carthage to illustrate another pivotal consideration for Roman imperial expansion – that of international security.[11] The similarities between the decisions that Rome had to take and those of our own modern super-states gives the subject a reality and gives the study of the political dynamics faced by the Roman senate a tangible feel in our world today.

The Carthaginians were the beneficiaries of a thousand years of history. To the Romans they were known as the *Poenici* (Latin for Phoenician) or *Punici* as their roots were Phoenician and their strengths were seafaring, manufacturing and trade. Phoenicia was situated along the modern-day coast of the eastern Mediterranean (Israel and Lebanon) and they had traded and co-existed alongside their ancient Egyptian neighbours for hundreds of years, sharing social and cultural identities through their Egyptian trade. Their long-established sea routes needed ports and the city state of Carthage, built around a wonderful natural harbour on the north coast of present-day Tunisia, enabled their many merchant ships and warships to traverse the Mediterranean on their way to and from southern Spain. By 300 BCE, when Rome was itself emerging as a powerful player in the region, Carthaginian and Roman merchants were already well known to each other, sharing the same market places, ship building technology and competing for minerals and markets. However, by 149 BCE when Cato the Elder is supposed to have dropped a Libyan fig on the floor of the senate building, apparently by mistake but more likely by contrived, impactful design, and announced: '*Ceterum (autem) censeo Carthaginem esse delendam*' ('Furthermore, I consider that Carthage must be destroyed'),[12] major transformation was taking place both in the relationship not only between

Carthage and Rome but also in the psychological and political horizons of Roman statesmen and the people of Rome. This 150 year period had seen the outbreak of two of the three Punic Wars and Cato was expressing the view, and he did it many times before his death, that the final destruction of Carthage was essential if Rome was to survive.

The first war developed largely by accident when, in 289 BCE, a small mercenary army named the Mamertines took control of Messana. Some twenty years later, fearing attack by the forces of the powerful Syracuse, they appealed for support from both Carthage and Rome. Rome had been expanding northwards and south towards Sicily for the past decades and we can see these movements as clear signs of an imperial policy in the third century BCE – part of a *metrocentric* plan of expansion. However, how far to go and how quickly were questions that strangled further quick action. Carthage were quickest from the blocks and arrived to help and seal control over not only Messana, but also stationing a garrison on Sicily indicating that they were there to stay and expand. The slower reaction force from Rome did eventually arrive but only after significant debate in the senate, mostly led by Appius Claudius Caudex. It was Caudex that put the matter to a vote of the popular assembly in 264 BCE and as such we can infer that, as far as Sicily was concerned, this is evidence of no overriding policy but instead a defensive move in seeing a Carthaginian threat to the mainland and trading routes around Sicily – a *pericentric* approach.

Caudex was given command of an army which was successful in evicting the Carthaginian presence from Messana, but it also triggered off a draining and exhausting war that was to last until 241 BCE with various battles both at sea and on land for eventual control over the whole of Sicily. The Treaty of Lutatius that was signed after the destruction of the Carthaginian fleet at the Battle of the Aegates Islands on 10 March 241 BCE led to Rome annexing the whole of Sicily as a new Roman province – to become the richest and most lucrative posting for any proconsul looking to fill his coffers. Furthermore, all prisoners taken by Carthage were returned to Rome and a vast indemnity of 3,200 talents was to be paid over the next ten years. The later acquisition

> Evidence of the Battle of the Aegates Islands in 241 BCE was most recently exposed in 2018 and 2021 when a team researching the site off the north west coast of Sicily discovered six bronze ship rams as well as some iron helmets and pottery. These finds made a total of 25 rams so far identified – most of them Roman, which is a surprise given that Rome claimed victory – although this has been explained by the fact that the Carthaginians had captured over ninety Roman ships in a previous battle.

of Corsica and Sardinia from the Carthaginians further enlarged the Roman empire in the third century BCE and again provided valuable provinces to the state to administer.

One conclusion therefore is that the First Punic War demonstrates a Rome uncertain about expansion beyond her mainland and even more concerned about taking on a Mediterranean super-power. It was one thing sprawling across the mainland, strangling fellow Latin tribes into submission and giving them Roman citizenship for their compliance, but it was quite another going to war with a powerful neighbour such as Carthage, and it took over twenty years of military struggle to secure Sicily. While the eventual treaty may have gone some way to alleviating these concerns, in the senate at least, concerns and reservations remained.

A Carthaginian historian, if we had one whose records had survived, would no doubt relate to us that Rome was a bullying power, with ideas beyond its ability to enforce them, trying to find excuses to expand. The selection of Sicily and trying to squeeze the Carthaginians out by enforcing a blockade does represent a change of approach from Rome. However, the closest reliable Roman historian we can refer to is Polybius (who was in fact a Greek hostage to Rome) who has been described as 'a remarkably well informed, industrious and insightful historian'.[13]

The accounts of the wars by Polybius are almost contemporaneous with events (written about a century after the first war) and considerable, and unusually firm reliance is placed on his narrative of events. Polybius is renowned for his forty books named *The Histories* – the first of these deals with the First Punic War and reveals much about the Roman concerns on the periphery of their territory as they came up against the first super-state of the ancient world.

A second conclusion regarding the impact of the First Punic War on Roman imperialism therefore might be that those concerns raised in the senate that held back action on the periphery of the Roman state were well founded. The results of the First Punic War were stark. The historian Adrian Goldsworthy in his book *The Fall of Carthage* cites Roman manpower losses as 'appalling' – Rome was also close to bankruptcy and the number of adult male citizens available to man the new navy and legions had dropped by 17 per cent over the course of the war.[14] Going to war was easy to say but far harder to endure and this was to be a hidden consideration. No one in history likes to be recorded as the naysayer or killjoy in a debate on honour or military prowess, either in the *domus* (family home), the forum or the senate, but the reality was that wars can be costly, they can be long and they can be lost. These were factors that, although absent now in the remaining documents we have, were no doubt argued over in debate and not all Romans were therefore imperialists at heart.

Lest we make the dangerous assumption that the Roman military machine was invulnerable to defeat, we should look at the fine print, and throughout the life of the Republic the Romans suffered nearly 100 military reverses or outright defeats on the road to creating an empire – whether through accident or design.

Another consideration for decision makers in Rome, whether or not imperial policy was being made in the centre of Rome, reacting to events on the periphery or taking strategic advantage of opportunity, was what happened in the post-war phase. We have the perfect analogy that politicians learn little from history – and even less if they do not know their history – with the 2003 US invasion of Iraq. Here was a clear case of total focus on war and almost no concern regarding the responsibilities winning that war might bring. A country has been destroyed, tens of thousands of lives lost and millions of lives changed for the worse as there was and is no idea of what to do with a country you do not want once you have defeated it.

After 2004, Iraq split asunder in reaction against the American onslaught and became and still is a costly debit on the balance sheet – except of course for the oil companies. BP, or 'Blair /Bush Petroleum' as it has been called, had not produced oil in Iraq for forty years prior to the 2003 invasion. By 2023 over £15 billion of oil has been pumped from Iraqi wells under amazingly flexible licences granted by the US and UK. It could be argued that the huge tax revenues from this exploitation of Iraqi raw materials more than paid for the initial costs of the war – unless you are of course one of the mothers or fathers, sisters or brothers, or indeed children of the 655,000 Iraqis killed between 2003 and 2010 (90 per cent of which were violent deaths), or the 4,492 US military deaths or the 187 journalists or 179 United Kingdom servicemen who gave their lives for Iraqi oil. Clearly the main target was not Saddam Hussain but the oil his country contained. Two thousand two hundred years ago we have no real idea how many Roman or Sicilian civilians, Carthaginian soldiers, or Roman legionaries died in the Punic Wars, nor do we know exactly why they were fought and there is the rub – perhaps it was the grain supplies that flowed from Sicily that was the clinching decision to support Caudex in his attack on Carthage, just like it was oil in Iraq in 2003.

But the war against Carthage did not end there. The Carthaginians had not gone away and they would be forever angry, there was no real peace now between the two protagonists; armies on both sides needed maintaining, warships needed provisioning, and only a spark was needed to ignite the simmering tension throughout the Mediterranean that perhaps neither side wanted. The costs of maintaining full-time troops and garrisons in Sicily were now a permanent cost to the Roman state treasury and the border had to be defended over a much larger coastline.

Another war came, and this time in Hispania in the late-220s BCE. The uneasy friction between two rival nations erupted when the Carthaginian general Hannibal took centre stage in a revanchist revival against Rome which almost saw the complete destruction of Rome itself. The Battle of Cannae in 216 BCE was a rout of the Roman forces, with estimated losses for the Roman state of 55,000 according to the Roman historian Livy writing towards the end of the first-century BCE, or 70,000 according to Polybius.[15] However, the Second Punic War ended with the decisive Battle of Zama in October 202 BCE, where the legendary Scipio Africanus destroyed Hannibal's army and his eighty or so elephants in what is now northern Tunisia. Rome was able to once again dictate terms and added the huge Carthaginian territory of Spain to its imperial possessions, as well as the coastline between Spain and Italy – including the first stages in the assimilation of southern Gaul. Carthage, now reduced to a minor state rather than a Mediterranean giant, still existed until men such as Cato the Elder dropped their figs.

Chapter 5

The Importance of a Single *Ficus*

In this assessment of the difficulties of identifying the differing types of imperialism that can be attributed to the growth of the Roman empire, it should now be clear that there was never one over-arching political policy or plan that each new generation of senatorial leaders had to follow. Instead, it seems, on balance, that all three main theories have their place and that Rome acted, or reacted, as events presented themselves and as leaderships changed. For modern day rulers to idolise the creation of the Roman Empire as some kind of role model or paradigm of strategic success is therefore folly, based on ignorance of the evidence or a complete lack of historical knowledge.

This is, however, not the case when we look at the Third Punic War. In this case we have the evidence of both Polybius and the later Greek Appian of Alexandria, known to history as Appian, who wrote his *Roman History* in the early decades of the first century CE.[16] A large part of the accounts of Polybius regarding the details of the Third Punic War are lost, it would seem forever, but Appian used Polybius as the basis of his narrative so Polybius is somewhat still preserved – although through a second pair of hands. Between these two authors we are able to identify a profound change in approach amongst those in power in respect of their regard to imperialism and imperial affairs, and it's through the life and actions of Cato the Elder, for example, that we can see through this glass rather less dimly.

The elder Marcus Porcius Cato (as opposed to his grandson Marcus Porcius Cato 'Uticensis' – or the Younger – who figures so highly in the last century of the Republic in his political clashes with just about everybody) had been raised in the epicentre of the Republican ideology of the *mos maiorum* – the duties and responsibilities of a Roman man. For this Cato, born around 234 BCE and pre-eminent until his death in 149, the notion of devotion to the state was the central theme of his life. Born in Tusculum, he followed in his father's footsteps of being both devoted to agriculture and his Sabine (ancient) farming roots and service in the army. Here was no nobleman, but someone who rose from the rural ranks of the well-to-do and arrived in Rome, where his talents and intelligence propelled him forward through the *cursus honorum*, the ladder of political steps that lead through the ranks of the Roman magistracy, and where he was almost unique in being a new man or *novus homo* reaching the very top as consul in 195 BCE. He experienced both envy of his rise and admiration of his plain-speaking talents, and it was Cato the Elder that was also able to witness at first hand the ravages and costs of war as the Second Punic War was part of his life.

Cato was at heart a man of simple tastes and he loathed the growing evidence of avarice and luxury being displayed by the new wealth being created from a growing empire – he was concerned that *luxuria* and *avaritia* would so erode the fabric of traditional Roman values that he came to the attention of Marcus Fulvius Flaccus. Flaccus was the real deal, a Roman general and a nobleman of real influence from a senior patrician family. They joined together with Flaccus, extolling the virtues of '*Cato's energy, his military talent, his eloquence, his frugal and simple life and his traditional principles*'.

The transition that was developing within the upper echelons of Roman society was noticeable to all and this was a direct result of the impact of imperialist growth; material wealth was now an objective, as was ostentatious display – and with this came demands for more wealth for all, and the politics of envy took on a new dimension. Gradually a major division became evident in the senate between nobles wanting exclusive control over wealth and *luxuria* and a more conservative, austere grouping with a love for the traditions of the old order centred on loyalty, simplicity, integrity and order. This was a conflict that would now last for decades and become part of the reason for the eventual fall of the republic. But as one delves more deeply into Roman character in this and later periods it is plain that the Romans found no conflict between being critical of unbridled wealth on the one hand, living an austere lifestyle on the other, and plundering overseas possessions for every silver coin they had. It was not a question of taking it, but more with what you did with it later.

A Dichotomy of Values – Roman integrity combined with Roman barbarity

In 195 BCE, Cato the Elder achieved the highest rung on the *cursus honorum* and was elected co-consul with his patron and colleague Flaccus. As both a *novus homo* and aged only 39, his rise had been meteoritic and his one-year term was equally turbulent to the point where he was perhaps grateful to leave Rome for his proconsular province in 194. At this time, and in the future, these postings were a reward for achieving a consular rank, but also a convenient way of removing the influence of the immediately-retired consul from Rome while the new men had their turn. In later years, when corruption and electoral bribery was rife, a proconsular posting – providing it was to the right province – was also a way of refilling coffers emptied by having given out significant bribes.

Cato received Hispania Citerior as his provincial gift – this was the north-eastern section of southern Spain that led south east down the coastline to Hispania Ulterior and the Gibraltarian region – and then north eastwards towards the southern coastline of Gaul (modern day France) and what was soon to be known as Gallia Narbonensis. Today we would see Catalonia and Valencia as the main components of Hispania Citerior.

After making offerings to particular Gods that he wished to protect his family and himself, Cato the Elder would have left his luxurious residence in Rome and all his other farms and rural villas in the hands of trusted servants and members of the family. Then, with a very significant retinue following him – his close family, his lictors carrying their distinctive leather strapped bundles of rods with the blade of the axe seeping through (eleven men for a proconsul), a retinue of *scribae* (scribes) for the daily flow of correspondence, servants, slaves and then a significant baggage train, he left for Spain. There was no doubt also an armed guard from a cohort of legionaries – perhaps on their way back to their unit – because we should not forget that, while this and other provinces had been taken from Carthage by treaty, it was an enforced exchange of rulers and rules that was being imposed on the 'province'. Indeed, the boundaries were very blurred between those who now fell under Roman law and those who spat at it.

On his journey to Hispania Citerior Cato could have taken one of two routes – either by land all the way along the northern and then south western coastlines to Spain or by sea to Sardinia and thence on to Spain. Either way the Stanford University ORBIS tool informs us that Cato and his column would have taken at least twelve days to make the journey, and probably more than that should he choose to stop along the way to meet with friends, so it could have been a number of weeks before he arrived in the hot climate of Spain.

Becoming the governor of a province was a new experience for every proconsular appointment, not because these men had not travelled before but precisely because the empire was so new. They were being thrust into governing lands that had no map, often no boundaries, that were full of rebellious and often savage enemies of Rome, and where the administration was weak to say the least. Rome had not been able to dole out provinces on this scale ever before. The empire that was accruing – for whatever reasons historians might judge – was a new stage in the development of what we now know as the Roman empire.

Naturally there had been provincial roles in the past as Rome conquered or assimilated tribal areas or city states within the peninsula, but whole vast tracts of lands, cities and people seized both from a defeated enemy and from an indigenous population was a new phenomenon. Hispania Citerior, as a new Roman province, had only been formed in 197 BCE – four years after the end of the Second Punic War in 201 BCE – and what we might call 'the rules of engagement' with the local population and oligarchies meant a very permissive approach to governance. Crucial to success or otherwise was the character, attitude and ambitions of the person now in charge of the province. It was not until Cicero, some 150 years later and, prophetically with the support of Cato the Younger, that a series of scandalous court cases against unscrupulous governors of provincial commands led to some sort of codification and guidance being put in place.

A second point to recognise at this stage is that, while Rome had acquired significant tracts of land from Carthage by dint of defeating them in war, the ruling classes and the people of Rome – the decision makers – were still wondering what benefits would flow, as opposed to the problems and new costs of administration of these new territories. There was no Roman administrative structure worth speaking of at this time – roads and communications were rudimentary, crime, ambushes and revolts by local tribes were commonplace, tax collectors were murdered while they were still working out what areas they were 'farming', and local inhabitants had to learn a new language for trade, for legal disputes, and for simple discussions with their new rulers. Writing between c. 165 and 235 CE, the historian Lucius Cassius Dio wrote in his *Histories of Rome* that the people of Hispania Citerior came from many different tribes that had no common language and nor did they share any form of common government, which gives a flavour of the measure of the tasks ahead for successive governors of the province.[17] This was a pattern to be repeated elsewhere in the embryonic empire.

Just as importantly the local nobility and influential power brokers in what had been a Carthaginian state now had to adjust to a whole new way of doing business – working with Romans – and this required a whole new approach. From the earliest days of the growing empire, we can see that Rome relied on supporting local oligarchs if they wanted a successful and peaceful period in office. Local oligarchies were an essential tool of control and administration – why reinvent the wheels of administration if it was not necessary? This of course meant that some provincial governors were more adept at working with their real masters in their province than others, as we shall see, but equally many local rulers saw this as a chance to reclaim their independence and influence and so, with control over a new province, came provincial rebellions.

The third aspect to bear in mind is how Cato saw the development of empire once his term had been completed. It is certain that his period as provincial governor would have opened his eyes not only to the problems of managing imperial possessions but also the advantages for Rome. He was by all accounts ruthless. In Book 34 of his History of Rome, Livy recounted how:

> *'He* [Cato] *proceeded to Spain and pacified Nearer Spain [Hispania Citerior] in a war that broke out at Emporiae … Several colonies were founded. Marcus Porcius Cato triumphed over Spain …'*[18]

But a more expansive account was written by Plutarch in his *Life of Cato the Elder* which adds to the colour of Cato's complex, often insensitive and brutal personality, and therefore how he was to treat his new Province.[19] If Cato was typical of the Roman senator of his time, then it is no surprise that he arrived with subjugation on his mind. His predecessors since 206 BCE had been fighting many of the local tribes and Scipio Africanus had advised the Senate that Hispania Citerior and Ulterior needed firm handling and that troops needed stationing there permanently. Just prior to Cato's arrival a Roman Army under the command of Gaius Sempronius Tuditanus had been routed by a combination of local tribes and the praetor killed in action – initially these provinces were praetorian commands until Rome had made all the necessary changes required to make them consular commands. New forces were sent and the alarm bells rang in Rome amongst those who professed concern about imperial expansion, whether it be planned, by chance or reactive.

At the end of 196 Livy tells us that a proconsul was dispatched to calm and control the province and, with his military background and determined, authoritarian demeanour, they selected Cato the Elder. His journey therefore was as part of two legions and 15,000 loyalist local infantry plus twenty ships that were sent. Of the two available routes, Cato selected the sea route and landed first near the base of the Pyrenees at Rhoda (modern Rosas), where he threw out the local Hispanic garrison, and then again by ship to Emporiae (Ampurias).

Rosas (Roses in Catalan) is located on the Costa Brava in Catalonia, Spain. To the north is the home of Salvador Dali some 22km in Cadaqués. Originally like most communities in the south, it was founded by Greeks as a trading colony and developed links with the already established port of Marseilles. Roman remains can be seen from the second century BCE, indicating that a Roman presence arrived quite late and was coterminous with the new period of imperial expansion. There is a small museum in the town with numerous Roman artefacts.

Having drilled his troops, one presumes in the vicinity of Rosas, in how he wanted them to fight, Cato then advanced and as Livy says '*spread terror and flight in all directions*'. Roman rule arrived in all its glorious barbarity – in the area of southern Catalonia villages were burned, fields plundered, inhabitants murdered and prisoners sold into slavery – any conceptions that the arrival of Roman rule would bring culture, civilisation and peace were quickly dispelled and we must be under no illusions that, while these things did happen in time, it was to take decades and even centuries for this to unfold. Cato returned to Rome to a Triumph – the traditional and highest honour for a victorious general, but he left behind simmering anger, discontent, famine and resentment, as well as many who had lost everything to the looting carried out by the soldiers with Cato's blessing. In these events we have the enduring conundrum of how we see Roman rule in provincial governance – how could a man so blessed in learning, skilled in oratory and the law, determined to conserve the honour and legitimacy of the past in Roman history, a family man, an honourable man, still command such savage armies and actions on those Rome was supposed to be adding to her empire? This dichotomy of values is all the harder for us to understand as we view them through the prism of twenty-first century values, with liberal sensitivities to woke issues and concepts of justice. To Cato there was no dichotomy and the provinces of Rome had many painful lessons to learn before they could understand the answers.

One part of the relatively short-term efforts to establish longer term control was the founding of colonies. As Livy tells us, colonies were formed wherever Romans went and these were often places selected for their strategic importance and settled by simply taking land from local people and giving it to retired or retiring legionaries. These *coloniae* sprouted all over the Roman world and it is through these new settlements that Romanisation partly began – this was true in Hispania Citerior, as it would be in the new province of Gallia Narbonensis. Cities taken by force were simply handed over to local Roman control, men who had decided that their fighting days were over or who had come to the end of their service and found a place in which they wished to settle and live out their days. They constructed local Roman rule and processes, dealt with local disturbances and welcomed new troops and commanders each year as they arrived for their turn.

But a return to his homes in and around Rome did not mean that Cato had finished with Carthage. The Carthaginians may have lost almost everything to Rome who, by 150 BCE, was the dominant power of the Western Mediterranean, but Carthage itself was still intact. A strongly fortified city that had never fallen, and with a menacing fleet still to protect it, Carthage continued to be a thorn in Rome's side. Unlike previous Roman approaches to expansion which are uncertain, hidden and shrouded in smoke and mirrors, we can see a clear policy developing to deal with Carthage. Both Polybius and later writers taking Polybius's work at face value, seeing the Roman senate as simply waiting for a pretext to finally finish Carthage once and for all. Cato's *Ficus* or fig was a symbolic act to the senate – if they thought Carthage was no longer a threat, they were wrong. If a fig from North Africa could fall from his toga onto the floor of the Senate in Rome and still be fresh to eat, then Carthage was too close an enemy to ignore – '*Ceterum censeo Carthaginem esse delendam*' – 'Furthermore, I advise that Carthage must be destroyed.'

The questions for us are numerous. It seems likely now that Rome was indeed practising defensive imperialism – seeking out threats to the future political and strategic hegemony that they desired. This was quite new in its apparent openness. A senator persuading the senate to exploit any failing in their enemy may not have been new, but it was now a policy – and a policy of going to war was again a new dimension for Rome – dispelling risks and sensing their superior might and willpower to fight.

Then there was the way Carthage was dealt with. Once the Roman forces arrived, upwards of 50,000 Carthaginians are thought to have died, either in battle or of starvation. The city, with centuries of history, heritage and the culture of the Phoenicians was burned to the ground and apparently the fields for hundreds of acres all around were sown with salt so that they could never be used again to provide food for the local population. Those that were left were savagely treated and sold into slavery. Carthage was erased from the map of living cities and its ruins sit there today as totemic images of the barbarity that Rome could employ against those it had decided were its enemies.

> '*Even in retrospect, Roman authors did not conceive of their city's rise to dominance as the result of a policy, let alone as the result of greed or ambition, but rather the reward of virtue and wise decision-making, along with the favour of the gods and the occasional piece of good fortune.*'

This is how Neville Morley in his work *The Roman Empire* assesses how historians of the era understood the actions of their forbears. Almost 100 years on from the destruction of Carthage, Cicero was vociferous in underlining this view and extolling the virtues of past heroes of the Republic who, in his eyes, evolved an empire not in defence of Rome but of its allies. In *De Officiis*, Cicero tells his son Marcus that it was the highest duty and ambition of magistrates and generals to defend the provinces and allies with justice and honour.[20] Again, we must be wary of evaluating how accurate this assessment was with our twenty-first-century passions and values, but it does seem to me that there is something of the hyperbole of self-delusion to see the destruction of whole populations and their erasure from history as justice. Furthermore, to attempt to persuade an entire national audience that everything they did was honourable, was as inversely dishonourable as writing a 'moral' guide with this perverted sense of superiority for one's own son.

There is one final potential motive for early Republican imperialism worth exploring – if for no other reason than it could be the moving target we have been looking for by way of a convincing explanation for the expansion and creation of the Roman empire.

Part II

The Conquest and Settlement of Gallia Narbonensis

Chapter 6

Economic Opportunities and Political Realities

Avaritia v. Magnificentia

Greed was not endemic to Roman society but it grew in abundance in direct proportion to the increasing availability of wealth flowing from imperial possessions. The French philosopher Voltaire said that: *'Men hate the individual whom they call avaricious only because nothing can be gained from him'*. For Voltaire, all men were out to gain from all others and we have in that quotation the essential ingredient of greed – hatred. In Republican Rome it was a hatred of losing one's place in the social order that was the driving energy behind the greed that was such a large component of the dynamics that drove imperial expansion.

There is no agreed starting point where we can point to for evidence of a changing nature amongst Roman men of power and influence, where *luxuria*, *avaritia* and greed replaced honour, duty and loyalty. To help us narrow down the centuries, we can draw on the work of Livy, whose first fifty books dealt with the history of Rome from the earliest times through to the fall of Carthage but thereafter he devoted his time to assessing the history of the fall of The Republic. It was as if Livy saw business as usual in the Roman Republic until their final victory over their great rival and then it was the start of the decline of Rome. Historians across the centuries have devoted vast volumes to research and innumerable books sit on the shelves of libraries around the world dedicated to the task of understanding exactly why it was that the Roman Republic collapsed, but could it really be that the fall of Carthage opened the gates to the unbridled greed of man on such a scale that it consumed an entire

> The ruins of the city of Carthage can be seen in a series of sites outside the city of Tunis. Before the Romans destroyed the city in 146 BCE, Carthage was a wonder of the ancient world containing centuries of Phoenician history, culture and trade from across the Mediterranean. Less popular to visit than those cities such as Rome, it equals Athens in its grandeur even now. Its UNESCO World Heritage status means that the site is well preserved and visitor friendly.

state and political system or was it just a natural step in a development that had been long under way?

The avarice of man has been in evidence since the earliest times and the Bible would be a far shorter book if it did not moralise on greed in all its forms. Greed was not a new phenomenon in Rome; far from it, it was an essential component of the thirst for political power – it was the scale of greed that was new. The acquisition of vast new imperial territories opened up new horizons of understanding of what the true power and wealth of Rome could be. The traditional value system of familial history and birth became eroded by the power that came with wealth to infect concepts of merit. New sources of wealth created new men of power – the two did not need to go together, but they grew like giant leeches around, through and into the decent men in the senate. Bribery in political elections was also not new. What was new was the scale that these bribes could now take – instead of influencing a portion of the crowd or a certain voting tribe, why not bribe the entire electorate?

For Morley this new relationship can be put into simple terms: the cycle of accumulation of the Roman elite:

> *'The ultimate goal was family power and prestige: material resources were accumulated as a means of gaining status and, especially, of gaining the opportunity for military glory by holding political office; political and military power were used as a means of accumulating material resources. There was no logical end to the cycle, no point at which a family or individual might conclude that they had amassed sufficient wealth and honours, only an incessant comparison with the success of other families and other individuals in accumulation.'*[21]

In respect of 'incessant comparison' it was not just the individual head of the family that made these assessments but also the wives and indeed the children. For Fulvia, living in the first half of the first century BCE, it was probably the power and wealth of each of her three husbands that attracted her. We know so little about the power women of ancient Rome, but we can imagine only too well how, some of them at least, drove their husbands on to greater glory in pursuit of greater prestige for themselves and the family. For children too, especially the young men of the second and first centuries BCE, the comparative wealth of their family compared to others was now an important consideration as to whether they could hold their heads up high in society or compete for electoral success. At one time, their birth guaranteed their place on the first rung of the *cursus honorum*, but times were changing and now it was not automatic but based on the grubbiness of money. The sons of wealthier men without status but with huge financial power were now propelled forward at faster rates into the legions as young tribunes and onto the *cursus honorum*. If wealth lay in conquering overseas lands, then that is what had to happen.

Greed therefore began to fundamentally distort Roman society and the objectives of the classes. Merit alone would not be enough – even the highest birth was no longer a guarantee of success, as it was wealth that became the determining force. It was thinking of this kind that created much of the early hatred for the Republic that infected the spleen and psychological state of mind of young ambitious and envious men like Publius Clodius Pulcher, Julius Caesar, and hundreds if not thousands of young, ambitious men who saw their futures thwarted by a lack of substantial family fortunes. Such feelings of injustice and the disproportionate allocation of wealth drove wedges between the traditional class structures and accepted norms of social harmony.

In Cicero's lifetime, spanning the last century of the Republic, he was to witness men like Clodius and, more violently, Catiline not only threaten the new financial classes and the state itself, but also gather around them in protection, anger and rebellion dozens of similarly displaced young nobles and aristocrats. It was greed and the inequalities of the distribution of the new wealth of empire that created this seismic division, and senators like Cicero were not blind to the ravages of greed and jealousy and what these new emotions were inflicting on the stability of the state. Cicero spoke in glorious eloquence about the madness of these young men in his *Catilinarian Orations*. When Cicero spoke, all men listened and his attack on Catiline was a vehicle for his attack on the changes he was witnessing all around: '*Shame on the age and on its principles*'.[22] So spoke Cicero, and when Cicero spoke men also wondered who he was going to attack. Cicero's career ascended to a point in the 60s BCE where he was not only acknowledged as the greatest orator of his time but also with proconsular authority. He knew the senate; he was sensitive to its growing impotence and lust for money, and he was therefore also aware of how he felt the Republic needed his leadership to block further decline:

> '*...he* [Catiline] *is watching and marking down and checking off for slaughter every individual among us [the senate]. And we, gallant men that we are, think that we are doing our duty to the republic if we keep out of the way of his frenzied attacks*'.[23]

For his part, Catiline was a divisive and scandalous figure and his leadership of the attempted rebellion against the moneyed classes was always tainted by his more scandalous background, but he was remembered well by the poor for his sacrifice on the battlefield in the name of greater equality and this was a reflection of the changing times brought by empire. Catiline's dreams of righting the perceived wrongs of greed, political power and *luxuria* amongst few hands ended in death on the battlefield of Pistoia in Tuscany, where Catiline was found near his standard surrounded by his followers. What Mary Beard calls a 'clash between ideology and ambition' might also be seen a clash between preservation and modernisation.

Rebellion, resentment and death were just some of the effects that stemmed from the replacement of codes of morality and conduct, across the whole of Roman society, by those ignited by *luxuria* and *avaritia* in the post-Carthaginian imperial era. This is not to suggest that a desire for luxury, money and prestige had not always been there, of course they had, but, for the vast majority of Romans, they were unobtainable as lifestyle choices – indeed they were not a choice – until the arrival of Empire, when the equal potential for sloth and luxury amongst the governing classes permeated down to distort traditional Roman values. Governors were not immune to the lure of the treasures of imperial expansion – take for example the prosecution of Verres as governor of Sicily as R.T. White pointed out in his article on the Luxury at Rome:

> *'The critique of luxury is exemplified quite early in the first century* BCE *by Cicero's attack on Verres. Verres was accused of 'acquiring' a vast range of artworks and precious luxury objects both from private individuals and – even worse – from temple buildings and their treasuries, and keeping them for his own private use.'*[24]

But Verres was part of a trend, not an aberration. Many contemporary writers, poets and historians of the times littered their discourses with words and phrases associated with luxury – the rhetoric of Cicero was not alone in mentioning greed (*avaritia*), drunkenness (*ebrietas*), vulgar ostentation (*etra modum sumpta et magnicentia*), corruption (*licentia*), effeminacy (*militia*) and debauchery (*stuprum flagitium*). It is also possible that the majority of trading goods tended towards luxury items the larger the empire became – Rome could feed itself but was a glutton for marble, gold, Greek sculptures and luxurious precious stones from Egypt. Even Pliny the Elder was able to identify the start of this drift into a demand for luxurious goods from overseas when he spoke of amber, pearls, silk, exotic timbers, exotic beasts for the arena, jewellery, spices, pepper, slaves (especially educated ones such as doctors, teachers, cooks, scribes and translators) and of course art. Another contemporary history book, The Holy Bible, talks in Revelations of Babylon the Great, ie. Rome, as: 'The great consumer of cinnamon, and odours, and ointments, and frankincense, and wine, and oil, and fine flour, and wheat, and beasts, and sheep, and horses, and chariots, and slaves and the souls of men'.[25]

Opportunity for Acquisition

Apart from the jealousy and envy aroused amongst the poorer nobility and aristocracy, there were many other ripple effects stemming from the destruction of Carthage and the inheritance of vast new imperial territories. The pace of economic change was already increasing well before the final fall of Carthage, and to the east Rome viewed another major rival amongst the Greek City States – Macedon. The legacy of Philip and Alexander, fourth-century Kings of Macedon, was strong and throughout the third and second century BCE, Roman armies had been engaged in a series of attempts to either pacify, defeat or police a series of kingdoms in Illyria. Eminent historians such as E.H. Scullard saw these policies as reactive and having no imperialistic designs across the Adriatic, while others view these measures as consciously-planned steps to dominate the Greek peninsula.[26] Whatever the lack of consensus in this area, the outright defeat of Macedon by the armies of Rome in 167 BCE placed Rome on the threshold of wholesale changes in society, culture, politics and history.

These matters are important and, while this is not a book on the economic impact of empire, we do need to be able to reflect on the backdrop that a new imperial demand and energy gave to the settlement and control of new provinces such as Gallia Narbonensis. We would do well to remind ourselves that the Roman people, at all levels, may have lived in a different age, spoken a different language and have a myriad of different customs, but they were still people very similar to us. Their emotions on family, friendship, parenthood, death and all the other emotions of humanity were the same as our own. By extension, therefore, just because these chapters seem to identify greed as all-consuming it does not follow that greed consumed all. Just as in our own world, there are many whose lifelong motivation is the acquisition of wealth, it is all they live for, but they are not typical of the majority. So, in the era of Roman history the same was true. What is also a fact is that when the opportunity for new and fantastic plunder came along – whether in Iraq in 2003 or Macedonia in the mid-second century BCE – there were many whose lust became heightened to a whole new degree and who shared the same motivations of avarice and greed despite the gap of two thousand years.

Just as we have members in every culture and society in the world today who feel the need to display their wealth and luxury, so too did the Romans – but there was a difference. The Roman *domus* or home was more or less open all the time and very public in character. The client-based system of order and obligation meant that each morning the homes of the wealthy and famous would be opened at dawn to welcome the arrival of visitors on all manner of business, and these may have been making calls across a number of homes throughout the morning. This is where the real work of the day was done – in the *atriums* and hallways, in the gardens and on the terraces – gossip exchanged, meetings planned, coups organised, letters agreed, endorsements received, trials discussed and all manner of political business decided. Consequently, even Cicero recognised the need to display his power, wealth and ostentatious ownership. The X or Instagram of the day – the Roman baths – would be dominated by gossip over the latest fashions that were seen in a home either at the morning *salutatio* or at the evening dinner. The demand for objects of luxury increased with the size and wealth of Rome, and the demand was insatiable.

Consequently, the end of the Third Macedonian War in 168 BCE, not only saw over 70 Greek cities sacked and plundered with the full permission of the senate, but also vast amounts of booty taken from royal palaces and treasuries being taken to Rome. It is estimated that over 120 million sesterces flooded into the Roman treasury, and thereafter out into investment in the growing empire. Many officers and men were made fantastically wealthy by this event, which laid the foundation for the attitude against Carthage only twenty years later, and the combination of these two successful wars changed Roman history forever and would, in turn, have a profound effect on Gallia Narbonensis in the coming years. But there were still other attractions for a successful expansion of empire.

Military Experience and Political Advancement

Earlier we established the fact that political success increasingly became dependent on the ability to bribe. Coupled with this was the long-established need for military or political experience in the empire. These two expectations now created a constant demand for service overseas, either in one of the older or newer provinces of the empire or by serving on a campaign to conquer new territory – or at least quell any disturbances or rebellions within them. One such young man who served Caesar was Gn. Sallustius Crispus – the Roman historian Sallust – and he wrote often on the demands of young nobles carving out a career.[27] Any young man hoping for a political career on the *cursus honorum* had already been indoctrinated with the ideas of service to the state and the requirement for glory:

> *'As soon as the young men could endure the hardships of war, they were taught a soldier's duties in camp under a vigorous discipline, and they took more pleasure in handsome arms and war horses than in harlots and revelry. To such men consequently no labour was unfamiliar, no region too rough or too steep, no armed enemy was terrible; courage was everything. Their hardest struggle was*

> *with each other; each man strove to be the first to strike down the foe, to scale a wall, to be seen by all while doing such a deed. This they considered virtue, this fair fame and high nobility.*'[28]

The battle-hardened centurions of the republican legions were set the task of making men out of noble boys, and the boys led the rest of their lives in awe and respect for the Legions that took and created the lands for them to govern in later lives. In the same way, the non-commissioned officers of armies of the last 2,000 years have emulated the Roman model, with men of the Landsknechts in the Swiss guard of the sixteenth century, the Krieg Schule in Prussia in the nineteenth century, or West Point and Sandhurst today putting the young men of good or noble background through various versions of misery to toughen them up for political life.

The increasing need for junior roles in a legion was met by the increasing demand for men to police and govern the new provinces – with the increasing wealth of Rome this was something that was going to become a problem after the Augustan period and the first century CE. This mutually complementary relationship ensured that not only did the army grow, but that it also became more professional with the retention of experienced men, part of the substantial Marian reforms of the 90s BCE, now being funded by the vast resources and funding of the state. No longer did legions get disbanded after service, but they established their own existence, battle honours and legends. For the very committed and very talented, youthful exuberance and survival could lead to a military career before entering politics – even rising to the rank of military tribune after around ten years before taking the first step onto the *cursus* as quaestor. Thus, military service needed military opportunity and the intention was to sustain the honourable, courageous and loyal nature of senatorial ranks – the intention lasted many years but not forever. Military service interspersed with political appointments was not uncommon and not only did the empire provide for both, but also supplied the opportunity for glory and wealth to attract support for the highest office of all – a consulship in one of the two positions available each year. Ultimate glory came with the senate awarding the magistrate or general a Triumph through the streets of Rome and into the heart of the city – the forum itself.

The *Fasti Capitolini* were a series of engraved marble tablets discovered in the forum in the 1540s. These preserved records were once on public display and updated every year in the *forum Romanum* at the core of the empire. These tablets form one of the core sources of chronology for the study of Republican history, but alongside these were also discovered the *Fasti Triumphales*. This later group of tablets, with some exceptions, record every Triumph awarded down to

19 BCE. A study of this later group provides vast amounts of information – most notably how the empire was growing, where the new campaigns were being fought, the peoples being defeated, and the gradual increase in military actions overseas. The *Fasti Triumphales* are in fact a window into the military campaigns of Rome and evidence of the sustained growth of empire where election to the highest offices depended on financial resources, but also on popularity with the people of Rome. Military success was popular and commemorated with the building of new temples, the building of triumphal arches, and the dedication of new altars to give thanks to the Gods.

Although we cannot point directly at what the mass of the Roman people felt about war, they certainly saw the benefits and the glorification and occasionally deification of their leaders as a direct result of success in war. The Triumphal procession was not just about celebrating the hero. In the columns that followed him were successful legionaries, heroic centurions, popular officers, and thousands and thousands of newly-taken prisoners soon to become slaves. Within the majesty and iconography of the procession, paid for by the person awarded the Triumph by the senate, were blatant references to what power and military might could achieve. All powerful Kings of realms were now in chains to Roman superiority, the people could rally to join the army where they too could earn their own glory and turn an ordinary life into an extraordinary one somewhere in the existing empire or in a new part soon to be added by conquest. Hitherto, the Roman senate had been careful not to commit to war, to arrange treaties, to agree to mutually-beneficial annexation where local rulers wanted the protection of Rome to maintain their stay in power, or alliances against a common enemy, but increasingly Rome became dragged into wars and found herself benefitting beyond their dreams of avarice. Thus, imperial concerns also began to make up more of the daily business of the senate until the concerns of Rome, its people or the people of Italy had to shout to be heard.

The Rise of the *Equites*

Further economic considerations of the causes of Republican imperial expansion are evident in the rise of the *equites*. At one time, the primary role of these larger landowners whose social position was just below the senatorial class, was to provide cavalry for the army. As trained and skilled horsemen, they were the equivalent of the medieval Knight and they carried out many feudal-based functions for their overlords, and through smaller magistracies managed the rural and smaller provincial areas throughout Italy. With the growth of the army their numbers became insufficient to provide enough cavalry detachments and, over time, they began to populate the senior officer ranks of the legions where experienced, trained and intelligent officers were always in need.

Conterminously, the *equites* reaped the rewards of fortune when, in 218 BCE, the *lex Claudia* restricted the commercial opportunities available to senators – feeling that 'trade' was beneath their dignity. This opened up a wealth of opportunity for investment-minded *equites* that stemmed from the new provinces. Equestrians very quickly became the dominant tax collectors in the provinces – becoming known as *publicani* – they also invested their reserves into mining copper, gold and silver, buying out the local mine owners – or simply forcing them out of business. Shipping, road building, brick making and the huge logistical costs of supporting each legion now became profitable businesses for the *equites*. The gap between the senatorial class and more ambitious *equites/publicani* closed and the latter were often to be found pressing, bribing or intimidating provincial governors to allow them to raise local taxes and live in great splendour – they fulfilled valuable functions and were richly rewarded for their service. Imperialism suited them well and some even had their eye on political power at the very highest levels. In time *equites* wore their own version of the senatorial tunica under their toga with their own single red stripe (the *tunica angusticlavia*) very similar to the broad stripe of a senator. Political power struggles between the two classes in Rome naturally developed, and they became ardent supporters of wars and the imperialist policies from which they would benefit further.

In the speeches of Cicero, an equestrian himself, we can often see traces of sympathy if not blatant bias towards the equestrian order. Cicero was criticised for being of humble birth, as certain members of the aristocratic orders saw it, and he was at the forefront of trying to represent his order whilst at the same time becoming a member of the senatorial class – an almost impossible task. By the time that Augustus took power and the era of the Principate replaced the Republic, there was an urgent need to realign the classes, so Augustus introduced a series of reforms that created a chasm for equestrians to jump should they wish to join the ranks of senators.

Commercialism

Given that the Roman economy was founded on forced labour, another economic necessity and driver for expansion was slavery. Estimates vary between 10 and 30 per cent for the number of slaves that made up the total population in the later republican period. One of the factors that was a key player in the increase in personal wealth was the availability of slave labour, and with increased imperial provinces came captives, sometimes tens of thousands, who were then sold into slavery.

But the mercantile class were not just interested in buying and selling slaves. Merchants followed the legions into new territories or stayed with them in old ones, they built roads, aqueducts, baths and spas, taverns, stables, brick-making sheds, marble extraction mines, ran sandal-making shops, mass-produced weapons for the new legions, or replaced those lost in battle; they made helmets, manufactured steel, sold jewellery, ointments, statues, good luck charms; they provided services such as writing and carrying mail, stone masons were needed everywhere to note mileposts, engrave funeral stones, erect arches – the list is almost endless and the empire needed more of everything.

In the nineteenth century, eminent historians such as Mommsen were convinced that the demands of the merchants throughout Italy pressed on the senate to go further and to open up and thus exploit more territories. How far and how fast this happened is a point of conjecture as the evidence is scant but again, archaeology is adding to our knowledge and each generation of researchers is adding to our core knowledge. To what extent Romans saw themselves as commercial is another key question – we know for example that many, but not all, of the senatorial class looked down on trade and dirtying their hands with making money:

> *'A state that would prohibit its nobility from engaging in carrying on trade could hardly be called a commercial nation.'*[29]

Nevertheless, the senators were not averse to making money through conquest, nor did they hold back from almost extinguishing the small peasant farmer in Italy itself by creating massive landholding estates. Perhaps it was a case of their public protestations and their private actions. The process of expansion quickened as the Republic aged and was especially prevalent in the last century of its life, when barriers and social expectations and propriety were a thing of the past. There were also prime movers in the commercial sector, increasing numbers too as the Republic neared its end, and the 'richest man in Rome' created much of his wealth in the first century BCE by exploiting trading in property and loans – Marcus Licinius Crassus. It was no mistake that Crassus, Pompey and Caesar created their political alliance – the First Triumvirate – because of their huge financial power. Caesar and Pompey inherited some but the majority of their wealth had come in war and the exploitation of victory in far flung provinces – this was considered noble. Crassus was a trader – irrespective of his noble birth, his money came from unrivalled commercial success.

So, we have a mixed picture, but it is most likely true that commercialism took off randomly and at different rates depending on the character of individual personalities living at the time. Floods of traders followed each legion, sometimes died with them if they lost a battle deep inside enemy territory, but a victorious campaign would soon see couriers riding hard back to Rome in haste asking for more trading goods to be sent – or indeed road contracts to be negotiated for routes into new provincial honeypots. New roads, built by entrepreneurial merchants using the slave labour from the captured areas, were vital if trade, communications or the movement of the army were to flourish, and these were huge investment endeavours similar to our motorways, freeways or autobahns today.

Merchants have existed as long as man has been able to walk and there would have been an uneasy tension between the old conservative values of the past, where Romans liked money but did not want to be seen indulging in making it, or the new opportunities that the empire provided. It is Polybius who continues to remind those who read his legacy, that the senate was especially sensitive to public relations and image at home and abroad and they were always reluctant to be seen as an immoral aggressor – the good opinion of the civilized world was vital to their sense of honour and *fides*, and despite pressures from *equites* or merchants they were not going to allow their decisions to be regarded as based on greed.

Another fact worth noting at this point is that, once a new province had been established – either through war, treaty or alliance – commercial exploitation both by the political class and the mercantile class had a free reign to grab what they could while they could. Hence it is no coincidence that Cicero and Cato the Younger devoted much of their popularity into becoming unpopular by their reforms designed to make the Roman administration of the provinces fairer and to attack those whose exploitation was the most grotesque.

Taxation as a Motive for Expansion

One of the remaining economic motivations for imperial expansion was the almost infinite potential for taxation. In the early centuries of the Republic taxation seems to have had a gentle touch within Italy ranging from a simple 1 per cent to 3 per cent in time of war in order to equip and provide for the armies raised for a particular campaign. Naturally with the expansion of the empire and the creation of a large standing army of legions, this was simply not going to be anywhere enough income for the state.

One of the many changes in both republican and imperial taxation came via the move from taxation on wealth and property and instead to direct taxation on personal income under Augustus. The administrative foundation for this was the census, and by the first century CE the Roman census was in full operation, enshrined as it is in the Christian Bible.[30] This is not to say that taxation was a homogenous exercise – it certainly was not. Indeed, the raising of revenues was highly permissive, often based on the character of the province and their willingness to pay. Many other factors played into the efficiency of tax collection. The early years of imperial rule were characterised by slow moving administrative processes – even finding good administrators was a challenge, and finding good and honest ones even harder. This made the early Roman empire highly inefficient in contrast to popular portrayals of Roman organisation. Tax collection was heterogeneous, convoluted, open to abuse, and complicated, and this must sit at the background of our understanding of how many decades it would take for the Roman empire to create a Roman administrative system worth its name.

As the empire grew, it was to be the *publicani* that benefited most from taxation – certainly up to the Augustan reforms based on the individual census. These men or groups of businessmen turned up at well-advertised auctions in order to bid substantial amounts for the state contract to collect the taxes. A risky venture depending on their ability to squeeze revenues out of the unwilling, but the rewards could be substantial. The money paid at auction for a contract was in fact a loan to the state which was claimed back from the money they collected. In addition, they were allowed to charge interest on this loan which was again payable from the taxes they collected. It was commonplace therefore for there to be a close partnership between the provincial governor and the *publicani*, often based on greed and bribery, and, with the backing of the governor, there was virtually no limit on the methods that could be used to exact the taxes. There were endless disputes regarding all aspects of tax farming, not least of which was where the civic districts began and ended – to sit in the centre of a disputed area meant tax being collected by competing groups or individuals. Cities were not exempt from this and they too needed clarity of where they sat within the new provincial estate. Over time, it would even be left to the emperor himself to often mediate or arbitrate over boundary disputes, as well as set the momentum for improved levels of efficiency and the eradication of financial corruption – something the Roman state never achieved.

The contradictions between Roman justice, peace and good government, and the systematic enslavement of the provinces are prime examples of the dichotomy between the oft-lauded glory of Rome and the reality for its subjects, who were often exploited, abused and ignored.

The ending of tax farming by Augustus heralded the new age of taxation on personal income and this not only became a very painful process for many wealthy Roman citizens, but also a very expensive one to administer creating even higher demands for income. The heady days of exploiting the gold and silver mines of Hispania could not last forever, inflation returned and became a new terror for the state, and debasement of the coinage followed in an effort to maintain economic stability. Many taxes came and went across the expanding empire but the thirst for income to sustain the ever-increasing state was unquenchable. In Gallia Narbonensis, as elsewhere, Roman administration developed as best that it could, centred around Narbo Martius, modern day Narbonne, and the residence of the governor.

Slavery

Given that the success of the Roman economy was founded on forced labour, another economic necessity and therefore motivation for further expansion was slavery. Roman society was built upon a range of foundations, one of which was the pivotal role that slavery played in the economic and social structure of the Republic – estimates vary between 15 and 30 per cent, or around ten million, as the proportion of slaves out of the total population in the later Republican period.

In his 1980 article on the Roman slave trade, William Harris theorised that the growing empire had an ongoing annual need for 500,000 new slaves each year to replace the high mortality rates in slave labour.[31] Harsh conditions building roads and tilling fields across the provinces, as well as the average age of death being between 20 and 25 years of age, meant that the death rates amongst slaves were staggeringly high. Only those sold into slavery in the wealthier families could expect a longer life, especially if they had an educated background, and this group also could be the beneficiaries of manumission – freedom into Roman society with Roman citizenship.

The demand for slaves in ever increasing numbers was serviced by a range of suppliers but by far the largest numbers flooded into the various market places from victory in war. Cicero himself left us a clear example of enslavement as a direct result of victory in one of his letters to his close friend, confessor and ally, Titus Pomponius Atticus. Of the thirty-two letters he wrote to Atticus in this one-year period as Governor of Cilicia between 51-50 BCE, Cicero exposes his own dissatisfaction with being away from Rome, which he sees as a second exile, but also takes the opportunity afforded to him to dispense justice fairly yet also to make money. Cilicia was hardly a plum appointment for the man who proclaimed himself as having saved the Republic from collapse, but it was still an opportunity to add military glory to his already full list of legal and political achievements. Equally important as anything else, Cicero writes about the appalling, exhausted state of the province that he inherited from his awkward and testy predecessor Appius, and again this gives us a valuable insight into Roman provincial government, first hand and through the eyes of a participant.

Thus, Cicero led his small legionary army to a number of victorious engagements against the partisans and tribesmen of the mountainous regions to the east of his province – the people Atticus called mountain bandits but whose image Cicero polished up into *Eleutherocilices* – 'Free Cilicians'. Successful, but not enough to secure a Triumph in Rome – much to his chagrin despite considerable efforts to pave the way with his colleagues in the Roman senate – Cicero relates to Atticus how he had reduced a series of strongholds and taken Pindenissum. His letters to Cato and the two consuls for 50 BCE, Marcellus and Paulus, dripped with intimations of how he deserved a Triumph, how his victories were to be equated with any other great general, and must have almost been seen as comic in their desperation; he recognised that time was not on his side, especially if the Parthian threat further to the east became real – that would have been a real test:

> '*hanc gloriam iustitiae et abstinentiae fore inlustriorem spero si cito decesserimus*': '*I hope that this glory of fairness and self-restraint* [in his administration of justice] *will shine the more brilliantly if I do get quickly out of here.*'[32]

In his private correspondence to Atticus, letters that he never dreamt would be read and preserved for posterity, Cicero bragged that he made 2.2 million sestertii from the campaign and that large numbers of prisoners were sold into slavery – valued at some 12,000 sestertii – depending on the price they fetched per slave, we can estimate numbers were in their thousands, and Cicero provides us with an invaluable opportunity to look at the practice and motivations of Governorship in the provinces to which I will return later in this book. Of course, greater victories over larger, more populous provinces always yielded greater numbers of salves. The third and final defeat of Corinth saw some 50,000 people sold into slavery, but this was easily eclipsed by the crushing of the Jews by Vespasian and Titus in 66-70 CE, which yielded 97,000 – this according to Josephus (B.J. 6.9.3) – while Trajan's Dacian wars produced 400-500,000. Thus, slavery was not only a vital sub-structure of the Roman economic model, but was also hugely profitable, allowing for free labour to subsidise both state and public ventures and capitalism.

Chapter 7

The Early Foundations of the Province, 118–27 BCE

Geography

The earliest references to settlements in southern France are Greek in origin. The Mediterranean was dominated by Greeks and Phoenician traders long before the Romans became a major power, and it was Greek and Phoenician settlements that originated along the length of the southern coasts of France. In his 1988 detailed analysis of the settlements of this region, A.L.F Rivet lays out the approximate boundaries of the area which later was to become the Roman province of Gallia Narbonensis – Rivet emphasizes the logical extent of what would become the new Roman province by referring to the physical geography of southern France.[33]

To the north are the mountains of the Massif Central, and more specifically the southern region of the Massif known as the Cévennes. The Cévennes is characterised by gorges and steep granite schists, high forests and fault lines. The geology is a mix of granite and limestone through which seven major rivers flow. In pre-Roman times, the Cévennes was home to a number of Gaulish and Celtic tribes of whom the Arverni were one of the most powerful and who lived in the modern Auvergne region, but they were neighbours with others: the Ruteni in the west, the Gabali in the north, the Helvii in the southeast and the Vellavi in the northeast. Together, in the third century BCE, these tribes formed the Arverne Confederation – a defensive alignment of tribes that remained solid for nearly 150 years – it was the Arverni chieftain Vercingetorix that led a major revolt against the presence of the Romans in 52 BCE and whose tribes were eventually defeated by Caesar in his Gallic Wars.

To the east of the region are the Alps. These run northwards from the sea towards central Europe and, with their often deeply snowed-in and frequently impassable valleys which can both defend Italy and prevent her from advancing, they present a major benefit or obstacle to traverse. Along the southern coastline was a series of coastal roads – originally a series of unlinked mountain pathways that was to become the Via Julia Augusta, running from modern Piacenza (Placentia) to Arles (Arelate), west to the edge of the valley of the River Po, then south into the Ligurian coastal area and past Genoa. Thereafter it clings to the mountains through Ventimiglia (Album Intimilium) and through the small but pivotal mountain village of La Turbie (the Triumph) with its impressive Augustan monument overlooking Monaco. Later this road ran all the way to Nice and joined the newly-constructed Via Domitia and so on into Hispania. One can imagine an almost continuous line of traffic trying to navigate this route, ever onwards frantically hugging the sheer cliff faces, with generals, senators, families, slaves, legionaries, wagons, walkers, merchants all gazing eastwards back towards Italy sitting in the azure blue Mediterranean Sea – which was often directly below them too.

To the west are the south-western Pyrenees and here we find more direct references to the presence of the ancient Greeks alongside the Celtic tribes of the valleys and hills. In Greek mythology, Pyrene was a princess whose name was allocated to these mountains. Herodotus, the Greek historian, wrote that there was a town in 'Celtic Europe' called Pyrene and her story is that she was the virgin daughter of a powerful local King named Bebryx who supported Hercules in his famous 'Labours' only to discover she was raped by Hercules. In his grief, Hercules called her name across the land and the mountains returned his cry of 'Pyrene, Pyrene'. The flat-topped mountains spread across the Pyrenees north west to the Bay of Biscay but in the south, where they drift into southern Gaul, the slates, limestone and granite mix of stone have been transformed into marble and, over time, this area would be popular mining territory for Roman businessmen and engineers. The southern Pyrenees also contained numerous hot clear and saline springs much loved by the Romans as grottos, places of worship and enjoyment.

Finally, to the south was the Mediterranean – the cradle of human trade from Africa to Europe and the centre of so many early civilisations. Along the southern coastline of Gaul, hundreds of small inlets provided a home to seafaring communities from the earliest times. By the eighth- and ninth-centuries BCE there were already established trade routes from west to east and back again – not on the scale of future years but certainly not as rare as archaeology once suggested. One of the communities that grew most rapidly was that of the *Massaliotes* – their home was Marseilles and it was here, in one of the dominant deep water ports and trading posts of the whole Mediterranean, that the Roman interest in southern Gaul began.

Towards the end of 221 BCE, the Carthaginian general Hannibal took command of all the forces of Carthage and determined to rid the Mediterranean world of Rome completely. Two years later, once his army had been reorganised, re-equipped and reorientated towards a land-based victory with African elephants in tow, he crossed the River Ebro in Hispania and sacked the city of Saguntum – an ally of Rome – and precipitated the Second Punic War. The Roman senate was in uproar and the Carthaginians had provided the moral groundwork underpinning Roman honour that enabled a war to be declared on Carthage in the name of protecting her allies – a pericentric policy of action. The Roman senate quickly dispatched a high level group of senators to Carthage – numbered amongst the embassy were Q. Fabius, C. Licinius, M. Livius and L. Aemilius – the last two being the most recent consuls of Rome. Livy captured the importance of their mission in his *Ab Urbe Condita* and it is from Book 21 that we can follow events in such detail as to feel so fresh and vibrant despite the 2,000 year gap since he sat, for over thirty years of his life, dictating what he had discovered from Polybius. In Chapter 17 Livy recounts how and why the Romans first made plans to go to war.

First, the usual annual bargaining for the vastly attractive proconsular and provincial appointments for the coming year of 218–217 was completed. Once egos and political infighting had been satisfied, then the senate agreed to the creation of a vast army of six new legions – this involved enrolling and equipping 24,000 volunteers – as well as cavalry made up from volunteers amongst the *equites* to act as officers. To these were added over 200 new ships quickly constructed around the coastline in all of Rome's ports such as Ostia in Rome, Brundisium in the south and Misenum in the centre, and again volunteers asked to enrol as naval crews for the campaigns ahead.

> '*When these arrangements had been made, in order that before going to war, they might observe all the formalities, they dispatched into Africa* [heading for Carthage in Tunisia] *an embassy consisting of certain older men….*'[34]

Livy records that the Carthaginians were unimpressed with the attitude and high-handedness of the Roman delegation and the meetings ended, as they were designed to do, with declarations of war. The Romans had intended the mission as a face-saving propaganda exercise which was vital to their *dignatas* and moral superiority of the Roman cause rather than trying to prevent a war. For our purposes however, interest lies in the next chapter:

> '*The ambassadors, conformably to the instructions given them in Rome, crossed over from Carthage into Spain for the purpose of approaching the different states and winning them to an alliance, or at least detaching them from the Phoenicians* [Carthaginians].'[35]

Part of the Roman interest in this region stemmed from their need to traverse the mountains and plains of southern France in order to trade and communicate between Italy and Spain, but at the time of the Punic Wars it made strategic sense to be able to hold up any enemy approaching from the west by having alliances or at the very least agreements with the many tribes of the region. Livy tells us that the tribes of the Ebro River basin, such as the Bargusii, were welcoming and desired to revolt against the Carthaginians – whether this was through a desire for freedom or as a result of Roman gold it is impossible to know, but the task of gaining allies became far harder as the senators approached the Pyrenees and through into Celtic southern France. Here, according to Livy, they arranged a meeting with one of the larger tribes or nations of the region, the Volciani:

> '*…who gave them an answer that was carried all over Spain and turned all the other states against an alliance with the Romans. For the eldest of them replied as follows in their council: "With what face, Romans, can you ask us to prefer your friendship to the Carthaginian, when those who did so have been more cruelly betrayed by you, their allies, than destroyed by their enemy, the Phoenician? … To the Spanish peoples the ruins of Saguntum will constitute a warning, no less emphatic than deplorable, that none should trust to the honour or alliance of the Romans.*'[36]

Not unsurprisingly it was widely believed that an alliance with Rome could indeed be a protection but at the same time a curse – when Rome went to war it was by no means certain that anyone with an alliance with the Romans would not then become a target themselves – and it was also never certain whether the Romans would actually come to your assistance: '*Accordingly, having traversed that country to no purpose, they passed over into Gaul.*'

If we close our eyes for a moment, perhaps we can picture the next stage of this long, arduous journey for the senators. The warm hot winds of the southern coastal region where one crosses from Spain into Gaul made the air heavy and hard to breathe, slightly tempered at night but so very hot during the day. Their senatorial robes would have been thick with the dust of the journey – these were not Roman roads but worn tracks across rock-strewn fields – their constant sweating having long ago changed the bright white toga to a dusty cream – the shuffle and clanking noise of trudging soldiers who had protected them on this journey accompanied by the steady clop of numerous horses, some carrying officers with their heavy red cloaks and others pulling wagons of supplies, tents, poles and the wooden boxes of wax, wax tablets, paper and ink for the scribes *(scribae)* to do their work in the evenings – writing out messages to friends and family hundreds of miles ahead of them in Rome. Despatch riders arrived at all hours of the day and night having ridden ten or twelve days from Rome;

camp fires and flies, always flies, and innumerable slaves and attendants for each of the signatories on this mission. The volcanic lands in this region of the Spanish/Gaulish border created a dark rolling countryside, hills as far as the eye could see, very little green, hot low hills on one side and the sea breezes on the other that occasionally reached inland. Having completed this next arduous leg of their long journey, safe in the knowledge that Rome was at war and their armies would soon be on the move towards them, the senators:

> '*...beheld a strange and terrifying spectacle, for the Gauls, as was customary with the race, came armed to their assembly. When the envoys, boasting of the renown and valour of the Roman People and the extent of their dominion, requested the Gauls to deny the Phoenician a passage through their lands and cities, if he should attempt to carry a war into Italy, it is said that they burst out into such pearls of laughter that the magistrates and elders could scarce reduce the younger men to order – so stupid and impudent a thing it seemed, to propose that the Gauls should not suffer the invaders to pass into Italy, but bring down the war on their own heads, and offer their own fields to be pillaged in place of other men's. When at last the uproar had been quelled, the Gauls made answer to the envoys that they owed the Romans no kindness, nor the Carthaginians any grudge, to induce them to draw their sword on behalf of the former or against the latter; on the contrary, they heard that men of their own race were being driven from the land and even out of the borders of Italy by the Roman People, and were paying tribute and suffering every other humiliation. In the rest of the Gallic councils their proposals and the replies they got were to substantially the same effect, nor did they hear a single word of a truly friendly or peaceable tenor until they reached Massalia* [Marseilles].[37]

The relevance of these extracts from Livy is that they paint a picture of southern France in the second century BCE that was certainly not Roman and quite largely anti-Roman. Wherever this Roman mission travelled to speak to local chieftains, kings or elders they were met by the same fiercely independent mentality but, more than just a strong sense of courageous strength, there was also a degree of anger. If the Gauls of this region were forced to choose one side or the other, it was likely that it would be the Carthaginians, for these had clearly not given rise to any offence nor had they been systematically ethnically cleansing people of Celtic ancestry out of northern Italy and seizing their lands. The tribes of southern France were well aware of how Romans treated allies – they gradually enslaved them.

Polybius and therefore Livy take any assessment of the Roman imperial foreign policy into a new direction. As dignified and honourable in their decision making with neighbouring peoples that the Romans would like to be seen, we cannot ignore the evidence of Livy compared to the propaganda with which the Romans liked to infuse their history. The accounts of how the Celts in Gaul viewed their Roman neighbours go further and show us that not only was there a strong sense of independence amongst the Celtic peoples of southern France in this period, but also a unity of resistance to Roman influence. This was accompanied by an open and bitter recognition of what the Romans were doing to their brethren only a few hundred miles eastwards in northern Italy. If this area was as important to the future of Rome as it seemed to be, then it would require strong methods to bring the area around to the Roman way of thinking.

Having endured the fruitless meetings with the Gallic tribes of southern France, the long wagon train of the dusty senators had to travel two-thirds of the coastline before, as Livy reports, at last they came across friends in the bustling and culturally diverse port of Massalia. These senior and elderly political leaders of the Roman senate were under no illusions about the enmity of the Celtic areas they had just passed through and they would be able to report this to their friends and colleagues in Rome. But after they had washed, rested and recovered in Massalia, they would also become privy to new information: that these Celtic peoples had already been visited by the Carthaginian generals – some had given their support rather than become an ally of Rome, whilst others had taken Carthaginian gold for their loyalty.

> *'Hannibal had been beforehand with the Romans in gaining the good-will of the Gauls, but that even he would find them hardly tractable – so fierce and untamed was their nature – unless from time to time he should make use of gold, of which the race is very covetous.'*[38]

Resuming their journey back to Rome, at least the climate and geography started to become more welcoming and familiar as their coastal route took them closer to the sea towards Massalia, Toulon, Hyères, St Tropez, Cannes, Antibes, Nice and Monaco before crossing into what would become the new province of the Alpes Maritimes and then into northern Italy, which as the Gallic tribes had already complained, was already absorbed into Italy as Cisalpine (on the Italian side of the Alps) Gaul. Instead of the endlessly hot and dry days, the senators now experienced cooler days, fresher winds, a view of the sea on their right-hand side almost every day, and fresh fish from the local villages, before they finally rode, were carried, or walked what was, at that time, one or other of the few major roads of the Roman world – the Via Cassia from Genoa down the centre of the peninsula, or further south along the coastline the Via Aurelia.

Roman Massalia (Marseilles)

This was one part of the region of southern France that would not need conquering. Seen as the first large scale Greek settlement in France from 600 BCE, the port of Marseilles developed into a cultural centre for the whole Mediterranean, and by 200 BCE there were five major ports of a similar standing around the Mediterranean. It was trading traffic to and from these ports that secured the communication across the ancient world. Roads were either non-existent, very rough and dangerous and also slow, but fast ships, like those of the Phoenicians and the later Greeks, could traverse long distances far more quickly – although it was also a very dangerous mode of transport and unfavourable winds could stop convoys from leaving port for weeks.

Alongside the four ports in Athens, there were two in Alexandria, another two in Carthage (until its complete destruction by the Romans), and Rome, recognising where its future prosperity was to be paid, had built four ports of its own. Marseilles in Narbonensis was the newest arrival and provided an excellent deep-water gateway to Gaul and northern Europe. The Romans recognised this and, while they did not make any move on the rest of southern France, they did have close links and protective alliances with Marseilles. Current archaeological work in and around the city reinforces the fact that Marseilles is probably the oldest city in France and that the Romans had a strong presence here centuries before Q. Fabius, M. Livius and the rest of their senatorial party arrived here on their way home to Rome in 218 BCE.

The concern of the Roman senate about the strategic intentions of Hannibal were well founded, as he marched his army eastwards through southern Gaul unhindered by the tribes. With the military support of some of the Gallic tribes at the Battles of the Trebbia (a river in northern Italy in the Ligurian region) in 218 and Lake Trasimene in 217 BCE, Hannibal terrorised the Roman peninsula and won his most famous victory of all at Cannae where Hannibal destroyed the largest Roman army ever assembled. The result of this disaster saw the dispersed Roman forces fighting on for the next ten years and in 202 BCE, the

The Musée des Docks Romains in Marseilles was especially constructed to display the thousands of objects from the sixth century BCE onwards that relate to the Roman occupation of Marseilles. Vessels including Dolia – large jars for wine and Olive oil – coins, treasures and all sorts of shipping instruments are on display.

Musée des Docks Romains, 10 Place Vivaux,
Marseilles, FR +33 049 191 2462

hero of Rome – Scipio Africanus – destroyed the Carthaginian army at the Battle of Zama. The vulnerability of Rome to attack from an army sweeping through southern France, however, was never to be forgotten and established a strategic imperative to either control or acquire the land between northern Italy and eastern Spain.

Chapter 8

The Geography of Southern Gaul – the Journey of a Military Courier

What A.L.F. Rivet refers to in the third chapter of his book as 'Towards the Formation of a Province 153-100BC' was a period of mixed but steadily intensifying success for Roman imperial expansion.[39] There was no desire to fight or dominate but there was a recognition that somehow, and over a long-protracted period, Roman dominance over southern Gaul was essential to both future prosperity and security.

The Route of a Military Courier from Rome to Narbo Martius (Narbonne)

As far as we can assess, for the majority of the second century BCE, Roman commerce seems to have been able to travel to and from Hispania without major difficulty using the long twisting paths westwards through southern Gaul. Minor conflicts sometimes developed into localised uprisings but there was no strong sense of national identity and the worst the Roman garrisons had to face were small confederations of tribes. It was not until 153 BCE that the Romans were forced to intervene on a major scale when their ally city Marseilles was attacked.

If we were to imagine the route of a Roman military courier, perhaps around 140 BCE, taking personal letters from Q.Fabius in Rome to friends he had made on his embassy to Carthage, or from the senate to the leaders of military units in southern France, then the ultimate destination could be Narbo Martius – modern day Narbonne. ORBIS tells us that such a journey would take around twelve to fourteen days by fast horse, along the coastal route, stopping most nights and using the existing paths and roads.[40] If the despatches were of vital importance, and early horse relay points were available en route (later, these places would be vastly expanded across the empire with the *cursus publicus*) then this travel time could be cut to nine days by horse relay with possibly three different animals being used. The course and directions were difficult the whole way and, with only occasional sign posts, an inexperienced courier would need to ask for directions the whole way – if Latin was his only language, then the trip could be complex and often not be completed.

Having packed his saddle bags and setting off with a group of riders, he made his way north out of Rome along the Via Aurelia which would take him through modern day Tuscany and into the colder, more mountainous regions around Genoa.

The Romans were a very mobile people – especially keen to meet and greet friends and business contacts and the roads, whatever their condition, would usually be busy. Here and there would be the occasional cremation and ritual along the side of the roads or in nearby fields as death en route was a distinct possibility and part of the risk of travel, and there were always soldiers going somewhere in their distinct red cloaks either on foot or horseback. Our courier would have to overtake all manner of vehicles from curtained and exclusive litters carried by slaves, past carriages or *plaustra* carrying farm produce or building materials, wood and stone, or perhaps the large iron wheeled carriage, the *carpentum*, with up to a dozen people on board – like a slow-moving stagecoach from the wild west. In overtaking he would often only just miss the children running all over the road from families trudging to make a new life in Rome or a column of slaves being marched, and whipped, in chains. The building blocks of the roads would be covered in horse manure, human waste and urine from the traffic – until it rained and washed this detritus into the gutters. The Roman mile was 1,478.5 metres, and *milario* and massive carved granite stones could be found recording how far it was to the next parking place or *mansio* or the roadside inn – *taburna* – or to the next settlement. There were often signs to inform the traveller what he could expect if he stopped there for the night – jugs of wine or perhaps a penis. The further north he travelled, the less information there was – but there was always traffic.

Then our rider would veer west into the large and comparatively new Roman province of Liguria where his journey really began. Passing through the lowland hills from northern Italy into what we know as the Côte d'Azur or the French Riviera, our young soldier with his leather dispatch case on his saddle, red military cloak/blanket, food, helmet, sword, and water could see the stunning blue seas of the Mediterranean over his left shoulder – taking care that his horse navigated the rocky roadways carefully and even more so in places where the drop to the sea was only feet away.

As he approached the border areas where Liguria was deemed to end and the lands of the Gallic tribes begin, he would have passed through Ventimiglia on the modern Italian border with France. Our rider would have known this place as Album Intimilum which later became Vintimilium and eventually be called 'the twenty (Roman) miles' or Ventimiglia (the distance to the French border). A high plateau sloping down to a large flat sandy bay made this a beautiful place to rest, before pressing on along ever narrowing roads edging closer to the cliffs and through Menton and then Monaco – the latter being nothing but a tiny collection of white houses at the foot of the cliffs. The etymological derivation of the name Monaco is from the Greek *Monoikos* or 'single house', which perhaps tells us how tiny the early settlement was. Our rider could have led his horse down to the water's edge or stayed up high on the mountain road which today runs through La Turbie – it is here, in the early years of what would be the reign of Emperor Augustus, that a massive Trophy of the Alps would be constructed: we will come to that in a later chapter.

Onwards, Nicaea (from *Nike* – named after the Greek goddess of victory) was his next destination and he would have noticed that it was already a small port with a bustling Roman and Greek trade. If our rider chose the lower paths, then he would be able to trot around a long arc of sand and shingle passing fishing and trading vessels anchored out in the bay and the blue azure sea lapping at the occasional large rock outcrop where Nice airport stands today. However, the true Roman settlement was not in Nicaea at all but slightly north of the modern city centre up on the hills that overlooked the bay from the east.

Originally named the Kemenelon Hill in Greek, this was translated to Cemenelum Hill in Latin and was the base of the Celtic/Gallic Ligures Vediantii tribe for the previous two centuries and an excavation of a hill fort near the site was carried out in 1943.[41]

Here on the hills, the Roman town of Cemenelum developed – which today, in its turn, also lays under the modern-day suburb of Nice named Cimiez. Cemenelum was advanced and select even at this point, perhaps heralding its future as a tourist destination for the rich and famous of all eras – including the Romans. Much of the site remains unexcavated due to modern housing that was built over the site of the Roman town, however this was a town that would one day have over 10,000 inhabitants, an arena and a wonderful bath complex with white marble floors and glass windows. As an indicator of local wealth and status of the town, numerous dedications to various deities – such

> Artefacts discovered in Cemenelum date as far back as 1100 BCE which establishes this settlement as one of the oldest in the south of France. The Musée d'Archéologie de Nice Cimiez in Nice contains thousands of artefacts, including many amphorae that once stored wine, and the harbour of Nicaea is littered with wrecks that underscore just how active this area was in pre-Roman and Roman times. The Roman ruins are impressive, with numerous architectural layers built over each other charting the development of the Roman town.

as to Jupiter, Hercules, Mars and Silvanus which cements the settlement as a locale for religious devotions with priests and a *flamen*.

The Cemenelum bathing complex was substantial and was composed of three inter-connected baths – a *Tepidarium* which was a warm room, followed by the dry heat of the *Laconium*, and finally the *Caldarium* which was as hot as the slaves and managers of the baths could make it. After sweating for anything up to an hour, it was then a swim in the *Natatio* or warm water pool, and a final bath in the cold room or *Frigidarium*. Toilets and massage rooms completed the complex. It would be Augustus who would name Cemenelum as his capital of Alpes Maritimae – a sub division of the province of Narbonensis and the most important city on the Ligurian coastline. Rivet also refers to the inscriptions found for various legionaries in the Augustan and later periods who were either recruited from Cemenelum or perhaps were serving there when they died.[42]

Due west of Cemenelum is modern day Vence, but in this period it was known as Vintium. Worth mentioning, as this beautiful small walled town contains numerous inscriptions – some of which remain cemented into walls. Although not the size of its larger neighbours, Vintium would have been as lovely a place to live in Roman times as Vence is today.[43]

Leaving Cemenelum, and a few kilometres further on around the other side of the bay, our rider would arrive in modern day Antibes. Our dispatch rider would have recognised this settlement as Antipolis – meaning 'opposite city' in Greek given its location on the other side of the sweeping bay from Nice. The Greek historian Strabo wrote of Antipolis and the bustling community with its iron age settlements still visible alongside the signs of a thriving Greek community with an increasing number of Roman residents around the small port. Archaeology suggests that the earliest Roman buildings date to the second century BCE so there were already Latin speakers and residents in fine houses where our rider may have dropped off a letter or two – even though as yet they wait to be discovered.

Heading south back towards the coast was another embryonic Roman settlement. Fréjus was founded in a strategically important position, sitting as it did with its own deep-water harbour and protective bay. It would be here that a Roman presence was again already well formed and the famous poet and later military commander Gaius Cornelius Gallus was born here in 67 BCE. A few years later, and as Gallus was growing into a talented young man destined for greatness, Julius Ceasar was so attracted to Fréjus that, in around 49 BCE, he re-named the town *Forum Julii* or 'market of Julius'. In his *Histories*, Tacitus would refer to Forum Julii as '*claustra maris*' – gateway to the sea.[44] Consequently, the community was to expand during the last century of the Republic into a sizable and influential Roman settlement. It was also to be here that Gn. Julius

Agricola, who later became a renowned general and conqueror of Britain, was born in 40 CE.

Fréjus also had the peculiar honour of being the place where shipwrights built dozens of galleys that were subsequently used as part of the fleet of Mark Anthony – when he lost the Battle of Actium to Augustus in 31 BCE, many of these ships were repatriated to Fréjus and it was to become a *colonia* (military home) for the veterans of the Eighth Legion – and renamed as Octavianorum Colonia.

> Given the rich Greek and Roman presence in Fréjus, it is no surprise that the Archaeological Museum contains thousands of Roman and Greek artefacts and is well worth a visit – as are the remains of the aqueducts built nearby. Fréjus is still a lovely French town with a feel for antiquity, even though some of the Roman remains are in a sadly decayed state.

Just prior to the arrival of our rider in the area, in 153, when the Deciates and Oxybiens tribes (branches of the Ligurians to the east) of eastern Gaul had combined to attack both Antipolis and Nicaea, it was the Massaliotes, the loyal allies of Rome in Massalia, that sent for help – and Rome responded. A Roman army was raised and sent under the command of the then Consul Q. Opimius and entered Gaul. After a successful campaign, a sizeable chunk of the central coastal area around Marseilles was now firmly in Roman hands, and what would soon become the Province of Gallia Narbonensis began to take physical shape. Polybius tells us:

> '*Having become masters of these peoples, Quintus* [Opimius] *handed over as much of their territory as he thought fit to the Massiliotes and compelled the Ligurians in future to give the Massaliotes hostages for certain periods.*'

With the Roman foothold expanding inland around Massalia thanks to the victories of Opimius, it was inevitable that after 153 further clashes on the periphery of this new border area would arise and more requests for aid would arrive in Rome. Perhaps our courier, as he made his way south west, carried just such communications from the senate. The harbour in Forum Iulii was originally formed from a lagoon and remains impressive today with signs of the Augustan developments around the quay and the canal which was built in the first century BCE. Much of the Roman wall that surrounded the town is still evident, as are the impressive gates. Similar to Nîmes, it is clear that Forum Iulii exercised considerable military and administrative control over the surrounding district and again the tell-tale signs of the expansion of the town – quarries and villa sites – litter the area to the north. Roman potteries have been identified all around Fréjus, as have brick works which would be needed to for the later aqueduct that would be built to serve the water needed for the town.

From Fréjus our rider resumed his journey, either taking a northern route through the great valley via Vidauban, Le Luc, Cuers and then arriving in Toulon, or following the rocky and, at times, difficult coastal route via St Tropez and La Londe-les-Maures and arriving also in Toulon. This would be a particularly difficult part of his route because of the topography of the region. Either way, Telo Martius was his destination – modern day Toulon. Another large town with a Greek and Phoenician past, Toulon was also a favoured port with thriving trade routes in the western Mediterranean. The great harbour was a perfect shelter from the sudden storms for coastal shipping and it was famous for a local sea snail called murex. Somehow the shell of this snail mixed with local acorns created a rich purple dye – a dye that was traded with Rome for the purple colour used in imperial robes.

Massalia or Marseilles was the de facto 'capital' of Roman activities in southern France until a formal capital was founded for the first governor and once a *provincia* had been founded. As we read earlier, Massalia had welcomed the senators on their return journey from Carthage as the premier city-state of the entire region. Massalia went on to support Rome in the Second Punic War (218-201 BCE) and grew both in size and independence during the last century of the republic – gathered as it was around the wide and deep waters of the old harbour.

The city was a natural conduit between inland Gaul and northern Europe. Commodities manufactured in Rome were sought after in Europe and an expanding Rome wanted and needed increasing quantities of statues, granite, glass, silver, wine, olives and other products from the estates of the south of France.

It was the influential men of Massalia that called out for help from Rome, on the periphery of empire, when the Allobroges and Averni tribes, led by Bituitus, invaded in 123 BCE, and it was the defeat of these tribes by the forces led by Fabius Maximus and Gn. Domitius Ahenobarbus in 121 BCE that began the new era of Roman colonisation. The city sided with Pompey and the republican senate against Caesar in the Civil War of 49 BCE. The city was surrounded and fell and gradually after that, lost its pre-eminence as the main city of the province. It was to Massalia that Titus Annius Milo had fled, to eat his 'Red Mullet', after his condemnation and failed defence by Cicero in 52 BCE – possibly because this was as close to a Roman environment that he could find but within a city state that still felt distinct and independent of Rome.[45]

Leaving Massalia behind, our courier once more mounted his horse and now had a choice – it was either a longer route heading north and then west via Aquae Sextiae – Aix-en-Provence – to his main destination of Arles, or head due west across some awkward coastal landscapes. Assuming he went north, arriving in Aquae Sextiae would allow him to rest his tired and dusty body in what would become the 'waters of Sextus', where the river had been diverted into a series of warm thermal baths. Surrounded by images of the gods, our exhausted courier could perhaps stay the night in what was another thriving Roman community built around and over an ancient Greek site and in the shadow of what had been one of the largest Iron Age civic centres – or *oppidum/a* – in the whole region. In Aquae Sextiae, indigenous local tribes had been living, working and marrying their Roman neighbours for some years. Merchants and traders liked to live in relative harmony with some still living in the *oppidum* of Entremont up on the hills – while others accepted the inevitable and came down from the hillside settlements and began to settle in the Romanised streets.

A Case Study in Roman Conquest and Colonisation – the *oppidum* of Entremont

Cassiodorus, a Roman historian writing over three centuries later in the fourth century CE, relates how Rome continued to send legions to quell occasional uprisings throughout this whole coastal region. Given that the Roman presence – and therefore Roman allies – were limited to the coastal areas, there was no need to venture inland, where far greater dangers awaited any Roman convoy, be it military or civilian.

One such operation was successfully led in 125 BCE by Consul M. Fulvius Flaccus in what seems to have been a genuine attempt to help its ally Massalia and other Roman communities from another attack by the Salluvii. Flaccus was successful enough to be granted a triumph through the streets of Rome in 123 BCE, although his campaign was not decisive and, the following year, another revolt broke out and this time it seems to have been more serious. Consul Gaius Sextius Calvinus headed onwards to modern day Aix-en-Provence determined to quell the rebellious tribes of Provence and to gain his triumph. Entering the territory of the Salluvii, Calvinus and his small army set about correcting the relationship between Rome and its so-called allies and Strabo relates how:

> *'These were the first of the Transalpine Celti that the Romans conquered, though they did so only after carrying on war with both them and the Ligures for a long time – because the latter had barred all the passes leading to Iberia that ran through the seaboard. And, in fact, they kept making raids both by land*

and sea, and were so powerful that the road was scarcely practicable even for great armies. And it was not until the eighth year of the war that the Romans succeeded, though only with difficulty, in opening up the road for a breadth of only twelve stadia [a stadium is roughly equivalent to a furlong] *to those travelling on public business.'*[46]

The Salluvii or Salyes were just one of the dozens of tribes of varying sizes and importance spread across France south of the Massif Central who were resisting the increase in Roman traffic. Ethnographically they are considered to have been Celto-Ligurian, which means that they dwelt both east and west of Massalia during the Iron Age and by the time of Roman expansion during the first century BCE, their religion was still considered to be 'barbaric', with the *téte coupée* (severed head) a central part of their religious cults.

Smaller tribes existed in tandem with the Salluvii, such as the Avatici, Tricores, Segobrigii, Dexivates and Anatilii, and they all came together in the Salluvian Confederation which emerged during the second century BCE. Their capital was built on a plateau today named Entremont and the *oppidum* was a fortified Iron Age settlement, a meeting place and hub for discussions, ceremonies and trade – this was the obvious target for Sextius and his legions. In 123, the Salluvii overran their smaller Roman neighbour some 3km below in the valley, and again an appeal was sent to Rome back along the route of our

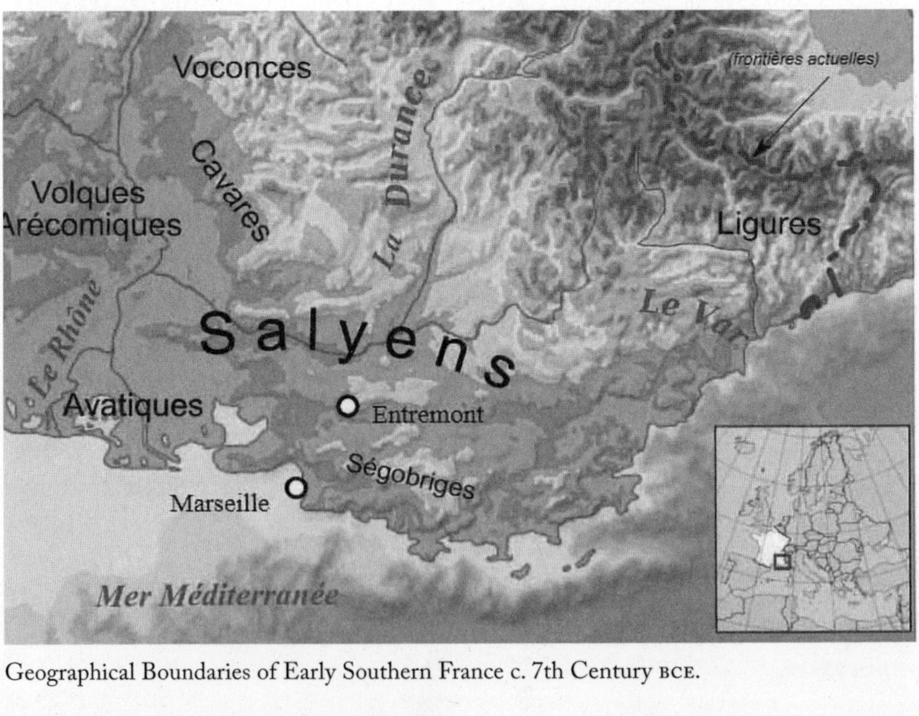

Geographical Boundaries of Early Southern France c. 7th Century BCE.

The *oppidum* at Entremont is located 3 kilometres from Aix-en Provence and is a nine-acre site that was excavated in the 1940s. The site makes for a fascinating journey back to a pre-Roman existence, and the many wonderful finds are now on display in the Musée Granet in Aix-en-Provence.

Another fine example of an *oppidum* can be seen near the village of Murvial-les-Montpellier, between Montpellier and Béziers. The site covers 20 hectares and is one of the largest hill forts in the region. At some point the Romans constructed a large temple here with Corinthian topped marble columns. There is a lovely little museum in Murvial-les-Montpellier which contains the archaeological finds from the site.

courier – maybe a seven- or eight-day journey – for help. It would have taken a few weeks to assemble a fighting force or collect troops along the way, but Gaius Sextius soon arrived and put a ruthless end to the uprising both around Entremont and further along the coastline. Rivet comments that large numbers of Roman lead and stone missiles from sling shots have been found around the site indicating stiff resistance to the Roman troops.[47] By these means – that of brutal conquest – a further extension of Roman control unfolded. There may not have been an explicit policy of imperialist expansion but we can see how the price of Roman assistance was Roman colonisation, followed by the subsequent stage of annexation supported by a rapidly appearing new road system to gradually build up the arterial infrastructure of empire.

After defeating the Salluvii, Sextius also oversaw the destruction of the Entremont settlement on the hills and beneath it founded the Roman colony of Aquae Sextiae – after the 'abundance of hot and cold springs and because of his name.' By around 90 BCE, and only twenty years later, archaeology tells us that the entire Entremont settlement, hundreds of years old, had been abandoned and the stone from its houses and halls plundered to create Aquae Sextiae – modern Aix-en-Provence.

Ethnic Cleansing

As the traces of the Iron Age existence of these Gallic tribes was slowly being erased, the Romans were practising a clearly defined strategy and policy of ethnic cleansing. The systematic destruction of the Gallic *oppida* was not just designed to eliminate the military opposition of the Gallic tribes but it was also intended to disrupt the oral and written history of the conquered by the relocation of cultural centres to where the process of Romanisation could work best. Cultural variations were tolerated, as was religious practice, but to get ahead in this new Roman world it would ultimately be necessary for the individual to succumb to the Roman gods and way of business. This benign imperialism cleansed the communities over time of their heritage and legacy, where the Roman language had to be learnt in order to function and survive and where Roman culture dominated. The rich, talented and cultured social history of the Gauls was to be erased via Romanisation: the Peace of Rome – *Pax Romana* – was thus established.

Contriving to pretend that their arrival was a blessing for the 'barbarians' where the Roman Gods had blessed the people with the wonder of Roman civilisation, could only be carried so far, with the result that the Romans knew full well that national resistance would continue for many years. The sheer size and numbers of the *oppida* is in fact evidence that there was a natural drift to urbanisation amongst the Gauls, and they were walking their own path towards city states before their natural development was brutally ruptured by the arrival of the Roman armies. The combination of Romanisation and urbanisation therefore was able to build on a process that was already well advanced amongst the Gallic tribes. In the modern world we see exactly the same causes and consequences 2,000 years later with the ejection of the Muslim Rohingya in Myanmar, the war between two ethnic groups in South Sudan or the treatment of the Christians and Yazidis in Iraq and Syria, where cultural destruction accompanies relocation and the carving out of new states over the ashes and bodies of the old.

Wherever an enemy was crushed, a new Roman colony was founded. It was commonly the case that there would be long-lasting and bitter unrest in newly conquered territories and, however we might imagine the glorious process of founding a new colony, it was in fact just a way of initially stationing a military presence in the form of a garrison until the forces of societal osmosis stepped in. Wherever the military remained the camp followers built settlements where Roman potters, leather workers, priests, carpenters, prostitutes and merchants followed to live off the wages of the legionaries and their officers, and gradually all the apparatus of local government arrived over time. There was no manual of colonisation, but the pattern was the same in any part of the expanding empire. The French archaeologist Jean Gascou concluded, *'the capital of the Salluvi entered by force into the Roman orbit'* and was a mixture of Romans, Greeks, and repressed Salluvians, all of whom now suddenly found themselves subject to Roman law and discipline – whether they wanted it or not.

One of the main reasons why the Roman senate seized upon the opportunity to send an army so far westwards led by a consul to 'free' a small repressed settlement such as Aix was that they knew very well that it was located at another strategic point along the road to Italy – thus able to protect the homeland – but was also a link with Massalia, creating a Roman enclave in the region to protect Roman communications to and from Hispania. Indeed, it is not beyond the realms of possibility, though backed up by no evidence whatsoever, that the Salluvii were 'encouraged' to rise up and unwittingly provoke their own demise. It is in the nature of their work that fifth columnists leave no evidence behind.

Recent ethnographic research has shown historians a lot more detail about the next stages of development whereby the old Gallic administrations were erased and instead a *praesidium* was established – an intermediary step when no Province existed – made up of notable local leaders of certain bodies, possibly the senior army officer stationed there, a notable professional, and maybe representatives of the local inhabitants. The representative of this last group was probably essential: Pliny the Elder, writing in the early first century CE, named it *Aquae Sextiae Salluviorum* – the 'Water Springs of Sextius and the Salluvii' – which suggests that the vast majority of the population were now suppressed members of the Salluvii and it was therefore something of an indigenous city made up of local people under Roman rule.

True to form, Sextius did not just create for the future, he also needed to punish the past and, while he was founding his new settlement and destroying parts of the old *oppidum*, Sextius displayed the true nature of collaboration with or subjugation by Rome. Diodorus, the Greek historian writing some sixty years later wrote:

> '*When Sextius had captured the city of the Gauls, and was selling the inhabitants as slaves, one Crato who was led in chains with the rest, came up to the consul, as he sat upon the tribunal, and told him he had always been a friend to the Romans, and for that reason had received many injuries, and had suffered many beatings from his fellow citizens. Sextius immediately released him from his binds, along with all his family, and restored all his possessions: and for his goodwill to the Romans, gave him power to set free nine hundred of the citizens, such as he himself thought fit. For the consul was more generous and bountiful to Crato than he expected, so that the Gauls could easily see how exactly just the Romans were, both in their punishments and in their rewards.*'[48]

One or two thoughts spring to mind from this quotation. Firstly, these events were within the living memory of participants so there is a fair chance that Diodorus was recording a true observation rather than just repeated whispers down the decades. Secondly, Sextius was no ordinary general, he was a consul of Rome and had jointly governed the whole empire from the senate in Rome

– his attitude towards the Salluvii could afford to be both brutal or lenient as he was very unlikely to be criticised. As a former consul, Sextius had a notion in his mind of what groundwork he was laying for the future prosperity of Rome in this region and knew full well that his actions would be reported throughout the length and breadth of Gaul in all directions. Finally, we know nothing of Crato but it is unlikely that he knew 900 residents of the town thus, the choice of who went free and who was lost into slavery for the rest of their lives, must have been extremely hard.

A formal founding of Aquae Sextiae would come shortly with the announcement by Sextius that these were his waters – the waters of Sextius. Later the nearby area would be the site of a famous, huge and bloody battle in 102 BCE between a Roman army led by Gaius Marius and the tribes of the Cimbri, the Teutones and the Ambrones.[49] After a series of tragic defeats and huge losses amongst the Roman armies sent to stop this mass of Gauls moving towards northern Italy, Marius became at once refreshed from the springs, and, having given devotions to the gods of the thermal, defeated the Gauls. All of this was in the future; for now, refreshed by the thermal waters, our courier would set off on the last leg of his journey and head for Arelate which was another stronghold of Roman presence in Narbonensis.

Arelate – modern day Arles – was a must-see stopping place even before the radical expansions of the next two centuries – and it remains a must-see place today. The great Rhône River divides into two just north of this strategically-vital town, which, thereafter, slows into the flatlands of the Camargue delta. Arles was to become a serious player in commerce across the region: boat building and transportation up and down the Rhône made it a thriving financial centre and a smaller version of Massalia. Arelate had already been a thriving port for hundreds of years and in 122 BCE, Sextius made sure that his legionaries also took Arelate into their protection. Strabo, writing at some point close to the birth of Jesus Christ, in Book IV 6.44 of his *Geographika* states that: *'On the Rhône is Arelate, a city and emporium of considerable traffic'*.

In contrast to Massalia however, the leaders of the town were to side with Julius Caesar in the coming civil war of the mid 40s BCE, and, for being on the winning side, Arelate received generous treatment, allowing them to eclipse their neighbours. Caesar conferred a new name on the settlement – that of *Colonia Iulia Paterna Arelatensium Sextanorum* and settled the loyal veterans of his VI legion – Ferrata – in and around the town. The commercial prowess of Arelate, with its wine trades and boat building, is exemplified in the city museum where a superb example of these times is the restored and spectacular 102-foot Roman trading barge in the Museum of Archaeology.

The Roman barge is one of the treasures of Arles and was protected from decay in the mud of a local river. The museum exhibit includes a 20-minute video with English subtitles. The museum is closed on Tuesdays.

From Arelate it was possible for our Roman rider to either head southward to the coastal waters and the small Roman settlement of Aigues-Mortes, possibly founded by Gaius Marius as a coastal fortification to defend the soft underbelly of the Camargue, or he could continue west and inland to the much larger and impressive settlement of Nemausus – or Nîmes.

In tiny Aigues-Mortes, salt production had been underway for centuries. Our rider may have ridden past a Roman named Peccius who was working on the salt beds as the small town of Aigues-Mortes became Romanised around 100 BCE. As he passed the salt pans, he could have glanced away to his right where he would be able to view the snow-capped mountains of the Alpes Maritimes rising inland over misty-green forests as he looked into Gaul. However, if he had letters to collect or documents to deliver then he would very likely ride to Nemausus. Modern day Nîmes is known as 'the French Rome', and even in 140 BCE it was already a Greco-Gallic city with a substantial Roman community making their play to invite Rome to subjugate the entire region and place them at the centre of administrative control.

For our rider, we can assume that he would have seen a large, bustling town with ambitious plans to grow, a cultural mix of Romans, Gauls and Celts. His route in from the north east, would have brought him down the valley past numerous quarries which were already being used to mine stone for walls and roads, and would also be used much later to provide stone for the huge Pont du Gard aqueduct – whose eventual route our rider would have traversed. For now, around 140 BCE, we must see Nemausus as an evolving Gallo-Roman town surrounded by Iron Age settlements up on the hills around the valley where Nîmes is situated.

Another Ethnic Cleansing Operation – Oppidum de Nages

Namausatis or Nemausus was the god of the dominant tribe in this area. The Volcae Arecomici would have continued in their ways of worship of their local gods and their way of life, although aware that, below in the valleys of the Vaunage region in which they had lived for hundreds of years, the world was changing. The Arecomici protected their way of life and their independence by reinforcing their hill forts, and six have been identified in the local area with the largest *oppidum*, that of de Nages, with large walls and earthworks. The remains that can be seen today are still impressive despite 2,000 years of weathering and human exploitation. But in the late-second century BCE, it was Roman troops who would do the most damage in the growing friction between the indigenous tribes and the ever more invasive Romans.

The area surrounding Nîmes remains one of the significant examples of Celtic influence and settlement and, for those whose interest lies in pre-Roman Provence, then this is a region of special merit. The hill fort sites, and especially the Oppidum de Nages, date to the sixth century BCE. Archaeological excavations have revealed a skilled civilisation of craftsmen and traders who networked widely, as well as with the other tribes and communities in the region of the Vaunage. The main Oppidum de Nages, only 10km from Nemausus, had a street system and large halls for the tribal chief, as well as metal workshops, potteries, jewellery makers and shops. The defences were of large walls of stone with protected gates, and population estimates range from 3-4,000 inhabitants – maybe more when the Romans began to ravage the area.

The Oppidum de Nages is situated in the lush rolling hills of the Vaunage area. Excellent wine and food characterises the region, and it is often ignored by tourists making it a wonderful destination for the historian.

Nîmes and the Vaunage: An opportunity for glory – Quintus Fabius Maximus

The senate, now sensing the need for continual pressure on the Gallic tribes, dispatched another general in 122 – Cn. Domitius Ahenobarbus. According to Appian, Bituitus, King of the Allobroges, asked for pardon and return of the Salluvian prisoners but not only was this refused, they were already on their way to Rome. Settled further inland to the north, the Allobroges and their allies the Avernii were determined that Roman control be restricted to the coastal areas. They met in battle at Vindalium somewhere near the River Sorgue – possibly a hill fort near Mourre-de-Sève north east of Avignon. Despite a crushing victory for the Romans, unrest was everywhere and Domitius moved on to become proconsul of the area – as yet one far from under Roman control – while yet another general thirsty for his chance of glory arrived.

Like so many other Gallic settlements, the hill forts around Nemausus belonging to the Volques Arécomiques (Arecomici) were also attacked and taken by the Romans in 121 BCE, but this time it was not Domitius who surrounded the settlements on the hills and Nemausus itself but Quintus Fabius Maximus who, in 120, had led a new legionary army from Rome, passed through the settlements dealt with by his predecessor, and set about completing the victory.

Fabius was another 'general' who wished to add military glory to his curriculum vitae despite having reached the zenith of authority as a magistrate on the *cursus honorum*. Initially, Fabius had been elected quaestor as a young man in 134. As part of his early training for political office, he needed military experience and his influential uncle took him to Hispania Citerior, where they fought together in the Second Numantine War – as a young noble in his twenties therefore he had already been placed in command of a unit of 4,000 volunteers, although he would have been guided and groomed by a cluster of more experienced officers to ensure that he did not lead them all to disaster. Given that Fabius would have travelled through this area before, with a military column on his way to Spain, it is more than likely that he had his eye on creating and defeating an 'enemy' in this area at the appropriate time. This of course accords well with the pericentric theory of Roman imperialism – seeking opportunities to expand on the peripheries of the empire when the opportunity arose. As propraetor in Hispania, he wasted no time in achieving another badge of honour in being censured in Rome for his exploitation of grain from a Spanish town.[51]

In 121 Fabius had been elected consul alongside Lucius Opimius. Lucius was a tough and uncompromising politician in the noble mould and, as we have seen, it was his father Quintus Opimus who had been victorious in southern Gaul in the 150s. Lucius would not be joining the family tradition of conducting war against the people of southern France – he was busy executing 3,000 Roman citizens implicated in the uprising led by the Gracchi brothers against the senate. It was the actions of Lucius Opimus that established the *senatus consultum ultimatum* – the ultimate power in times of national emergency which the senate could invest in an individual to save the state. Compared to events in Rome, Fabius must have felt he had the easier job, and he decided to stay on in Gaul once his consulship ended – perhaps he felt it was safer than Rome – and in 120 was appointed proconsul in Gaul: still not governor, as there was no province of Gaul – yet.

Fabius continued to seek out opposition from the Allobroges and the Averni and brought Bituitus to battle on 8 August 121 – we know the precise date through Pliny's account of the illness being suffered by Fabius who, we are told, directed the battle from his stretcher or a sedan chair. Apparently Bituitus, King of the Averni, boasted that the Roman force arrayed in front of him was barely enough to feed his dogs – brave or stupid, it would have at least been met with a roar from his warriors. It is possible though not certain that Ahenobarbus was also present to lend his military experience to the battle – although Fabius would still have been the senior military commander. The vast army of Bituitus (some references suggest in excess of 180,000) would have fought with their characteristic noise, from their screams and jeers, and of course their renowned great courage. Fabius and his men would have had good cause to wonder if they could win this fight; it was certain that no prisoners would be taken on this day. The Gauls were able to increase this concern amongst the legions with one of their most fearsome weapons. This particular weapon of war was in fact an instrument – the famous carnyx. Typically made of brass, this tall thin trumpet could be as much as twelve feet high and large numbers of them shrieked across the battlefield like agonising dragons from hell, striking fear into their opponents and conjuring up images of a gruesome death. Historians have been able to study this instrument as numbers have recently been discovered in an Iron Age grave. Replicating the design allows us to hear the echoing noise as if we were there, standing on the rocks and grasslands of battle, alongside the centurions stirring their men to kill even more of the enemy. Even Polybius referred to the:

> *'Countless trumpeters and horn blowers and since the whole army was shouting its war cries at the same time there was such a confused sound that the noise seemed to come not only from the trumpeters and the soldiers but also the countryside which was joining in the echo.'*[52]

However small a Roman military detachment was, their discipline to stay and move as one soldier often held the day, and so it was that the mass of Gauls dispersed and it was at this point, the Romans could and later did claim, that the province of Narbonensis had been founded.

A delighted senate awarded Fabius a Triumph through the streets of Rome and the spectacular nature of this particular parade went down in Roman history. Once he had left his army at the borders of the Italian state, as was the law, Fabius processed southwards to Rome along the great highway of the age, the Via Aurelia, and then, after meeting, greeting and receiving many visitors, planned his triumphal route.

In 2004, in Tintignac in Corrèze, France, archaeologists discovered over 500 bronze and some iron items in a shallow 'grave'. This was probably some sort of offering to the gods, a sacrifice of treasured objects donated in either gratitude or for their favour. Included in the vast hoard were 40 fragments belonging to at least seven carnyces – the fearsome bronze horn. French researchers reconstructed an original carnyx horn and, for the first time in 2,000 years, were able to listen to what instilled fear and panic into Roman legionaries before they battled against the Celts.

As much as the celebrated and renowned historians of our or any other age may try to interpret what it was that drove the Romans on to military aggression, it was the desire for glory that ranked perhaps most highly. In her 2007 book, *The Roman Triumph,* Mary Beard writes of how Rome needed Triumphs both to pacify the people and to celebrate military glory – as such, the Triumph was a motivator of conquest rather than a reward of defending the borders of the empire.[53]

Although the award of a triumph was politically sensitive and it was by no means certain that a general would be granted a triumph, the victorious *Imperator* sought to display himself as close to God-like. Riding in a chariot in full armour, his face sometimes stained red like the God Jupiter, the victor displayed not just the spoils of his campaign to the assembled crowds cheering every second of the procession, but he also celebrated his troops in their clean and shining armour, clanking in synchronised marching towards the very centre of the empire – the forum and Temple of Jupiter Stator – the stayer. Also in the procession were his captives – thousands upon thousands, in chains, in servitude, powerless in the face of the glory of Rome. Flowers, rose petals, immense noise and celebration, parties and public holidays all accompanied a Triumph and it was all very far removed from the lands in which victory had been gained. The Roman people could be forgiven for thinking that they were invincible – sadly they were not. In later years as the enormous wealth extracted from the vanquished enemies of Rome poured into the treasury, the Triumphs became more ostentatious and more extreme, for example with Pompey's three-day procession and the elephants pulling his golden chariot becoming stuck in a triumphal arch – the result of some poor event planning. So this is how the Romans treated their foes and King Bituitus, his family and many of his people saw Rome at first hand and experienced what it was to be an enemy of Rome.

Rome had changed her attitude quite markedly and quickly towards southern Gaul. After all it had only been some thirty years since the mission of Q. Fabius and his senators had travelled and met in councils with the leaders and Kings of so many tribes which they had now conquered, and it is likely that the Salluvii, Allobroges, and Averni were all part of those meetings. They had learnt the hard way that failing to become an ally of Rome equalled becoming an enemy. But Fabius had not yet quite completed his orgy of self-glorification. After his humiliation of the King of the Allobroges, Fabius now assumed the full name Quintus Fabius Maximus Allobrogicus in recognition of his triumph over the people of the Allobroges. Finally, Fabius used much of the plunder stolen from the tribe to build a triumphal arch, the Fornix Fabianus, over the Via Sacra in the forum itself – placing a statue of himself on top of the arch and fixing his place in the history of Rome at the cost of a tribe from Gaul.

As for the continuing story of Nemausus, although we are uncertain as to when it was officially named as a *colonia*, Rivet suggests that it was probably well before Augustus and possibly in the time of Caesar.[54] It was Nemausus that was given control by Rome over twenty-four *ignobilia oppida* – or smaller settlements whose names were listed and survive as testament to the power and influence of this expanding Roman city. A column found by chance near the centre of Nîmes in 1747, contained the following towns governed by Nemausus:

ANDVSIA
BRVGETIA
TEDVSIA
VATRVTE
VGERNI
SEXTANT
BRIGINN
STATVMAE
VIRINN
VCETIAE
SEGVSION

Rivet is clear that Ucetia is modern day Uzés and Andusia is Anduze – some 40km north west of Nîmes.[55] The entire area around Nîmes, for some 50km or more, also became peppered with dozens of Roman villas where excavations and finds indicate that this was to become a hub of real Roman activity, energy and life in the province of Narbonensis. Expansion was rapid and impressive and soon was able to claim to be the most distinguished city in the province, rivalling even those not on our dispatch riders' route – Lyon, Apt, Orange and numerous others.

Excavations have revealed over eighty mosaics that adorned new luxury middle-class and noble houses, and the speed of expansion was reinforced by the current number of inscriptions that have been discovered – currently over 2,000. Nîmes was also to be the town of birth for Plotina, future wife of the emperor Trajan, and home to numerous celebrities and political power brokers in the future development of Rome itself.

From Nîmes our courier had a clear and open ride due south west and on to his final destination of Narbo Martius or Narbonne. But, before his arrival, he would have passed through the town of Baeterrae or Béziers. Occupied well before even the Greeks, and before the Celts and Gauls arrived, Baeterrae was on the road that led between Italy and Spain, and Iron Age hill forts dotted the

Within the city of Nîmes today there are a range of some of the best Roman remains in Europe. The Amphitheatre is impossible to miss or ignore and is considered the best preserved of its kind outside Italy. The Musée de la Romanité opened in 2018 and, in addition to the superb mosaic floors and artefacts, the exterior design of the building is memorable and based on the folds of a flowing toga. The Maison Carrée is an ancient Roman temple and the Temple of Diana is an outstandingly well-preserved monument – as is the Pont du Gard aqueduct – see later chapters of this book. Surrounding the Temple of Diana are the remains of the extensive thermal spas and pools, now a landscaped garden, which made Nîmes such an attractive destination for visitors for centuries before and during the Roman era. The location of what would have been impressive baths remains elusive, but this is more than compensated by the rich variety of Roman history so well preserved.

area and were thriving in the 140s BCE and this is another prime area for the enthusiast of the pre-Roman period and what was erased by the Roman conquest.

Ancient traders and travellers would have paused here to water their mules and themselves and drink the local wines which, as the Romans took over the province, would be vastly expanded in both range and quantity to feed the thirst of the empire and Rome itself. Perhaps our courier took advantage when he rode through from one of the huge clay *dolium* (a large wine storage jar) that were transported to Rome. One such *dolium* that was discovered in an excavation near Rome was marked *'I am a wine from Baeterrae and I am five years old'.*

Almost any army passing to Spain or eastwards towards Rome, would have passed just to the south of the town – no doubt sending in troops to forage for what they could gather as they trudged past. Today most of the original Iron Age hill fort and the Roman town rests under new buildings, but there are still indicators that Baeterrae was special. Records and inscriptions show that it contained a number of *flamens* or priests to serve in what must have been a range of temples dedicated to the eighteen-or-so worshipped deities in the Roman world. Strabo mentions Baeterrae and calls it 'a strong city', which could refer to Roman walls around the town or the fact that it was largely on a hill.[56]

This unassuming city is pivotal in the story of the evolution of Narbonensis and stands as a vivid example of how much it was trade, every bit as much as glory and power, that truly drove imperial policy. Similar to so many other thriving Roman towns in the last years of the republic, it was used to recompense tired and surviving legionaries who had fought either for Rome or for a successful general and, in 36 BCE, Baeterrae was colonised by veterans and renamed *Colonia Julia Baeterrae Septimanorum.*

Chapter 9

The Evolution of the Physical Infrastructure of Southern Gaul in Two Case Studies – the Via Domitia and Narbonne

Just 38km further southwest from Baeterrae and Narbonne would have come into the view of the courier. Then, as now, this area is part of the famous Languedoc-Roussillon region of France where the grapes are freshened by the Mediterranean wind and salt air.

Likely to have also been centred around an Iron Age *oppidum*, Narbonne is first mentioned in the fifth century BCE and identified in various texts as a small Greek/Celtic community with a harbour and market place, but the key strength of this particular settlement was its location as a transport hub serving Gaul into Hispania and northwards into the Pyrenees via the historic Carcassonne.

The Via Domitia from 118

As the proconsular representative of the senate, it was Domitius who deserves credit for having the vision to plan out how the new 'province' could be best controlled. By 120 BCE then the Romans had now acquired a military dominance over all the major tribes of the area from Gallia Cisalpina in northern Italy down as far as Narbonne. Further west, trouble still loomed with the undefeated Volcae Arecomici, to the north were the powerful Helvii, and for the legions to travel quickly and safely, it was a road that was the most vital asset that they needed. There were roads of a sort built by the Gauls; they were far from the barbarians that the Romans liked to portray them and their road network provided a sub structure of communications for the new masters of the territory.

Before he returned to Rome, Domitius gave instructions for the construction of what was to become one of the greatest roads in Roman history. Named after him, initially the Via Domitia was surveyed to run from Beaucaire near Avignon, south west down through Narbonne – which was earmarked as a pivotal military strongpoint – and ending at Col du Perthus on the Spanish border – where it would then lead into the main road being built north-westwards from Toulouse on the coast to Bordeaux on the Atlantic, the Via Aquitania. Although history does not record which Roman ordered the building of this offshoot; it is possible

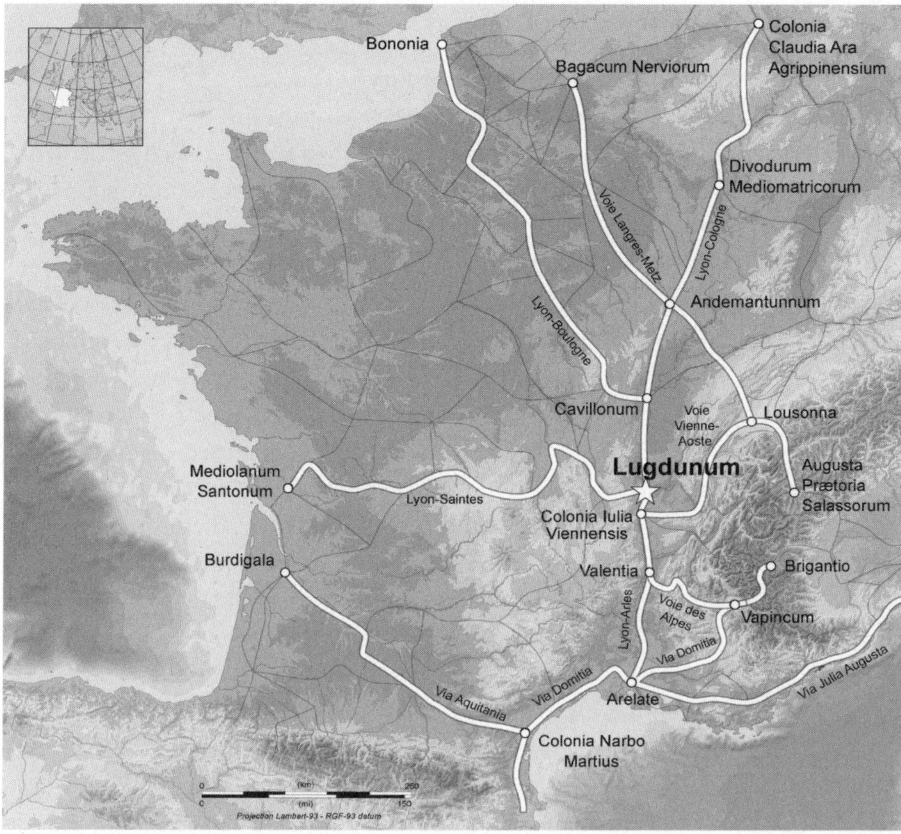

The development of the main Roman road system across the province.

that Domitian was also responsible, wanting a navigable road to the northwest to gather the much-needed tribute for the Roman treasury. Over the centuries to come, the Via Domitia was naturally extended to reach back eastwards as far as the Italian border but for now, a great deal of work lay ahead for Roman surveyors, engineers, stone cutters, wagon masters, camp followers, prostitutes, ditch diggers and thousands of slaves.

Tracing part of the ancient route said to have been trodden by the Greek hero Heracles, the Roman surveyors made use of any advantage they could – they were well aware that Hannibal and his elephants had come from the opposite direction on exactly this same route to Rome less than 100 years before. The process for excavating and laying a Roman road were well known, and experienced road builders would have been recruited to the task with legionaries overseeing the large camps of slaves forced into building over their own land. On the approaches to towns and *coloniae*, or through triumphal arches or across bridges, beautifully paved areas were more carefully constructed and many of these remain today, still grooved with centuries of traffic.

New Roman Accommodation Built Along the Way …

Domitian founded not only the new military settlement of Colonia Narbo Martius (Narbonne), but also Forum Domitii (Montbazin) and both became central staging posts along the new highway, but in between the main settlements were a range of differing planned buildings. To provide a night's rest or pit stop for the thousands of governmental administrators, politicians, officers and dignitaries that would now start to flow through the new province, *mansiones* were situated at roughly every 25-30km – the average distance a man could walk on foot – but sometimes they were far closer if the terrain was harsh. Managed by a *mansionarius*, the initial small stone buildings that would have housed our courier gradually became extended, just like a modern day petrol station, and instead of just a bed for the night and some feed for the horses, over time new infrastructures have been discovered including small gardens and even baths – no doubt depending on the level of traffic and the initiative of the superintendent who was paid by the government through the local administration to look after the needs of government officials, and no doubt tips supplemented their pay.

But what about the unofficial traveller with little money? Less reputable establishments often sprang up near to the *mansiones* and these were the *cauponae* – they also provided a bed for the night but often the traveller was not alone. Prostitutes and thieves could and did frequent such places and graffiti decorates some of the remains which have been found. So what about the non-governmental traveller who also did not want to have his throat cut or spend the night with the local girls? For the more refined traveller there were the *tabernae.* Initially not Taverns as we may know them but similar to roadside houses that were, by law, required to provide hospitality on demand. *Taberna* is derived from 'shed' or 'board', and these could be very basic hostels, but they were clean and often with a family in residence who supplemented their income by offering a bed for the night. Over time, many did grow into taverns and some even developed renown as being quite the place to stop with good food and welcome. In his letter of 27 January 61 CE, Cicero mentions that he had received three letters from his friend Atticus – one of which had been handed over at 'Three Taverns' – clearly a complex of *tabernae* on the lines of an M25 complex near London.

> The small town of Montferrand Aude is situated 50km north-west of Carcassonne alongside the N113 to Toulouse, and the remains of a roadside *mansio* can be seen which was at one time converted into an early Christian church.

Lastly there were the *mutationes.* Given that the main mode of transportation around the empire, apart from on foot, was by horse, then they too needed looking after and a 'changing station' or *mutatio/nes* was an essential feature of any road, be it Roman or otherwise. Clustered around making a small living would be all the paraphernalia needed for travelling by horse – wheelwrights for that dodgy offside front wheel on the wagon, veterinarians to deal with sick animals – *equarii medici* – feed for their animals or in the case of a military courier, a new horse altogether to help maintain his speed with his despatches.

Milestones (*miliarium*)

Along the Via Domitia between Beaucaire and Le Perthus, over eighty Roman milestones have been discovered. This may indicate a Roman preoccupation with measuring time and distance which was certainly important for the army at least but it is also an indication of how, during the later imperial period, local administrators were keen to show their loyalty to the new Emperor – especially if he was going to be passing by. Stone masons were commissioned to carve into granite deep incisions that would stand the test of time and they would be pleased with the results. The ancient town of Alba is surrounded by small, remote villages and was, yet again, founded over the site of a large, 30-hectare Iron Age *oppidum* – likely to have been the capital of the Helviens territory and the home of their King Bituitus. Once conquered by the troops of Fabius Maximus, Roman colonisation continued and in the centre of the town are a number of Roman remains that indicate thriving trade with Rome was already well under way before the final invasion.

Building the Via Domitia

Building Domitius' new road was going to involve all the best technology and skills that the early years of the last century of the Republic could apply. The skilled professionals that built roads were known as *agrimesores* and, alongside numerous other skilled roles needed to build an empire, this was a well-regarded profession requiring literate and numerate men of intelligence. There was no college of training as far as we know but the skills and workmanship was clearly passed down through generations, and especially so from the late-first century onwards when road building blossomed throughout Roman Europe.

In Roman Gaul there are many examples of Roman road building that has defeated the ages and, apart from laying out the best routes through thousands of miles of French countryside, they also survive in their original form. Many parts of the Via Domitia, the Via Julia Augusta (which later linked eastwards to

Leaving Alba and heading east towards Le Teil on the main road to Montelimar, there is a visible milestone from the first century which is one of at least twenty on the road from Nîmes indication that this Roman 'B-road' was indeed a busy highway northward from the coast. The deep inscription states that it is four Roman miles from Alba and indicative that Alba, though deceptively quiet today, was once an Iron Age and then Roman centre of much activity.

the Roman border) and the Via Aquitania – both in its earliest incantation and later – can still be walked along today. Specialists were needed in considerable numbers as parts of the route required bridges to be designed and built or forts laid out for the military, and of course the massive aqueducts required to provide water for all the uses the Romans needed in their new *colonia* – a bucket from a well was not going to sustain a population of thousands nor clear away its waste.

The main tool of the trade was the *decempeda* – a surveyor's rod of 'ten feet' which allowed distances of twenty feet to be covered, with two rods leap-frogging each other, very quickly. The *groma* used geometry and lead weights suspended from a cross-piece and was the surveyor's main instrument for laying out the grid patterns of towns or ensuring the road ran straight and this, together with an array of other tools and skills, allowed the surveyor to mark out a landscape that we have used for over 2,000 years – these roads are their legacy to us and testament to their skill, vision, dedication and hard labour under canvass for years on end. Indeed, their ashes lay lost and forgotten alongside the roads that they constructed.

Section of the Via Domitia is preserved in Narbonne at the Hôtel de Ville. Fascinating design means that you can stand on the modern-day road system and see opened up below where fellow travellers walked and rode over 1,000 years ago on the same spot.

The *Colonia* at Narbo, 118: by 23 BCE the capital of the new province

It would not be until the first emperor of the new imperial age, Augustus, visited Narbo Martius in 23 BCE that it was formally proclaimed the capital of the new province and given its name Narbonensis – almost 100 years after Domitius recognised Narbonne as a vital strategic link with Spain and the north Atlantic coasts and it was here that the two new roads – the Via

Domitia and the Via Aquitania – took shape. Narbo was not only at a central point on the routes to Spain but also was already a bustling port, ensuring that military supplies and reinforcements could be injected into the heart of the region rather than having to fight their way through from northern Italy. Thus, it is no surprise that Narbonne and the area around has plenty of evidence of Roman occupation and the many inscriptions around Aix-en-Provence deserve a special mention.[57]

As they mapped out where the new highway would run, Roman surveyors looked back to whence they had come and built back towards the east and the Italian border but this time well inland, through Nîmes (Nemausus) and cutting through the territories of the former tribal lands. Tradition dates the founding of Roman Narbo as 118 BCE and initially the small settlement of Greek and Celtic influences received the stationing of an army garrison to guard the building of the new highway from attack. Later, as the town grew, it became a full colony and the name was changed to Colonia Narbo Martius and, in 23 Augustus formally named the entire province Gallia Narbonensis – the nexus point and capital of the whole province.

The Via Domitia passed through the centre of Narbo Martius. Armies traditionally love to parade directly through cheering crowds, even though this may have proven to be a bottleneck as larger formations arrived. While the Romans were quite rightly focussed on the conquest of southern Gaul – both along the coastal routes but also forging northwards inland – they were also gradually extending their grip on Spain and an increasing number of large, legion-sized, troop movements passed directly through and around the outer limits of Narbo until even whole armies marched along this route and over the *pons* (bridge) to the south of the Roman settlement.

It is still unclear where the exact centre of Roman Narbonne was situated. Climate change is not new and the local river systems were already changing in this period, which meant that settlement patterns were changing too. A.L.F. Rivet rightly established that not only were there numerous Iron Age *oppida* on the surrounding hills that could have been used to site the first Roman *colonia* in Gaul, but also that Narbonne itself today yields little pre-Roman evidence of occupation, which might mean that the earliest site was in fact a Roman fort with a garrison which, with the usual practice of a town expanding around the fort to supply the soldiers, was in fact the genesis of the colony.[58]

Writing in the very early years of the first century CE, in his *Geographika*, Strabo states that: '*Narbonne is situated above the outlets of the Aude and the lake of Narbonne. It is the principal commercial city on this coast*',[59] which suggests that, even though evidence of Iron Age prosperity is elusive, not to say invisible, it is likely that a sizeable settlement was situated here well before the Romans arrived and that is why they selected it for the capital of the entire province.

Today it is possible to zig zag around the town from one Roman site to another. The placid atmosphere belies just how frenetic this town must have been from around 110 BCE onwards as the population grew. Alongside the flourishing trade through the port, there would have been an endless traffic along the Via Domitia, with weary travellers choosing to recuperate from their journey in the town, government officials arriving to deliver or instigate administrative issues or a myriad of other reasons to stop over. Apart from the section of the Via Domitia which gives a sense of the numbers of commuters passing by the settlement, there is also the *horreum* or warehouse.

> The *horreum* (the town's public warehouse) is a stunning underground reminder of Roman architecture, and nearby the Musée Archéologique displays numerous busts, coins and artefacts of the everyday life of the Roman inhabitants.

Located underground, this somewhat claustrophobic and yet impressive structure is so impressive, not just because of the building techniques used in its construction, but also the scale. This was where the merchants of the emerging commercial centre of Narbo stored their goods safely prior to sale. Grain, olive oil, wine, food, clothing and even marble for building would have been unloaded here and kept under guard. Larger towns may have numerous *horrea*, with each room rented out to a different merchant or trader. More like a cellar (*horrea subterraneum),* the cold air acted like a semi-cold fridge to keep food fresh, and the doors on each room were protected with locks and bolts, and fire risk was reduced by the use of only stone walls.

The brickwork design was not random but, just like the surveyors building the roads, followed a strictly prescribed pattern. Inside the vaults the bricklayers created excellent stonework with the traditional square stone blocks – which would have been cut outside by the masons – laid at an angle or *opus reticulatum* which was very popular in the first century BCE. Once completed, the *horreum* was named after the owners, dedicated to an emperor, or after the items they stored. Some of the most impressive in the whole empire were those of the great port of Ostia on the way into Rome itself, some of which can still be seen today and no doubt goods stored in Ostia were shipped to Narbo across the Mediterranean from *horreum* to *horreum*. In fact, one particular mosaic that survives in present day Ostia shows the existence of a special type of sailor that was skilled in trade on the route between Ostia and Narbo, such was the extent of frequent trade with the new provincial city that exploded with conquest and absorption into the empire. Dating of the Narbo warehouse suggests that it was constructed around the time that Caesar settled his Tenth legion there in the mid- to late-40s BCE and this would fit with the need to export a considerable amount of goods for the new inhabitants as the town swelled.

In the first century, the River Atax flowed through the town. At that time the banks would have been natural and wide with no embanking, so the river today only bears a very scant resemblance to the original, however one of the original seven spans can still be seen and is testament to the beauty of Roman mathematics and design – as well as to the brick workers and builders.

Another wonderful representation of the Republican period in Narbo is the House of the Genius. Situated within a cloister or *claustrum*, this small enclosure reveals part of what Narbonne would have looked and felt like in the first century.

> The House of the Genius can be found just south of the main cemetery inside what is also known as Le Clos de la Lombarde – a small area or cloister of the original Roman town.

The house is an impressive building covering nearly 1,000 square metres and compares favourably with those in Pompeii both in style and design – indicating that the rules of fashion permeated the empire through word of mouth and no doubt parchment plans, plus having their roots amongst the noble houses of Rome. Porticos surround a garden and atrium which served as the usual semi-public meeting place so important to a well-known figure or official, the early morning meetings with clients being as much about display as functionality. There are also remains of the dining room (*triclinium*) as well as many fine black and white mosaics and, naturally, the colourful winged Apollo carrying a cornucopia is the image from which the house takes its name. Clearly building and the layout of Narbo exploded within fifty years of becoming the centre of the province, and majestic large houses such as this no doubt covered the centre of the new city. James Bromwich tells us:

> *'From inscriptions, a list of buildings that impressed the fifth-century writer Sidonius Apollinaris and fragmentary archaeological finds, it seems that there were two forums and their associated buildings; the largest amphitheatre in the province, found in 1838, but badly excavated, poorly drawn and then built over; a large public bath next to the amphitheatre and probably a Flavian provincial cult centre; a theatre, though its site is totally unknown; and a number of temples. There were also fine houses, as wall paintings and mosaics*

indicate. M.Gayraud in his major works on the city suggests that it extended over 100ha and had a population of 35,000.'[60]

As soon as the provincial governor's residence was built in the town, we can imagine how the traffic to and from Narbo Martius must have blossomed and how vital the new roads were – adding more pressure on the slaves to work faster, harder and to die for Rome – just in case we are swayed by the magnificence of public building and forget the other side of Roman rule. Instead of one military courier passing through occasionally, there would now be many arriving each day and heading off in all sorts of directions, stepping up the pace of control and exploitation. At the same time, however, other sites across southern France had been long identified as places for growth and very soon Narbo would be competing for building materials with Nîmes, Arles and a whole host of smaller new Roman settlements. The army too needed supplies of building materials and they would have to argue their case by letter via the couriers to and from Rome.

As a final testament to the seismic changeover between tribal Gaul and the arrival of Rome – or the eradication of one civilisation and the implantation of another – just 4 kilometres to the north-west of Narbonne the remains of another *oppidum*, this time at Montlares, can still be seen. Only 56m high but

The Pont des Marchands (Merchants' Bridge) is a bridge over a canal in Narbonne. This remaining arch is one of what would have been the main Roman bridge over the Atex Flumen (River Atex), which became redundant with climate change and as the course of the river moved. What is left now is a single span of what would have been six or seven arches of this very impressive bridge over what was, then, a very wide and flat river. The remaining arches still exist but they have been built into the foundations of what are medieval buildings over what is now a refilled and banked river bed – the Canal de la Robine. This is one of only two bridges in the whole of France that are still 'inhabited'. If one stands back and imagines the bridge in Roman times, removing the housing from our gaze, then one can see that the remaining span is sloping away indicating that it was on the ascending slope of the huge bridge – at the same time we can imagine the hundreds of thousands of Roman soldiers, carts, wagons and hordes that would have traversed this bridge over hundreds of years – a testament to our imagination if we can do it, as well as to the Roman engineers. One final point to note is that the bridge span seems very low. In fact, the building and embanking of the canal raised the water level by 3-or-so metres, so in fact we cannot really see the full grace of the design.

still overlooking the plains around, this was the home of the Elisyces tribe. Now extinct in reality and almost extinct in history, it is yet another of the *oppida* mentioned in PART II of this book, where a civilisation once existed and was subsequently and gently erased by Romanisation. It was here that the tribe, once overrun by their neighbours the Volcae, tried to survive for a second time but, even after a brief spell believing they could work alongside Rome – and where they could try to benefit from the new prosperity of trade – they gave up and were assimilated into Narbo Martius. If you visit, it is still possible to see where a civilisation lived, worked and died amongst the nature that still survives, amongst the smells of many summers that they too would have recognised. Below you, overlook Narbonne, another civilisation that overlays even that of Rome.

> *'I met a traveller from an antique land,*
> *Who said – "Two vast and trunkless legs of stone*
> *Stand in the desert...Near them, on the sand,*
> *Half sunk a shattered visage lies, whose frown,*
> *And wrinkled lip, the sneer of cold command,*
> *Tell that its sculptor well those passions read*
> *Which yet survive, stamped on those lifeless things,*
> *The hand that mocked them, and the heart that fed;*
> *And on the pedestal, these words appear:*
> *My name is Ozymandias, King of Kings;*
> *Look on my Works, ye Mighty, and despair!*
> *Nothing beside remains. Round the decay*
> *Of that colossal Wreck, boundless and bare*
> *The lone and level sands stretch far away.'*
>
> Percy Bysshe Shelley

The exact date of the founding of the *colonia* is still a matter of debate amongst historians and an excellent analysis of this can be found in an article by Barbara Levick in *The Classical Quarterly* for 1971.[61] The use of numismatic dating suggests a possibly slightly later date when compared to the dating of consulships in Rome and decisions made within those periods of office, but we are safe to assume that 118 BCE is a strong contender as the date most normally associated with the establishment of the *colonia*.

As what would become a *colonia*, enlarged after 118 BCE, archaeological evidence shows that Roman houses were built all around the central squares of the town layout and Narbo became the effective, if not the official, capital of the whole province. Equally, a map of the surrounding region shows that the flat alluvial plains surrounding Narbo Martius become dotted with all manner and shape of Roman villas, most postdating the control that Rome exerted over the region after 118. The whole area exudes an abundance of Roman remains, good fortune, fine climate and agricultural and commercial vitality. In his *Pro Fonteio* (for or on behalf of Fonteius – a propraetor for Gallia Narbonensis, charged with extortion in 69 BCE) Cicero talks of Narbo Martius and the whole area as a major wine producer in the region, and certainly the port of the 'town' – as Cicero referred to it at that time – would have already been a vibrant centre of exchange and trade which could only have expanded hugely with the influx of people to what must have become a city before the end of the first century BCE.[62]

Part III

How Did Rome Govern and Exploit Gallia Narbonensis?

Chapter 10

Settlement by Osmosis – People Not Policies Make Provinces

The Tenth Legion (Legio X) – *Equestris*

In 45 BCE, seventy-three years after its foundation, Narbo Martius would eventually become home to another major influx of Roman citizens. When Julius Caesar fought his Civil War for control of the state and the establishment of his dictatorship, he found many enemies rose up against him in the region of southern France – especially the citizens of Marseilles. Consequently, once the war was successfully won, he decided to award his veterans of the Tenth Legion lands all around Narbo Martius.

The Tenth was no ordinary legion. Originally raised by Caesar in 61 BCE, when he was the governor of Hispania Ulterior, the Tenth became his most trusted and one of his most victorious and brutal legions with an unequalled battle record. The men of the elite Legio X fought for Caesar all over Spain, modern day Portugal, and Gaul in some of the most brutal battles against the largest

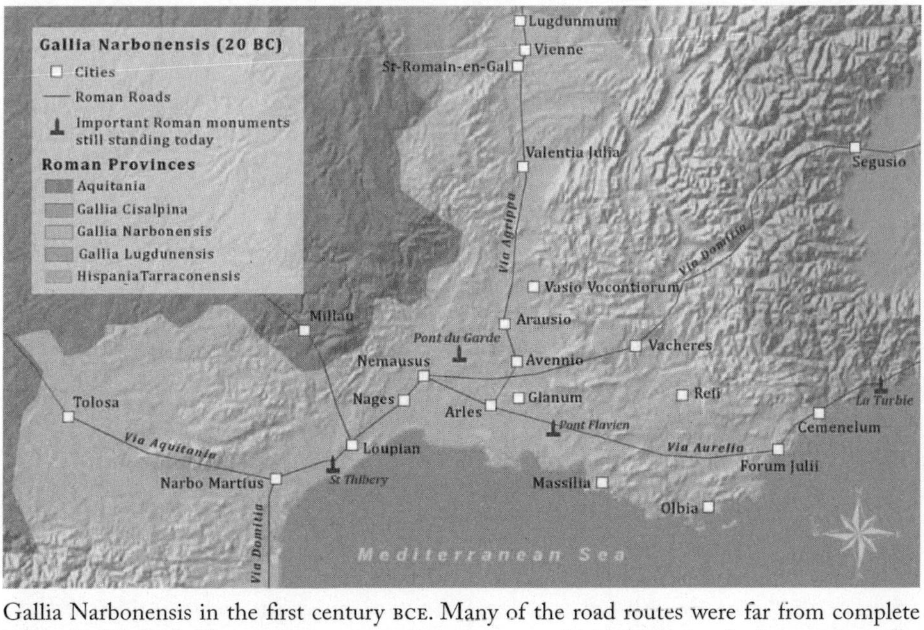

Gallia Narbonensis in the first century BCE. Many of the road routes were far from complete and it would take half a century to construct these into navigable highways for large scale traffic.

armies the Gallic tribes could muster and they often feature in his account of the wars – *The Commentaries*. Legio X took the Spanish Bull as its emblem and Caesar counted many personal and trusted friends amongst its ranks.

It was in 45 BCE that Caesar finally disbanded the legion after sixteen years' service and awarded Narbo as their retirement home and with this, the whole area surrounding the colony became home to some of Rome's finest soldiers. For some, their flirtation with civilian life would be fleeting. With the assassination of Caesar the following year, the Tenth was reconstituted for the civil war against the *Liberatores* – the murderers of Caesar – and some, no doubt, never made it back to Narbo Martius.

However, with those that did survive and settled, the pace of Romanisation quickened. Marriages and children brought communities together, one language declined and another took over, customs merged and religions cohabited. The saddlebags of gold and silver harvested from their campaigns were used by the legionaries to grow new crops, turning swords into ploughshares, and the lands around the *colonia* were neatly divided, drawn by lots, and farmed.

The practice of rewarding legions with the promise of free land for their retirement was a central strategy for the Romans – it kept men motivated for sixteen years of long service, kept their loyalty and support for their general, and secured new provinces with loyal citizens of Rome.

One can only imagine the network of new relationships, children, families, buildings and social constructs that flowed from this unique form of colonisation. With a legion consisting of around 5,000 officers and men, even if 50 per cent took the opportunity of free land, to never return home, then it would have felt like a Roman tidal wave had arrived. Caesar renamed Narbo as *Colonia Julia Paterna Decumanorum* – 'the ancestral Julian (his family gens) colony of the soldiers of the Tenth.' Within fifty years it was a city of 35,000 and this was one aspect of Roman governance – the establishment of loyal colonies in the earliest days that dominated local elites and laid down firm, familial roots. It may have been dangerous for women especially to be seen to be willing to marry into the conquerors, but over time such misgivings would have evaporated in the knowledge that the Romans were here to stay.

If it was the army that claimed a territory for Rome and ensured its security and early governance, then who made the lands into a province? The historical focus was traditionally to look at the obvious evidence, the great figures, inscriptions, buildings and historical accounts of great events and the men and women that shaped them – a sensible and understandable approach to the historiography of the Roman empire. However, in the last two decades, it is the lives of the ordinary people, the diaspora, the almost invisible but dominant force that created empires that have become the central focus of our true appreciation of how

Rome functioned as a society. Whatever the policies, strategies and underlying motivations of those who held power, it was the ordinary citizens of Rome who had the real job of colonisation and Romanisation, created the experience and set the newly conquered worlds alight. But who were these ordinary souls and what do we know about them?

No matter how many slaves were forced into hardship and worked to death building the new roads, or how many surveyors were employed, nor how well they agitated for building materials for their surfaces, bridges and aqueducts, travellers increased alongside them. As soon as word escaped that the region was open for business, then the flow of traffic increased too. Along the ancient Gallic pathways that had been used for centuries, Roman feet now trod along in droves. More than likely even before a section of new road was complete, a whole host of new travellers to southern France began making their way on the new surfaces – perhaps the Roman equivalent of the traffic cone not having been invented yet.

The Romans are noted for innumerable things one of which was their ability to write and shout insults – Pompeii has shown us much in that vein, and we are well aware of various profanities. Cicero too is very informative. In his *Epistulae ad Familiares* (Letters to my Friends) he is able to outline and establish the obscene status of many Latin words and phrases.[63] No sooner had the final layers of powdered cement been watered down through the top layer of cobbled stones than new travellers started making their way along – unless a legionary was stationed there to tell you to *Perite* or 'fuck off', to which the wagon master might respond *Futue te ipsum* or 'go fuck yourself'!

Some less aggressive travellers might be families joining their son or husband who was now a new landowner in Narbo having retired, alive, from his military service, so wagons and children would make the long journey towards the west and along the old coastal paths that our senators of the Punic Wars rode along, or where our military couriers once stopped. But also getting in the way of the surveyors would be a whole host of other visitors on their way to the new towns and cities being established either on the Via Julia Augusta from Italy which led onto what was becoming the Via Domitia south towards Hispania, or north-westwards to the Atlantic coastline on the Via Aquitania or perhaps due north from Arles into central France on what was to become the Via Agrippa towards modern day Lyon.

The Commercialisation of Gallia Narbonensis: oysters – power and morality

We can look to the evidence of the whole Roman empire for clues as to the identity of our fellow backpackers of the age and, if we do, we come across men like Gaius Sergius Orata – 'the oyster man'. It may not seem immediately obvious how the sale and cultivation of oysters impact on our assessment of how the Roman takeover of the province was conducted or what impact would have been felt by the indigenous Celtic/Gallic/ Romano population, but sea shells can tell us much more than one might think.

We know that Orata was active around 95 BCE – around the same time as the Roman stranglehold was being enforced around Arelate, Narbo and Masallia – and we also know that he was highly regarded as a wealthy and 'creative' businessman. His wealth stemmed from cultivating oysters on an industrial scale to feed the growing numbers of people able and willing to buy this popular part of the Roman diet, and he is also credited with being the inventor of the hypocaust method of heating buildings and baths.

Orata was no fool and, with the expansion of *luxuria* that was a key feature of the last century of the Republic, he created his oyster beds at Baiae to provide for the opulent living now going on in the mecca of new villas and recreational facilities, temples and baths. Now only visible with a snorkel, the underwater playground of the Republican super-rich that exploded into life around 70 BCE became the cult retreat for the super-rich of Rome. Here Orata could supply all the great men and families of Rome with freshly harvested oysters in whatever quantities they required – he could also network and build an extravagant lifestyle for himself. Even Cicero is noted as describing Orata in numerous texts as symbolic of the moral dilemma now facing the Roman elite. For example, Orata was a sharp businessman not afraid to use the legal process for his own business ends – such as two court cases over property on the Lucrine Lake, which he first sold then wanted back to farm oysters – and then when the contract for oysters was given to the *publicani* – wanted to sell again and recoup all his losses. Using and trying to bend the law was damaging:

> *'Potentially, then, Orata manipulated the legal system both by personal influence and by strategic interpretation of the law. His legal strategies had an economic payoff, allowing him to recoup some of the costs of the lost opportunity to farm oysters on the Lucrine Lake. Orata's lawsuit illustrates a potential moral problem that commerce posed to elite morality by raising the incentive to put self-interest ahead of the common good. Cicero disapproved of these practices and attitudes and he hoped to correct them with an appropriate philosophical reorientation.'*[64]

Whereas in Italy oysters, mussels and scallops were seen as a delicacy for the wealthiest classes in society, in Narbonensis shellfish had been a part of the staple diet for hundreds of years. As one drives and cycles around the coastal plains of southern France one can often come across long, flat and seemingly open-ended stretches of water. Like a lake but inland from the nearby sea, these reclaimed areas are full of brackish water – not fresh water but lightly saline. Known as *étangs,* these salty lakes and ponds had been farmed for mussels and some oysters well before the first Roman ever travelled through France to Spain and were consumed locally in Massalia, Arles, Narbo and wherever they could be transported before they began to rot. It was therefore hardly a revelation to discover that the Roman soldiers in the *colonia* and the settlers arriving from all over the empire created a demand for all sorts of shellfish – but most especially oysters. When we think of Pliny and how he saw Narbonensis as becoming an extension of Italy, he was perhaps not as aware as he might have been of how Narbonensis had already become a cultural draw and inspiration for Rome itself. The cuisine and pace of life that we associate with this region today was already well known and very attractive to Romans, with a cultural exchange both in and out of the region of those aspects of life that made existence more sensual and fashionable:

> *'What we are observing here has nothing to do with the transfer of a particular elite Roman food custom to Provence, but instead the creation of a new cultural phenomenon arising from the congruence of Roman and indigenous, Provençale culture and locally favourable economic circumstances.'*[65]

The demand for oysters became gradually wider with the new colonies stimulating a need for oyster farming on a large scale by the manipulation of existing food sources. While the nobles and wealthy families of Baiae were paying large bills for oysters to Orata, local markets in Narbonensis were able to supply at a fraction of the price. There are tales of fishermen towing baskets of oysters behind their boats to fool the shellfish into thinking they were still in the sea and one has to wonder if some intrepid oyster salesmen saw the opportunity of substantially undercutting Orata and sailing, for example, from Sardinia or even Marseilles to sell their catch and undercut the great oyster millionaire Orata himself. But a salient point here is that Roman sharp practice in the shape of ruthless businessmen such as Orata, would have seen endless opportunity to exploit the new province for commercial greed and brought with them the 'Roman' way of doing business, which the locals of Nabonensis would have to battle with from an inferior position from the start.

The olive – *oleum* – the oil of empire

Peace was the essential prerequisite for government to work and for commerce to flourish, and merchants and their business interests were carriers of peaceful intent. When Adolf Hitler invaded the Ukraine in 1941 he had the opportunity of following the Roman model of initial military conquest followed by magnanimous attempts to work to establish jointly beneficial interests. Instead, he chose barbarity and domination – thus he miscalculated on a tidal wave of hubris and the chance of enlarging his armies with a new voluntary resource of manpower dissolved. Forever at war behind his own lines against a people in continual rebellion, a recipe for certain disaster and erosion of resources – this is not a mistake that the Romans made. Although we may struggle to find the evidence, Orata symbolises the arrival of a commercial spirit designed to subjugate new territories by opportunity of shared success – an offering that appealed to the courageous and the ambitious but also to the conquered – why rebel when your standard of living had never been better and when your new masters gave you every opportunity to share in the magnificence of empire?

In 2020 alone, the Italian people consumed 11.5 litres of olive oil per head – nothing has changed except the quantity has perhaps declined. The joint enterprise that characterised the Romanisation of the new province was equally well illustrated in the case of olive production. Olives were and still are, perhaps, the major culinary image that comes to mind when considering a Mediterranean diet, and the image of an aged and gnarled olive tree is timeless and their cultivation has been dated to at least 6,000 years BCE. Thus, all the many Greek settlements along the south coast of Narbonensis, along with oyster farming, would have been experts in farming olives for food and the 'liquid gold' of olive oil. The influx of Roman entrepreneurs were able to blend in their own skills with those of the Gauls on the chalky soils of Narbonensis and set about increasing production and exports back to the Roman mainland.

Although Pliny the Elder, in his work 'Natural History' – *Naturalis Historia* – noted that the Gauls preferred lard and butter to using oil for cooking, the Romans were dependent on *oleum* – the oil from olives. Roman women used it to nourish their hair, every Roman kitchen needed olive oil, kings were anointed with it, masseurs in the bath houses used it to clean skin, ointment makers needed it for their creams, doctors used it in their treatments and the Temples of every town were lit by lamps filled with olive oil for burning – especially because it was odourless.

It is Cato the Elder that, along with his image of the fig, also left us the recipe for olive tapenade or *epityrum.* In his work called 'On Farming' – *De agri cultura* – Cato tells us:

> *'Epityrum album nigrum variumque sic facto. Ex oleis albis nigris varrsque nuculeos eicito. Sic condito. Concidito ipsas, addito oleum, acetum, coriandum, Cuminum, feniculum, rutam,mentam. In orculam condito, oleum supra siet.*

Ita utito: 'White, black, and mottled epityrum *is made this way. Remove the pits from the white, black and mottled olives. Prepare them as such: break them down, add oil, vinegar, coriander, cumin, fennel, rue and mint. Arrange it in a small jar, pour over oil, and it thus.'*[66]

Cato also tells us down the centuries that his estate workers were fed on bread, olives and wine all from his estates.

In Moulin des Bouillons in the Vaucluse, due west of Apt, an old farmhouse remains in the Calveron valley. Bromwich tells us that it is a sixteenth-century building but that the inside has a massive and ancient olive press of 'Gallo-Roman origin.'[67] Although this is disputed, what is not in doubt is that the surrounding region has been full of Roman finds and the technology for oil extraction is identical to that described by Pliny.

The two main types of Roman olive mill were the *trapetum* and the *mola olearia*, and examples of both are found throughout Provence. At the start of winter, olives would be harvested by hand throughout the farms and communities of Narbonensis, then laid on rush mats and washed before being soaked in hot water to make the extraction of the kernel effortless. Either animal or human power pushed the *cupa* or mill post around and the millstones did their job, with the oil from the olives of the first pressing producing the best quality. The pulp or *sampsa* was collected and stacked in baskets, dried and used for fuel, while the oil went into storage jars and amphorae. Thus, oil production was already an established part of the commerce of Narbonensis – certainly amongst the Romanised settlements and, over time, the Celtic and Gallic predilection for lard would be replaced and they too would succumb to the many uses that olive oil could be put towards. Those entrepreneurs, both Roman or Celt, that could see the potential for industrialising olive production in southern France were some of the same people that lived in the most opulent of villas throughout the region.

Tax Collection

Annius Plocamus – the tax farmer and collector – represents the inevitable arrival of the Roman state, reminding the Gauls, Greeks, Celts and Spanish inhabitants of Gallia Narbonensis that the peace and prosperity of Rome came at a price.

Although living slightly later than Orata, Plocamus was also emblematic of the type of new profession making its way into southern France. The role of tax farmer was risky, unpopular but also potentially highly lucrative and you needed to be a particular type of person to take on this role successfully. Plocamus is recorded in history by graffiti, and also by Pliny, who describes his activities. Interestingly, Plocamus was not a commercially-minded member of the *equites*, but a freedman – someone who had once been a slave but had been through the process of manumission and gained his freedom from servitude and had selected tax collecting as his job. This legal exercise, whereby their master assured their freedom either in their will or in front of a magistrate, created the *liberti*, another class of people within the multi-layered society of Rome and, although barred from reaching higher into new social classes, the *liberti* were created in large numbers and were able to carve out high levels of wealth and status of their own. In their turn, new lands meant new opportunities and men like Plocamus, who Pliny tells us travelled as far as Sri Lanka, could offer themselves as tax-gatherers or join a collective of such men to raise the funds needed to collect taxes within the new province. They may have done this due to their mathematical prowess, their sense of justice to the state, or more likely because they had the muscle and determination needed to extract money from greedy hands.

As Narbonensis became recognised as a formal province of Rome in 118 BCE, the system for collecting taxes was in a state of transition. For centuries, Romans had experienced very low taxes – between 1 and 3 per cent, levied on goods and property. With imperial expansion, especially into silver-rich areas such as Hispania, domestic taxes remained very low, but to compensate for the enlarged armed forces needed to create and maintain new lands, provincial taxes were inevitably to rise.

For some time, taxes were levied on communities rather than individuals, and this was often because the lack of information about exactly who the Romans now controlled was so poor and would take many years to create. Under these circumstances, tax farmers could do very well as there was no check on their demands from the Senate and it was they who decided what a community could contribute. Without any doubt this led to great friction between the conquered and the conquerors and the army was often needed to enforce the tax demands. Add to this the lack of strict guidelines to provincial governors – until the Augustan period, where expectations changed – and many a corrupt governor worked hand in hand with corrupt tax farmers and stripped their province clean in their year in office. There are numerous examples in the prosecutions and charges laid against corrupt provincial governors during the legal career of Marcus Tullius Cicero and Cato the Younger that expose the avaricious and brutal exploitation by men such as Gaius Verres and his tyranny over Sicily. What degree of early corruption there was in the governance of Gallia Narbonensis is more difficult to ascertain as it was still a province with an embryonic legal system. Provincial records remain very sparse – certainly compared to the treasure trove of material that we have been left by Cicero in the Roman courts – but it is certain that, in the early days of the administration of the province, the tax farmers played a significant role in helping provincial governance to evolve with a concomitant increase in anger and dissatisfaction with the same.

Dividing up the land – Cadastra A, B and C

Cadastration was the process of land division that attempted to delineate civic land holdings between private, imperial and civic. Property holding, the legality of ownership and proof of both were very important to the Roman psyche and was directly linked to states, wealth and therefore taxes.

A small army of surveyors were constantly travelling the various provinces of the empire trying to record the land holdings that they found or created. The role of *contemplator* or *mensor* both suggest a process of deliberation and consideration as part of their role and that is a reflection of one of the greatest challenges of the emerging and expanding empire – how to account for what existed, where it was, what was the value and who owned it.

There were various ways over the centuries of empire by which the Roman surveyors thought about land, discussed who owned it and then made their decisions. In Southern France, a common system seems to have been a stone marker or pillar. Often carved with the names of the owners and the year of the decision, many such stones have been plundered or ploughed away into the soil of Provence, but occasionally they are discovered. Another method was a hand drawn map given to each of the tens of thousands of retiring legionaries in and around the military *colonia*, with small parcels of land given as promised by their former generals after their service. This was also known as *centurinatio* which equalled 100 holdings at a time. When the land divisions had been decided, the parcels of land were drawn by lot to avoid any charges of favouritism, although without doubt there would be arguments over who received the best land, the ones near water and those full of rock.

However the most remarkable remains of Roman cadastration are what are referred to as Cadastra A to C. Found during excavations in 1949, these fragments are to be found in the Municipal Museum of Orange. The carved tablets would originally have been meticulously measured and carved before being put on display in the *tabularium* – the administrative office of any community – so that all the residents could see the plot divisions and all was above board. It was under the reign of emperor Vespasian (69-79) that the lands around Orange were designated for a revised survey which would expose which lands remained to be allocated, to discover what had been misappropriated and the parts that belonged to the community for the landless to try to survive upon. It was most likely the retiring legionaries of Legio II Augusta that needed this survey, as they were granted this area to colonise while their comrades returned to Britannia after the civil war in 69 CE. The legion had been loyal to Vespasian in the civil war and, given that it was he who emerged both victorious and alive in the 'Year of the Four Emperors' it was likely that the distribution of lands north of Orange was their reward for assisting him ascend the imperial throne.

Of the three fragments, it is Cadastra B that is in the best condition and refers to an area which is north of Orange and then reaches northwards towards Montelimar. One can imagine the intricacies of this survey work, the need to work around mountains and rivers and to try to only allocate cultivatable land. Tablets such as these may have been used all over Narbonensis and no doubt many remain in ploughed land across the province.

> The fragments cover an area that begins near Orange and then proceeds northwards towards Montelimar, where the Cadastra reaches the southern suburbs. The Municipal Museum in Orange contains thousands of artefacts from the many excavations in the area, including the Cadastra fragments and is opposite the theatre in Rue Roche.

The new tax collectors in Gallia Narbonensis not only performed a valuable service in collecting money for the state, but also in training the largely non-Roman population into understanding the new commitments they had to Rome – demanding the taxes they felt were due or felt the people could afford. They also helped to establish the role of local government in new provinces with the implantation of regular visits, translating the wishes of the governor, who in turn acted on the wishes of the central authority in Rome. This was government by osmosis – not by decree but by the regularity of local control. These roles were needed even after the Augustan changes of taxation based on a population census, so there were always jobs for the tax collector.

How Did the Rural Landscape Change with *Centurinatio*?

The past thirty years have seen significant advances in the science of landscape archaeology and the ability of historians to research the pre-Roman landscape of southern France. One particular area that has been intensively researched is that of the west bank of the Rhône River or eastern Languedoc. This area between Nîmes and Montpellier to the south west consists of a northern range of mountains, then southwards changing into rural farmlands and then the east-west coastal plain either side of the Vidourle and Vistre rivers. It is directly through the rural farmland area that the new Via Domitia would be built, with the hills to the north and the coastal plains to the south – linking already-established Gallo-Roman settlements.

The research by Francois Favory, Marie-Jeanne Ouruachi and Laure Nuninger published in 2009 investigates and assesses a wide range of scholarly investigations to produce an image of how at least one rural area of pre–Roman Gaul became reshaped by conquest and Romanisation.[68] If the expansion of urban areas under Roman influence tended to absorb the Iron Age settlements around them, leaving the landscape gradually empty of Gallic tribes, then the *centurinatio* of rural areas for the veterans of the legions did the same – with the exception that the French landscape had its own way of absorbing the new settlers. Either way, the pre-Roman landscape was effectively being cleared and repopulated and the changes were dramatic in the eastern Languedoc.

The Iron Age disposition of hill forts and settlements was not only ancient, by hundreds if not thousands of years, but it had not evolved as much by chance as design. Research shows that there was a hierarchy of settlement, from the largest *oppida* covering up to forty hectares down through those whose range was thirty to the smallest settlements farming or managing five hectares.[69] The average distances between the largest *oppida* was between 75-150km – or 3 hours walking distance – more than enough space to ensure that there was little direct competition or friction. With the desolation of these larger units, the land was free for the use of the Romans and *centurinatio* became a gradual process of taking the best lands first – those with flat cultivatable soils and available water – which meant that there were often large areas unoccupied – a number of patchwork quilts, some linked together and others totally isolated.

The process began around the time of Caesar, when the first legions were disbanded and lands allocated in the new province of Narbonensis, and continued apace through the Augustan period but it was a stop – start invasion. If legions were away fighting all the time and if the empire kept growing, then there were fallow periods where no *centurinatio* took place at all. The most common plot size within the century was 700 metres square – this was the small 'farm' promised to each legionary that survived loyal service – and they in turn built small agropastoral buildings for their animals and often their families to live in. One totally new rural landscape feature in this part of France – which may have been replicated across the province – was that groups of new settlers agreed to place their rudimentary buildings in a cluster together. Like settlers forging a new frontier in Canada or the Mid-West of the United States of America, these new settlements became *villae* or villages, and in places around them were located individual villas for those whose means were far more substantial.

Interestingly, the *villae* had few amenities or communications – they would have been reached across grasslands and rough ground: small tracks may have existed but nothing else. The protection and society they gained was just enough for a basic living and start of a new life, the weather was good, the soils rich and they could begin a family mixing the two or three cultures together. Later, when the 'motorway' of the Via Domitia cut through the landscape, and, certainly in the second century CE, the attraction of the road and fast communications between the many new town settlements saw these pioneering settlements disappear and it is their occasional remains that show as collections of rubble and rocks in the ploughed fields today.

The Building Blocks of Empire – bricks, tiles and concrete

Under the white marble of the columns and buildings of Rome were bricks, red, brown and black – the same was true of any great city in the imperial Roman era. With brick being the true symbol of Roman construction, it follows that brick and tile making was one of the largest industries of the Roman world.

When the Roman army evaluated where it needed to build permanent fortresses for their legionaries, it was with the background knowledge that the site would inevitably expand into a full civilian settlement outside the walls – thus it was necessary, alongside considerations of availability of water and communications, to locate the fort near to suitable soil or clay deposits so that tile and brick manufacturing could easily follow. Naturally, archaeologists have discovered brick ovens all over the Roman world, and from every era and in every conceivable size from small and local to the industrial scale that would have made the owners seriously rich individuals.

It was not just men that were entrepreneurially minded either, with women like Flavia Seia Isaurica being the owner and manager of her own brick works. We know of Isaurica's existence partly through the work of Piotr Berdowski. In 2007 Berdowski published his work on the economic activities of women in ancient Rome, and amongst his sources of evidence was the work of Isaurica who was the *domina* or owner of six clay beds and brick works to the south of Rome.[70] Archaeological research has shown that there were at least sixteen different *officiatores* or foremen in her employ – we know this through the various brick stamps found on her bricks. Just like a silver mark, these tell us where and who made these fine Roman bricks and, to date, ten different women have been found to have run brick works across the Roman empire. Although still invisible today, perhaps there were similar women working in Gallia Narbonensis.

Flourishing in the 140s CE, Isaurica may have inherited this business or built it up herself, but either way she ran it as the boss and we can only wonder how many women, and not necessarily just Roman women, began their own businesses in the new province on the back of new opportunity within a society still not Romanised. Iron age women were already independently-minded, queens and leaders of tribes were women, and priestesses too, so it may not have been too much of a leap forward to see women exploiting the availability of large numbers of new inhabitants – with cash in their pockets – to create their own economic futures and at the same time create jobs for workers, wagon masters, builders, architects, and engineers, so assisting in the pace of economic trade across the new province. If we consider for a moment just how many millions of bricks might be needed to construct just one aqueduct, and there were dozens across Narbonensis, then the brick works had to be everywhere.

It was the Roman dream not only to create functional and essential architecture that provided for sanitation and modern services to their cities, but also to make each *colonia* or urban – *urbs* – area a model of Roman prestige and power. The splendour of the Roman settlement was essential to convey notions of power, legacy and greatness and it is Roman concrete and bricks that have survived over 2,000 years to remind us of what the Romans achieved in their time on this earth.

The most ancient of Roman walls are often referred to as cyclopean – suggesting that only the giants of Greek mythology could lift them. Adobe bricks made of a mix of sand, silt and clay mixed with water and straw, dried in the sun, were used for the earliest Roman houses. In time cut limestone blocks began to be used for grander buildings and trophies, and then it was the turn of the *Opus caementicium* – a narrow brick composed of volcanic ash limestone and water. Discovered in and around the volcanic soils of Naples, these bricks spread throughout Italy in the second- and first-centuries BCE and then outwards into the new provinces. But it was *opus latercium* – brickwork – which we recognise as the most common format of rectangular reddish bricks that faced the walls, but were backfilled inside with Roman cement – hence they still stand today. Indeed, it is only the plunder in the post Roman period that saw many walls reduced to the size they are now. The vast tonnage of cement and back fill materials required for the largest projects would overpower even the largest construction firms of the modern world.

Slave women who had obtained their freedom were able to make their own way in business too, some even had their own slaves which enabled them to create a commercial future – such was the glory of the dream of Rome, far more than a city, an ideal and a calling. In Arelate (Arles) two such women certainly existed, and we know this from the salvaged and preserved inscriptions on a gravestone – one of 400 inscriptions of various types.

The Taste of the Roman Empire: *garum*

Following closely behind brick and tile production as one of the largest industries of empire was the production of *garum*. One of the most sought-after culinary products throughout Roman history – until salt became too expensive – was *garum*, a fermented rich-tasting fish sauce, and it was this trade or profession that made some Roman merchants become the most successful of all. Traded throughout the empire as a 'must have' condiment, *garum* and an equivalent called *liquamen* was as widespread as ketchup in our world. Hardly a *domus* or home existed without access to some variety of fish sauce, and this was because it added flavour to often very bland food, and all around the coastlines it would have been possible to see both small- and large-scale production – especially in the hot summers when the fermenting pots, jars or tanks would have been easy to spot heating up in the sun and giving off some pretty strong smells in the Adriatic winds.

The army was a massive consumer of the basic varieties of *garum* to help the cooks hide the bland flavours of their cooking, but there were also a number of different recipes or varieties which, because of the process of manufacture, could fetch incredibly high prices. Our focus here is on the trader of *garum* named Aulus Umbricus Scaurus, who is particularly well known to historians because archaeologists have identified both his home and family tomb amongst the remains of Pompeii.

Scaurus may have owned his own small fleet of boats, as some bearing his mark have been discovered in various places across the Mediterranean. Did Scaurus have time to expand his operations along the coastline of Gallia Narbonensis before his likely death in the catastrophe at Vesuvius in 71?

It is certainly possible that Arles was on the list of any entrepreneur seeking to trade inland. As we have seen earlier, the Rhône River was a major commercial artery, and also amongst the Roman inscriptions of the city are those related with *fabri tignarii* (carpenters), *fabri navales* (ship builders), *Architectus Navalis* (a ship designer), and also successful sea captains such as a man named Q. Naviculariens Victorinus, indicating that Arles was much more advanced in trade and ship building than most places in southern Gaul thanks to its position on the Rhône, and no doubt *garum* made its way up river to be unloaded in Arles.[71]

This is not to say that the *garum* industry was not already thriving amongst the Roman communities of Narbo, Nicea, Antipolis and of course the dominant port of Masallia, because it certainly was, but the influx of people on the back of newly-proclaimed Roman ownership would have seen normal commercial pressures break up what were, hitherto, monopolies. No doubt this happened in almost every trade, skill or shop, as new travellers seeking new fortunes spread into the new province and helped to establish peaceful co-existence where none had existed before. If Scaurus acts as a comparison for us, then his suite of shops, also identified by archaeological research, would have been mirrored.

Scaurus also appears to have owned at least six shops for his products, and family members, freedmen and slaves have been identified amongst the pottery shards, including Umbricia Fortunata – another businesswoman this time who lived and worked in Pompeii and produced and sold *garum.* Again, we are able to tell of her existence by the trade mark or *titulus pictus* which was a red and black mark on the neck of an amphora detailing the origin, destination and content of the product – Pompeii has provided thousands of these for us to study and understand.

Clothing the Empire: sheep

Another often-forgotten commercial activity that multiplied exponentially in the wake of the arrival of veterans from the legions and the founding of the *colonia* was sheep farming. Prior to the Romanisation of southern France, individual pastoral shepherding supplied small quantities of meat to the local *oppida* or Romano/Celtic towns and can be identified by the remains of small sheep folds and stockades on the smaller hills surrounding each settlement.

With the gradual increases in population with the wealth to demand larger quantities of meat and wool for clothing, sheep farming also became industrialised as farmers – no doubt many of them retired legionaries on their plots of land – took on the challenge of raising tens of thousands of new sheep. Landscape archaeologists using satellite imagery have studied the Crau Plain – a vast stony and grass area to the south of Arles – and have discovered far larger pens and sheep folds that could hold hundreds of sheep at a time. The research estimates that the animal population grew to in excess of 100,000 animals by the mid- to late-first century CE. With this increase in animal husbandry came not only jobs for more shepherds, but also for *macellarii* (butchers, and from where the word machete derives) and spinners to work the *lana* or wool across many settlements, certainly in the south of the province, and is further evidence not just of a commercial expansion but affluence with the region.

The Peace of Rome: mixing cultures, races and making them Roman

Immigration did not just bleed into Narbonensis from the east – what about the influx of new people from the west, from Hispania and from where the government of Rome was already understood and accepted? Once the new road stretched towards the Spanish border from Narbo, then the way was also open for increased trade with women such as Viria Acte, who was a Spanish entrepreneur who lived and worked in modern-day Valencia making statues for the Roman home and large stone monuments, restoring some others, and otherwise implanting the glory of Rome into the visual memory of the conquered.

But roads that were safe and easy to travel also invited tourism and we should not make the mistake of assuming that Romans were not also tourists – in fact the educated classes in Rome were endlessly interested in the far-flung additions to their empire. Those with the time and the means made their way on excursions – perhaps lasting years – exploring, exploiting and extracting riches from the conquered states. Even Cicero asked his closest friend and ally Atticus to collect books and statues for his homes from his travels across near Asia, Greece and modern-day Turkey.[72] Although incomparable to what we experience today with millions of photographs flowing through social media every day, the Roman tourist trade suggests a type of murky interface between conquest and intellectual interest, where goods were often purchased legitimately but at a price the owners hoped would avoid just seeing them seized for free anyway. To what extent the new settlements and the exploited *oppida* offered riches is debatable but the Gallic tribes were certainly far more skilled and advanced than history has given them credit.

Through a Glass Darkly: decorating the empire in glass

Finally, the Romans loved glass. Although rare and expensive in the early centuries of the Republic, by the mid-first century BCE the plain, transparent aqua blue-green glass that is associated with large scale production was spreading across Italy and the empire. No longer just an individual item of display, so important for the aspiring Roman family, glass was now being used to also feed the economy by being used to transport materials, perfumes, ointments, foods and even toothpaste and powder, and nowhere is this more evident than in the economic explosion of glass production in Narbonensis.

The major change in the production of glass came in the form of glass blowing during the last century of the Republic. It seems likely that there were a small number of sites, in the east of the empire, that produced large blocks of glass which was then sold and transported from the eastern empire to the western provinces and Italy itself. This was then cut and melted down – evidence for the production of raw glass in Italy and Gaul is scarce, but with blocks of imported glass and the introduction of blowing alongside the more precise glass casting, then production was able to vastly expand to fill the demand for cheaper domestic-use glass vessels.

It is the harbour area of Arelate (Arles) that has provided sub-aquatic archaeologists with a great treasure of artefacts. As we know from earlier chapters, Arelate was sited to the north of the massive Rhône delta, giving its port area access both to the south of France and allowing it to act as a gateway into the northern regions. We know that the volume of shipping in and out of Arelate was already substantial even before the Romans formally annexed the province, and that trade was active. Carefully peeling away the layers of silt and alluvial deposits from the eastern side of the harbour revealed the remains of at least twelve boats from the Roman period (including the 30m wreck that was recovered), but also masses of materials including shards of pottery, sculptures, thousands of amphorae – many perhaps dropped during the unloading process – and all manner of finds. However, over the twenty years of the excavations, there was noticeably little glass, even after the conversion of the town into a *colonia* for Legio VI Ferrata by Julius Caesar. Eventually it was recognised that in fact there were thousands of items of glass, but the nature of the dredging tended to miss the translucent glass fragments and when this was rectified over 4,700 pieces were found, including 1,250 complete items.

One of the best places to view a wide selection of Roman glass is the Musée de l'Arles Antique. Situated in the centre of the city and on the south bank of the river, Arles was and is ideally situated for any journey across the low flat plains of the Provence-Alpes-Côte d'Azur region, and the museum contains many items collected from across the area. The pottery and glass collections are some of the best in France.

The fact that the layers from which the vast majority of these glass items were recovered directly correlated to the Augustan and Flavian periods indicates that the influx, through trade, of cheaper aqua-coloured Roman glass was pronounced, and had become part of the new local commercial activity around Arles and no doubt numerous other Roman settlements. But it was not only fragments of the more affordable glass that were found. Alongside the scent and toothpaste bottles were moulded and blown ribbed bowls of the highest quality, delicate beakers with overlaid glass in differing colours, and imaginatively decorated bowls, and even the name of one workshop owner was inscribed as Titienius Iacintus – his name etched for eternity.

The same date range and abundance of glass was discovered in nearby Massalia (Marseilles). Widespread use and manufacture of glass was clearly another new aspect of Narbonensian culture during the Augustan age, but it was not only being produced in new workshops locally but also being imported in large quantities from shipping arriving from the ports of the Mediterranean. French archaeologist Souen Fontaine suggests that 80 per cent of glass arriving into the southern ports of the province was destined for sale north into further Gaul and Britannia, with 20 per cent of locally-produced glass transported from Arles, Lyon or Massalia back into the Mediterranean and, taken as a whole, the production of and trade in glassware is certainly another indicator of the increasing culture and wealth of Narbonensis.[73]

Subduing the Empire with *Romanitas* and Power

Culture is a mixture of inherited and created patterns of social life, fashion, the arts and scientific advances. The process of Romanisation was the manner in which the current, longstanding aspects of Celtic and Gallic culture were adopted and adapted and is referred to as *Romanitas*.

The extent to which the subjugated peoples of southern France accepted the gradual erosion of their own way of life and saw it replaced by the customs and practices of Rome is an area for ongoing debate and research. The rate of assimilation of *Romanitas* or Roman values and way of life depended on a number of variables, such as whether there were viable leaders of the indigenous people to lead revolts, or how entrenched a sense of national feeling existed in the conquered area. On the other hand, the role of the Provincial administrators, such as the Governor, could have a pivotal role in how attractive becoming 'Roman' was for the subjugated peoples, or indeed how present and alive a sense of *Romanitas* already existed – such as in the largely Roman settlements of southern France that our courier of the 140s travelled through. Equally important was the economy, and that was clearly changing and growing fast during the last century BCE and on into the Augustan age, and served to grease the wheels of integration and economic partnership between the resident Celtic/Gallic Romans and the new immigrants flooding in from both east and west.

On the surface it would seem that there is little evidence that the various tribes of what was now to become Gallia Narbonensis put up much of a fight once they had been beaten, and badly beaten, in battle against the Roman legions. By 115 CE it would seem that Rome felt that this was now their province and Domitian at least was setting about bringing his own version of *Romanitas* to the region. There was however one, very important exception that occurred early in the Romanisation of the province, where all that had been gained and planned for was in danger of falling apart – this was the invasion of southern France by the Cimbri and Teutonic hordes in around 110 BCE.

Ironically, history suggests that large numbers, though not all, of the Cimbri left their lands in modern-day Denmark and northern Germany due to climate change. Moving south east through Germany, they both defeated opposition and grew in numbers as they attracted supporting tribes in their search for new lands to settle and to plunder. By late 113 BCE, Rome dispatched Gnaeus Papirius Carbo, consul for that year, with a large army to turn back the invaders in the north. This ended in utter defeat for the legions, as did two further attempts under Marcus Junius Silanus, who met the hordes in the Battle of Arausio on the site of modern-day Orange in 109 BCE. What is now known to history as the Cimbrian War continued with the mass of Gallic, Celtic and Teutonic tribes numbering hundreds of thousands now moving south to Toulouse, and in 107 BCE the next Roman army also suffered defeat and alarm spread throughout Italy that they would be the next target. According to Plutarch:

> *'Soon however, all this envy and hatred and slander of Marius (for his being a novus homo or new man, his success in the Jugurthine War and his open condemnation of the aristocratic elites who had failed in battle so often) was removed and dissipated by the peril which threatened Italy from the west, as soon as the state felt the need of a great general and looked about for a helmsman whom she might employ to save her from so great a deluge of war. Then the people would have nothing to do with anyone of high birth or of a wealthy house who offered himself at the consular elections, but proclaimed Marius consul in spite of his absence from the city. For no sooner had word been brought to the people of the capture of Jugurtha that the reports about the Teutones and Cimbri fell upon their ears. What these reports said about the numbers and strength of the invading hosts was disbelieved at first, but afterwards it was found to be short of the truth. For three hundred thousand armed fighting men were advancing, and much larger hordes of women and children were said to accompany them in quest of land to support so vast a multitude …'*[74]

It was only the decision of the tribes to now head west to plunder Hispania, that perhaps saved a massive turning point in history, and may have even preceded similar events in the fifth century CE which saw the complete collapse of the Roman empire.

The Battle of Aquae Sextiae, 102 BCE

The appointment of Gaius Marius led to the rebuilding of the Gallic Legions that ultimately destroyed this threat, but one can wonder how many of the young men of the recently-conquered tribes of Gallia Narbonensis joined the horde and returned with them, hoping to throw the Romans out of southern France completely. As events turned out, the move towards Hispania gave valuable time to Marius not only to rebuild a Roman army of 30,000 men plus auxiliaries, but he also revolutionised their training. Based around Aquae Sextiae, as we now know right in the centre of the newly-acquired, if not conquered, province, Marius developed a new structure. Experienced soldiers and officers were now signed on for long service, their experience retained to train new cohorts around them. Men were trained to fight in new formations, to carry their own equipment so they were always mobile and ready to fight (the Marian Mules as they were referred to), and encouraged the corporate identity of the legion – something to be maintained and kept alive rather than disbanded after a campaign. Marius then led them to a bitterly- and brutally-fought victory at the battle of the same name in 102 BCE.

The site of the battle remains a mystery. Local legends name Mount St Victoire as the location, but this remains unproven. What is known is that a famed warrior of the Teutones challenged Marius to single combat, to which Marius very wisely replied that if the warrior desired death he could have it in battle – or better still, find a rope and hang himself. No doubt this duel of words was done via translators.

The Teutones and Ambrones tried to lure Marius and his army from his camp near the Rhône River, but this had been anticipated and the Roman camp was well stocked and protected and withstood heavy attacks on its defences for three days. Marius wished to frustrate the barbarian army, but also fight it on ground of his choosing, and he kept his nerve, despite complaints from his men, and then followed the horde when they left to ravage Massalia. Marius followed for many days and each night his army built a new defensive site until, at last, they came near to Aquae Sextiae. The River Atax separated the armies, with the Romans on the northern bank with hills to their backs, and the massed army of 150,000 Teutones and Ambrones to the south. A preliminary fight began between auxiliaries and Celts bathing in the river – apparently drunk on wine and confidence. This soon developed into a larger engagement. Marius was conscious that he had a smaller but better disciplined army and hoped that the barbarians would just charge and try to overwhelm his men. Sending Claudius Marcellus away a few days earlier to arrive hidden on the flank of the barbarian army, Marius held his ground for at least a day and then the attack came. Uphill, against a strong, better trained and equipped Roman force, the warriors of the Teutones and Ambrones were cut to pieces and fell back onto each other – there were so many in one place. When Marcellus suddenly appeared, the warriors collapsed into confusion and the Romans then marched downhill towards them, killing everything in their path. It was a slaughter.

Pliny again related the horror of fighting the barbarians as their huge numbers rushed at the front lines of the Roman lines seeking to overwhelm them like a tsunami of swords, spears, axes and shields:

> *'The greatest number and the best fighters of the enemy were cut to pieces on the spot; for to prevent their ranks from being broken those who fought in front were bound fast to each other with long chains which were passed through their belts. The fugitives, however, were driven back to their entrenchments, where the Romans beheld a most tragic spectacle. The women, in black garments, stood at the waggons and slew the fugitives – their husbands or brothers or fathers, then they strangled their little children and cast them beneath the wheels of the wagons or the feet of the cattle, and then cut their own throats. It is said that one woman hung dangling from the tip of a waggon-pole, with her children tied to either ankle; while the men, for lack of trees, fastened themselves by the neck to the horns of the cattle, or to their legs, then plied the goad, and were dragged or trampled to death as the cattle dashed away … more than sixty thousand were taken prisoners; and those who fell were said to have been twice that number.'*[75]

Marius' heroic status in Roman history was confirmed by his success on the battlefield. A much-relieved and grateful senate awarded him a consulship for the fifth time, lauded him as the saviour of civilisation, and his army idolised his generosity when the massive profits of his sale of tens of thousands of slaves was donated to them rather than to his own bank account. Marius secured his legacy in creating the standing legionary army of the future, as opposed to the traditional raising and then disbanding of forces as they were needed. For the defeated, the Gauls, Cimbric tribesmen and all the others captured, it was to be the traditional punishments – this was something that did not change, and the barbarity of Roman victory was as harsh as ever. Pliny records the suicide of around 300 Celtic women due to be sold into slavery – they showed their contempt for Rome and their own levels of courage by murdering their own children and then cutting their own throats or mutual suffocation until the very last was dead. The bodies of the thousands of dead husbands, brothers and sons were left to rot in the beautiful lands around modern-day Marseilles and Aix-en-Provence, where by many accounts they 'fattened the land' through their fertilisation of the soils.

Once this danger had passed, and Marius returned to overturn Rome to restructure the entire state through bloodshed and civil war, large scale rebellion across the new province seems to have come to an end. There were still significant numbers of tribes in the low hills and mountains of the Cévennes that remained independent of Rome, and local conflicts requiring the legions to control would last until after 27 BCE when Augustus decided to finally crush all opposition to Rome. In the meantime, colonisation by people – and not policies – continued. We have no evidence to determine exactly how fast the population of the new province grew, but we do have circumstantial and archaeological evidence from which we can make projections. We also have Cicero who, via his numerous speeches, books and orations, provides so much detailed information about Rome, its people of all classes and the empire.

Although most noted for his senatorial and political career, Marcus Tullius Cicero was a lawyer, and it was through the prism of the legal process that he saw and calculated all his strategies. Earning a living was, as we know, not only frowned upon, but shunned by the senatorial classes, and Cicero worked hard for most of his life acting mostly as a defence counsel and was 'paid' in kind by the clientele that he served and tried to protect. It was the huge benefits of networking that Cicero earned throughout his life that enabled him to travel as far as consul and beyond – even to becoming the saviour of Rome – for a short period.

Corruption in Narbonensis

One of the many notable figures defended by the great Roman jurist Cicero, was Marcus Fonteius. We know about the *gens* (family) Fonteia again from the opening of Cicero's defence. Originating in Tusculum just to the south of Rome and where Cicero owned one of his many impressive villas, the family was of plebeian class but nonetheless had successfully established itself as well thought of and respected, with many of its members achieving high rank on the *cursus honorum.* Marcus himself had achieved the not inconsiderable rank of praetor and then propraetor (acting on behalf of the magistrate which might be the Governor or a praetor) in Gallia Narbonensis from 76 to 73 BCE. It was in this role that he was accused of gross extortion and misgovernment, and found himself in the extortion courts facing *repetundae* – or money to be recovered having been obtained illegally. This was an increasingly common charge against the highest of Roman officials and senators who felt that the way to control the empire was to ruthlessly exploit it – hardly how *Pax Romana* was supposed to work, but the attitude towards avarice and greed was changing. Rome was arriving at a crossroads where tradition, nobility and the Roman ideal was butting up against money, greed and power – *avaritia* versus the *mos maiorum* – and the battles were played out in the provinces while the war would have to be won in Rome.

The partial fragments of Cicero's defence speech that have survived are a marvel to read, as are so many of his surviving texts, but the parts that are relevant here relate to the importance of Narbo Martius and the role of Fonteius in controlling the region when faced by rebellion. For example, in section 5 we have the following gold mine of information:

> '*Marcus Fonteius was in charge of the province of Gaul, which comprises a type of men and communities which to say nothing of ancient times have either within our own memory waged long and bitter wars with the people of Rome, or have been recently subdued by our generals, subjugated in war, brought to notice by the triumphs and memorials of which their conquest has been the occasion, and have lately had their lands and cities made forfeit by the senate; in some cases they have met in armed encounter with Marcus Fonteius himself, and have, at cost of much strenuous effort to him, been brought beneath the power and dominion of the Roman people. In this same province is the town of Narbo Martius, a citizen colony, which stands as a watch-tower and bulwark of the Roman people, and a barrier of defence against these tribes which I have mentioned … there is moreover a large body of highly respected Roman citizens.*'[76]

Apart from shining a light on how Cicero saw the acquisition of southern France as a military conquest – no treaties, alliances of client states here – this highly informative narrative illuminates just how troublesome the tribes of southern France had been to Rome over a long period, but also highlights the importance of the town (not yet city) of Narbo Martius in the strategic defence of the region – which further adds weight to the notion that Narbo was originally a military fortification along the newly-constructed Via Domitia – and finally notes that by 69 BCE Gallia Narbonensis was already very busy with a 'large body' of Roman citizens. Many predated the conquest of 120-102 BCE in the communities that we saw our courier ride through, but equally many had moved into the province in the previous fifty years. The commercialisation of the province no doubt created many new legal cases as well as opportunities for the mixed population to integrate and thrive economically. *Romanitas*, therefore, was already well under way across the province, spurred on by the economic revolution under way even before the Augustan age. We may wish to consider at this point where it was that Marcus Fonteius lived for his three-year tenure – it was almost certainly in Narbo Martius itself, although, as yet, no Governor's residence has been established by archaeology. However, wherever his residence was situated, he would be surrounded by a sense of prosperity, growth, expansion and a new sense of optimism in this vibrant province he was now to administer. We will return to the courts and Cicero's defence of Marcus Fonteio in the next chapter.

Legality of Rule: the development of Roman Law in Gallia Narbonensis

If, as this part of the book suggests, it is people that made the provinces for the Romans and not their policies, then it is important to recognise that perhaps one of the most divisive and at the same time unifying groups of new people making their living in the new province were the magistrates and lawyers.

The agents of Roman law covered the empire and came in many forms, with no consistency of application or knowledge, and it would take hundreds of years before Rome could assert a standard set of legal principles across its empire. Some of these 'agents' of the law were magistrates trained in the law by exposure to the courts in Rome, others were military officers with the authority to dispense justice as they saw fit. However, individuals specifically versed in the Roman judicial process or trained in the law were few in number and very rare in the provinces.

The profession of jurist or lawyer was evolving and often it was the wise man versed in the process of law that was consulted, rather than a fully-trained professional, and these men sought their living or indeed fame in the place with the most popular stage – Rome. Here the cases were complex, the protagonist's wealthy and very influential, and the costs of failure or success either terminal or well rewarded. The profile was far higher and the variety of courts plentiful. It was in Rome that Cicero regularly faced off against the other well-known legal names such as Hortensius, or worked with a close circle of specialist jurists who spent their lives interpreting the laws as they existed at that time, such as Gaius Flaccus or Lucius Sempronius Atratinus.

Naturally the administrator of justice present in any office in the provinces was the Governor himself, as the chief magistrate, alongside the *praetor urbanus* or, as in the case of Marcus Fonteius, as a *propraetor*. These individuals had risen to the senior offices of the *cursus honorum* through family rank, connections, bribery, or military glory – rarely through ability for the role. Very few however had climbed the ladder directly through the law – this was a profession, and professions were almost exclusively the preserve of the equestrian class. Cicero is a prime example of the jurist/popular personality who also forged a political presence in the senate. Here, senators, who were often former or potential clients, needed Cicero for his advice, guidance and indeed formidable legal protection. Cicero was a valuable insurance policy should he be needed, and he knew well that his currency as a jurist, legal scholar and supreme orator, crossed the boundaries of class, political affiliation and rank – his indispensability served him well – until he was not indispensable.

But in the provinces, especially in the early decades of Roman rule, there were few Ciceros – certainly the limited evidence we have to date suggests that the provinces needed to produce such men, and this would take time. Until then, Rome and the provinces had to make do with the agents of the law and the inevitable inconsistencies that this would bring.

Alongside the Governor came the twin roles of *praetor urbanus* – who dealt with legal issues in the provincial cities – while the law for Roman citizens was dispensed by the *Praetor Peregrinus*. This latter role was the magistrate for aliens or the *ius gentium*, and demanded a degree of intellect and understanding, as the magistrate was responsible for dispensing legal judgement, as it existed in local law and custom, amongst non-Roman citizens. This parallel structure of two legal systems running alongside each other should and did create confusion, but it also allowed the Romans to accommodate regional law within the overarching principles of Roman law. This very practical economy of effort demanded that as much of local custom and practice as possible be allowed to continue in each province under the umbrella of a steadily encroaching Roman state. In essence, Roman law operated within settlements where magistrates lived or where councils or assemblies met. Such a structure meant that the Roman view on the status of communities was the key determinant of where a case was heard – and who heard it. '*Romanitas*' meant educating the newly-subjugated people of Gaul, outside of the Roman settlements, into the joys of becoming a Roman citizen which would also give them the protection of Roman law as a really sought after inducement to leaving their own civilisation behind and immersing themselves into Roman life and culture. Engraved lists of laws and customs would litter every community and establish Roman law as the customary base for disputes.

The Lapidary Wall – Narbonne

Without any equal in any museum in the south of France is the Lapidary Wall in the Narbo Via – the latest new museum in Narbonne. The museum is a modern variation on the need to display civic pride. Just like the Romans, the citizens of Narbonne are proud of their history and heritage, but instead of a triumphal arch they have built a modern masterpiece at the centre of which is the wall of Roman engravings and stone memorials salvaged from the area, which includes numerous texts concerning local laws and rules of governance. An exceptionally important place to visit.

Thus, the law was a key example of the subtle, osmotic process of Romanisation – if you wanted Roman legal protection and to profit from the Roman presence, then become a Roman citizen and do what they do – use the law for your own benefit to persecute those that offend or stand in their way.

In the Roman view of how society should work, the citizen had the right to vote, the citizen had to work for the good of the people of Rome (Rome was not just a city but an ideology). Within the concept of *civitas* was the opportunity of self-government through political election and dialogue, as well as the responsibility for sharing and supporting the sorrows and fears when things did not go their way – in other words, democracy.

The communities of the new province already had a ranking in the administration of them in the eyes of Rome. The *coloniae* were at the top – places such as Narbo Martius which were outposts of Rome itself and where Roman law was pre-eminent. These were followed by the *municipia* – these were self-governing towns that assumed a contract with Rome to remain independent but loyal to Rome in return for Roman protection and privileges – here a mixture of local and Roman law was practised. The third and last group were tribute-paying cities or *civitates* – here no rights were recognised by Rome and the relationship was by treaty in return for cash. Thus, the various Roman communities across Gallia Narbonensis came into these three categories and moved through them as they grew in size and relationship with Rome, the mother ship. A change of status, especially the granting of the rights of full *coloniae*, had to be authorised by a vote and decree of the senate – and could thus also be removed – although as the traditions of and respect for the Republic declined, men such as Sulla and Julius Caesar simply ordained the founding of colonies at their own whim without asking the senate, and especially when they wished to settle their loyal retired legionaries in a specific area.

To allow the justice systems to work they had to be administered and it was down to the governor of each province to supply his own staff – the state spent very little in the early years of imperialism on staffing the provinces, instead they very much expected the provinces to run as a city state would do – with minimal civil service costs or the need for professional interference. Thus the *scribae* came into their own as part of the limited administrative infrastructure. As their salaries were paid for out of the largesse of the governor – who carried out his post-consular role not for glory (in theory) but as a service to Rome – one might expect the numbers of administrators recruited to be small.

However, there are two conflicting considerations to note in this respect. Firstly, one can begin to understand why late Republican problems with the exploitation of the provinces became such a problem. There were increasing numbers of provinces which created greater potential for abuse of office, but also if the costs of being governor could be met by stripping money from the people being governed, then why would they not get their expenses back by exploiting opportunities to abuse their office? In the earlier days, when the noble Roman saw his financial input as necessary for the further glory of Rome, this was not so much of an issue, but in later years – infected as they were by a thirst for money and greed – then why not grab expenses back however you could get them? Secondly, with a steady eye on glory and *auctoritas* – the intangible essence of earned and deserved prestige – the number of scribes began to equate to the status of the governor. The combination of these two competing forces would create an intangible cluster of issues for the senate, and later the emperors, to untangle in their search for good administration in the provinces.

Apart from the courts that may run in the *coloniae*, the Governor himself often went or was expected to go to his own assizes – a route would be arranged, letters would be written by the scribes informing city officials when the governor would arrive and to prepare a list of cases for him to hear as appropriate. In Gallia Narbonensis, this meant that initially such travels would be limited to the loyal and safer coastal settlements connected by the Via Domitia, but over time, as the reach of Rome intensified, so he would also need to travel further inland.

The *civitates* listed by Rivet include a number of smaller settlements that emerged later in the Roman imperial era but for the sake of completeness these are:

Tolosa	Toulouse
Narbo Martius	Narbonne
Ruscino	Château de Roussillon
Carcaso	Carcassonne
Baeterrae	Béziers
Luteva	Lodève
Nemausus	Nîmes
Alba Helviorum	Alba
Arelate	Arles
Glanum	St Rémy
Olbia	Almanarre
Aquae Sextiae	Aix-en-Provence
Massalia	Marseilles
Nicea	Nice
Athenopolis	St Tropez
Stoechades Insulae	Îles d'Hyères
Forum Iulii	Fréjus
Antipolis	Antibes
Alebaece Reiorum	Riez
Dinia	Digne
Vapincum	Gap
Apta Iulia	Apt
Cabellio	Cavaillon

Avennio	Avignon
Arausio	Orange
Augusta Tricastinorum	St Paul-Trois-Châteaux
Carpentorate	Carpentras
Volcontii	Vaison-la-Romaine
Lvcvs	Luc-en-Diois
Dea Augusta	Die
Segustero	Sisteron
Velentia	Valence
Vienna	Vienne
Genava	Geneva
Gratianopolis	Grenoble

All of these centres to dispense Roman justice would need to develop their own internal communication system where scribes were needed to send and receive the ever-increasing flow of letters, instructions, news reports and demands for information. Roman society was busy – the religious calendar alone created many festivals and public games and all of these needed organising and cataloguing, for example who won which events and deserved what prize. At the highest level in Rome, the position of *pontifex maximus* was a pivotal position, in so far as the calendar for the whole year was agreed and set by this figure, but one could hardly expect Julius Caesar, as one who held this position, to sit and write down and communicate with the whole empire. Livy records that a new post was created and this was named *scriba pontificus* – even more evidence of the role that writing, recording and communicating had in holding the empire together.

Even at the earliest stages of provincial control, the law courts of the main *civitates* would have been active in dealing with disputes between Roman citizens and also between Roman citizens and the indigenous population – *Romanitas* demanded that all be treated as equally as possible in the eyes of the law but how far this was upheld, we frankly do not know. What would be certain is that the brutality of Roman sentencing would have been standard and maintained across the region. Nevertheless, a sense of unity across the region would have developed where local and tribal laws and legal customs gradually became Romanised and replaced by a uniform set of principles, so, in this way, the law played a vital part not only in governance but in building the identity of the province.

How was Worship and Religious Practice used to Promote Peace?

Similar claims can be made about religion as it was commonplace across the emerging empire for local religious worship to be allowed to function alongside the growing implantation of the Roman gods. This polytheistic flexibility did however come at a price and that was the expectation of at least a show of loyalty to the Roman religion – even if it was as John Rogan put it: *'A pinch of incense or a libation at an altar, or before a statue, were satisfactory hallmarks of loyalty.'*[77]

Even the Jewish religion was tolerated until the strength of their feelings manifested themselves in religious revolts, at which point they, and their religion, were brutally crushed. Over time of course, the inhabitants of Gallia Narbonensis, as with all overseas provinces, learnt how far they could and could not push or exploit their masters, and in the matters of religious faith it was clearly advantageous to forsake the gods of old that formed the identity of the Celtic and Gallic tribes and to take on, at least superficially, the worship of the Emperors in the Augustan and later periods and the coming centuries. Recognition of the deification of Emperors was an important display of *Romanitas*, even if it was merely for show, and helped smooth the path for many an ambitious foreign merchant or political aspirant.

Across the region there are numerous remains of early Roman places of worship, especially temples such as that, probably dedicated to Apollo, in Riaz. Rivet suggests that it is a first-century tetrastyle temple 22-22m long and 10.75m broad. Four of the granite pillars remain and the rest had been plundered in the third century for building materials elsewhere. Some 350 miles due south of Riaz, another Roman temple worthy of note can be found in Antibes.

> The temple of Apollo in Riaz can be found on the western outskirts of the town once named *Coloni Julia Augusta Apollinarium Reiorum.* The monolithic columns of granite sit on Attic bases and are topped with Corinthian capitals of white marble. The design suggests that this was a four-pillar *prostylus.*

This is a relatively recent discovery, and archaeology has revealed another temple at Vaugrenier a short distance to the north of the current town centre. Although not as resplendent as those at Riaz, this would still have been an imposing tribute to the Roman gods. The square design included a colonnade on three sides as a walkway out of the sun, with a central shrine to enter at one end and three sets of ascending steps into the temple courtyard itself. Built in the first century BCE, it would have been one of the earliest examples of the arrival of Roman religion on a far larger scale than in past centuries.

Due west from Antibes and a journey of 145 miles across the northern region of Marseilles would bring one once more to Arelate (Arles), and here more evidence of religious worship can be found and seen in the wonderful Arles Archaeological Museum known as Musée de l'Arles et de la Provence Antique.

Here numerous Roman monuments can be found across the city in what is colloquially known as 'Little Rome', but the museum of archaeology holds a collection of over 400 stone inscriptions from all over this fine city, testifying to its Roman past and to the religious imprint of Rome. Reliefs in the museum of archaeology tell us that altars set up to worship Bona Dea, Isis, Mithras and Neptune existed, as they would have done in most Roman communities, along with the common statuary found in most Roman homes dedicated to Janus (doorways and beginnings) or Vesta (ritual and the hearth). In fact, the *lararium* or household shrine was central to the Roman *domus*, often situated in its small part of the atrium or embedded into a wall, sometimes with a small temple-shaped shelf:

> '*One of the most distinctive and easily recognisable features of Pompeian houses is shrines that we now call by the Latin word* Lararium, *shrine of the* Lares *or household Gods … some are quite elaborate affairs … But many others are much simpler … In many cases statuettes of Gods and Goddesses stood on the ledge or shelf of the* Lararium. …*Mercury is the most popular divine subject, closely followed by Egyptian Gods … with Venus, Minerva, Jupiter and Hercules, in that order, coming next.*'[78]

Perhaps the best preserved of all temples in the province, and perhaps the most important, is that built and dedicated by Marcus Agrippa in Nîmes – but more of that in the next chapter.

In time, as interaction developed between Roman and indigenous people moving into the urban areas, so these religious practices became more understood, accepted and adopted, and thus religion, and the way it was used by the Romans, was another key part of governance and acceptance by the subjugated. The widespread construction of Roman temples served two purposes – firstly, they provided the new Roman population with a familiar place to give thanks to their respective gods, but secondly, they were a visual embodiment of the power and authority of the Roman state. Building works associated with substantial temples could be found in all the main Roman settlements during the first century CE but they could also be seen in more remote towns and villages where the carved marble and Corinthian tops arrived to complete a fresh and imposing new structure dedicated to the true gods of the universe. One of the most impressive remnants as they now exist include the temple of Augustus and Livia in Vienna (Vienne). Marked out as a settlement going places within the new province, Vienna overtook Nemausus in opulence and style with over 500 inscriptions restored and on display in the city. The first Roman consul from Narbonensis was to hail from Vienna – Valerius Asiaticus – and the wealth of the city of Vienna was mentioned many times in the writings by Pliny and Plutarch, amongst significant others. Although it is often difficult to locate the original sites of forums in numerous settlements due to overbuilding in future centuries, this is not the case in Vienna and the temple sits on one side of what was clearly the town square. The bronze lettering above the main entrance has long since been pillaged, but the holes remain and provide a puzzle for historians and archaeologists alike. Obviously dedicated as part of the imperial cult to the first emperor Augustus, it was re-dedicated by emperor Claudius to Livia, Augustus' wife, Claudius being her grandson, in 41 CE.

> The Temple of Augustus and Livia in Vienne was originally built to honour the imperial cult. The temple is a masterpiece of Roman design and building techniques and almost intact – even having survived fire and plundering over the centuries. In 41 it was rededicated to Livia after her death by her grandson the emperor Claudius. Unusually, a sacrificial altar still fronts the temple.

But not all was new. The Celtic tribes who had occupied these regions for centuries had already learned to share their territory with Greeks, and before them the Phoenicians, and still managed to preserve their own religious identities and practices. The Celts had been particularly devoted to sacred places, and especially those located in woodland, and these were very similar to the altars and temples erected by the Romans to woodland Gods such as Silvanus or to nymphs. A *nemeton* replaced the Roman stone temple and the Roman poet described one such place for his master and ultimate nemesis, the emperor Nero, to read:

'*… no bird nested in the* nemeton, *nor did any animal lurk nearby; the leaves constantly shivered though no breeze stirred. Altars stood in its midst, and the images of the gods. Every tree was stained with sacrificial blood, the very earth groaned, dead yews revived; unconsumed trees were surrounded with flame, and huge serpents twined round the oaks. The people feared to approach the grove, and even the priest would not walk there at midday or midnight lest he should then meet its divine guardian.*'

Tactitus, son of a Roman officer wrote of the British Celts:

'*They deemed indeed a duty to cover their altars with the blood of captives and to consult their deities through human entrails.*'

If there was one reason above all others that caused the Romans to view the Celts and Gauls as 'barbarians', then it was possibly this aspect of slaughtering their prisoners above all others, even though – paradoxically – the Romans were happy to see Christians slaughtered by animals for entertainment in their arenas until well into the second century.

But another religious practice the Celts this time shared with the Romans was that of the divinity of water. Often referred to as cults, the reverence with which the Gallic and Celtic peoples treated water, especially anointed springs, mirrored the same beliefs of the Romans in terms of healing properties, the same as the Romans treated water. A fine example of such a special place that remains today and which has undergone successive periods of worship by different peoples can be found at the La Fontaine Sanctuary in the Roman *civitas* of Nîmes. In fact, Nîmes is an interesting example in that the settlement was not proclaimed as a Roman city until much later than Narbo Martius – nearly 100 years later in fact – and Narbo developed well ahead of Nîmes during the Republican period. However, it was Augustus that really initiated the expansion of Nîmes and, under the Principate, it developed into the largest Roman *civitas* in Gallia Narbonensis, reminding us that context is all important when we assess the development of the province or visit a site: we must see it within the long time period of development under the Romans.

In his excellent study of the Roman remains across southern France, James Bromwich tells us that the spring water poured from the ground with almost the force of the current fountain and the fountain, or spring as it was, originally formed the very centre of the original Iron Age settlement and *oppidum* and was dedicated to the worship of the Iron Age god Nemausus, from which the city derived its name.[79] Nemausus was possibly the name of a sacred wood belonging to the Volcae Arecomici who voluntarily surrendered to the Romans in 121 BCE. With Roman influence, the springs became even more revered and the cult of the spring expanded especially with the new imperial cult of the deified emperor Augustus, who had a particular love for the *civitas*, having visited at least once, and a *nymphaeum* (devoted to nymphs who were supposed to inhabit the place), theatre and a 'Temple of Diana' were built around the springs.

> The Sanctuaire de la Fontaine in Nîmes can be found just to the north of the current city centre, nestled nicely into a walled garden of baroque design. The original waters would have been worshipped here for thousands of years, many hundreds before the arrival of the Romans. The sanctuary was dedicated to Augustus – probably in gratitude for some favour to the city – and the remains of the *Augusteum* contains a sacrificial altar, temple and what may have been a library building.

This artist's impression of the Altar of the Three Gauls that once stood in Lugdunum (Lyon) – gives a sense of the magnificence of the marble and classical design.

Arles Rhone 3 was discovered in 2004 around four metres below the surface. A long, narrow trading boat, it would have been able to navigate upriver from Arles. When she sank, the boat was carrying limestone blocks – probably for a new building further inland. She was taken apart and raised in three sections, restored in Grenoble, and now sits in a purpose-built gallery in Arles (Arelate). (*Carole Raddato via Wikimedia Commons/CC BY-SA 2.0*)

The carnyx was able to strike fear into the hearts of enemies long before they were seen on the battlefield at Aquae Sextiae. The dragon's breath was a haunting melody that almost cursed the battlefield, and there would have been dozens in a Gallic army.

Remains of the monument dedicated to Arcanus in Arelate. This base would have been topped with a statue of the great man and was unveiled by the emperor Hadrian himself. (*Author's collection*)

Traffic congestion was an ever-present problem for Roman traffic. Bottlenecks caused by an over-abundance of slow-moving *plaustrum*, the noise of fast-moving chariots – the *essedum* and the heavy bus of the time – the *raeda* all came together in a cacophony of iron wheels on granite rock. The noise and smell must have been quite something at the exits and entrances of city gates, which we can see in the ruts of the roadways of the empire.

The 1st-century CE Roman amphitheatre in Nemausus (Nîmes). Scene of many gladiatorial contests, celebrations and wild animal fights, there were sixty arched spans and thirty-four tiers of seating to hold well over 25,000 Gallo-Romans. Eventually there were too many amphitheatres and not enough sacrifices. (*Adobe Stock*)

The world-famous Peacock mosaic found in Vaison-la-Romaine is breath taking. Dating to the mid-2nd century CE, it adorned the house of a very influential family and was designed to create wonder and awe – as it still does. (*Author's collection*)

The *Horreum* in Narbonne (Narbo Martius) remains one of the architectural gems of the Roman period. The design and function were such that one can almost hear the shouting merchants and their slaves moving barrels and amphorae to and fro each day as they bought, stored and then sold goods to markets and individuals. (*Adobe Stock*)

The amazing Pont du Gard aqueduct near Nemausus (Nîmes). (*Adobe Stock*)

The Trophy of the Alps at La Turbie. Overlooking Monaco and facing back towards the homeland of Italy. This was a constant reminder of the glory of Augustus and of Roman dominance. (*Adobe Stock*)

Remnant of the monument or tomb erected to Borysthenes by Hadrian in 123 CE. (*Carole Raddato/CC BY-SA 3.0 DEED*)

Aerial view of Glanum displaying just how close the original and later Roman settlement is to the rock faces that provided the silt to preserve the city.

The remains of the temples in Glanum underline just how impressive the town must have been at its zenith. The superb detailing on the tops of these Corinthian columns has survived the centuries and is testament to the amount of money the town was willing to invest in celebrating the glory of Rome. (*Courtesy of Decimus Claudius*)

Celebrating the heritage and history of their forbears was a strong theme under both the republican and imperial periods. Every Roman settlement would erect statues preserving the heroic deeds of their ancestors as well as the Gods that preserved their existence. These plinths survive in Glanum, although their carved statues have been plundered or destroyed over the past 2,000 years. (*Courtesy of Decimus Claudius*)

The original Gallic/Roman settlement at Glanum was based on the source of a warm water spring at the base of the cliffs where a religious and magical reverence was paid to the Gods of the underworld – perhaps originally a Greek place of mystery and healing. The Romans added their architectural grandeur to the spring and this Roman entrance would have provided access to thousands of people wanting to bath or drink the healing waters. (*Courtesy of Decimus Claudius*)

Artistic impression of the mills at Barbegal. (*Courtesy of Stephen Ressler*)

Remains of the mill complex as it stands today at Barbegal. (*maarjaara via Wikimedia Commons/ CC BY 2.0 DEED*)

The revealed section of the original via Domitian in central Narbonne (Narbo Martius). (*Didier Descouens via Wikimedia Commons/CC BY-SA 4.0 DEED*)

This bust in white marble is thought to be that of Livia, second wife of Augustus. Found at the foot of a well in Glanum in 1951.

The statues of Hadrian and his wife Sabina in Vasio Vocontiorum (Vaison-la-Romaine). (*Carole Raddato via Wikimedia Commons/ CC BY-SA 2.0*)

A section of the scattered columns of the aqueduct that fed Frejus (Forum Iulii). (*Adobe Stock*)

The stunning and inspiring temple of Augustus and Livia in Vienne (Vienna) which would have overlooked the great forum of the city. (*Jacques Mossot via Wikimedia Commons/CC BY-SA 4.0*)

The nine heads of the Villa of Chiragan.

The original Roman site was typical therefore, with a pool for holy washing and a square temple near to the water for the sick to sit or sleep in while the god secretly visited them. Priests would have been appointed with considerable status in the town to interpret dreams, and a high priest would have overseen the whole collection of buildings. This is a superb example of how Roman and Celtic worship dovetailed together in harmony. The imperial cult was something that sprang up in various settlements both during and after the death of Augustus – often less about religious worship and more about gaining political patronage – evidence of these cults can be found across Gallia Narbonensis. Naturally, the Romans encouraged this type of cult as it reinforced the devotion of the people.

The cult of the emperor brought with it a subtle but powerful method of propaganda for Italy and the provinces. There had been many religious cults in Rome in the previous centuries, but Augustus manipulated his own *res gestae* (achievements) and his legacy from his patron, the now divine Julius Ceasar, to support the imperial cult in spreading from Rome to the rest of the empire. Loyal citizens of Rome were selected for the special honour of serving in the temples and gardens dedicated to Augustus, and these *seviri Augustales* became new priests and cult leaders within their locality, preaching and solemnising, through ritual, total devotion to Rome and their emperor. Interestingly it was in Lugdunum – Lyon – that the first substantial regional cult centre was established by Drusus, the anticipated and chosen heir to Augustus, and it is in Lyon that the remains of the amphitheatre dedicated to the Three Gauls and Augustus can be seen. Here, Christians were martyred as late as the second century CE as part of the empire wide persecution of this opposing religious cult.

> The Roman amphitheatre of The Three Gauls in Lugdunum is a massive construction of the first century CE and a memorable reminder of the beauty and extravagance of Roman society. One can easily visualise the sorts of events held here over the centuries – the dedication, the visits of emperors, the plays, the meetings, the celebrations. It was here that the representatives of the 60 Gallic tribes met, and were no doubt awe-struck by the technological and visual brilliance of Rome in all its glory and power. Christians were almost certainly martyred here. Even though only part of the amphitheatre survives, it is a wonder of the Roman presence in Narbonensis.

In parallel with the divinity which Augustus now 'reluctantly' accepted, came a wider propaganda strategy. Statues of Augustus tend to carry exactly the same features, regardless of his age, and these were meant to *become* the emperor, present in every locality, every shrine and every meeting place for the cults devoted to his person. Gone were the craggy individualistic busts, replaced by Augustus, resplendent in his imperial armour, reaching out to the people of the whole empire.

The *Lex Narbonensis*

In 1888 a fragment of a Roman notice known as the *Lex Narbonensis* was discovered near Narbonne on which were listed some of the honours due to a retiring priest of the Cult of Narbonensis. Provincial cults have been long identified in the eastern parts of the empire and, by the reign of Augustus, there was such a cult also in Hispania – making it natural to see this extended throughout Narbonensis. The regulation of these provincial cults was, however, not local, but from Rome, indicating that the grip of Rome on the provinces and the flow of administrative requirements were consistent with an imperial age where the emperor needed to know he was supported and worshipped in every corner of his rule.

For those interested in the detail of these cults, the scholarly work by D. Fishwick from 2005 develops the subject into the greatest possible detail, within the evidence, and establishes that these priests and priestesses were most likely to have been between the ages of 40 and 50 years, drawn from the province itself, most likely residents of the provincial capital and were of good standing or well-regarded Roman citizens.[80] Recruited from the class of citizens above the equestrian rank but below senatorial level, this meant that they were possibly members of the provincial council – a priest was called a *flamen* and a priestess a *flaminica* and their own levels of personal wealth needed to be substantial enough to fund the celebrations and games that were arranged in praise of the emperor in their period of office.

The importance of religion at all levels of Narbonensian society is well illustrated at the other end of the scale with the story of 'Rapax' – the greedy. Bromwich tells us of the existence of a small sanctuary in Glanum – located just south of the town of St-Rémy-de-Provence, itself due east of Nîmes – which had a rich and varied history of Roman occupation, more of which later. The sanctuary area on the southern side of the site contains a spring which had its own cult but also a specific hole in the hillside devoted to the cult of Glan and the Glanicae. This place dates from the seventh century BCE as somewhere the sick and needy came to make their offerings to the Celtic god Glan and is a perfect example of how Greek, Celtic and Romanisation came together, and how the ordinary people, those at the bottom of Roman society, celebrated their worship, not in great temples with well-to-do *flamen* but with private offerings in very simple shrines.

Two inscribed altars still remain, one of which was used by a Roman legionary veteran of Legio XX to attest his thanks to Glan and the Roman god Fortuna Redux for his safe return home. Why 'Rapax' was so proud of his nickname we will never know – was it for the amount of food he ate in his cohort or the booty he had brought home with him to Glanum? – it does not really matter, his part of the story of Roman religious rites in Narbonensis is as important as all the rest.[81]

Chapter 11

The Governor under the Republic and the Principate

From 120 BCE onwards and with characteristic efficiency, once the Roman senate had decided that the area of southern France between Cisalpine Gaul and Hispania Citerior was now annexed to the empire, they began the process of organising the administration of the region. Historians have been in disagreement for many years as to which member of the Roman elite can claim to have been the first governor, and the debate swirls around a number of candidates. Chief amongst these is L. Licinius Crassus, who is recorded as consul of Rome in 95 and who, Valerius Maximus states, '*was awarded Gallia*' as his proconsular province. The problem here is that Valerius Maximus was writing under the reign of Trajan well over 100 years after the event and his style of writing, which includes some of the worst rhetorical flurries and tendencies, obscures the facts to the point where we are uncertain if 'Gallia' in fact meant just *Gallia Cisalpina*, or *Gallia Transalpina*, or our new province which, as yet, was unnamed and perhaps he therefore referred to it simply as *Gallia*. The claim of Crassus does have a certain advantage in that he was one of two magistrates (*duoviri coloniae deducendae*) sent to southern Gaul and who are credited with the official dedication of the colony of Narbo Martius – thus he knew the area well and had actually been there. Despite the lack of clarity, what is certain is that from 188 onwards a succession of magistrates would have been dispatched to the new province, which for the sake of our own sanity we will now refer to as Gallia Narbonensis, to manage the development of the province, push further inland where possible and meet the challenges that were presented.

The Matter of Boundaries …

By the 80s BCE, one would have thought that matters would have become clearer and Roman administration would have infiltrated enough into the new province to start to tie the administration together. This may indeed have been happening in a tentative way, with Narbo, Lyon and numerous other *civitates* contending for superiority in their own regions and across the province, but until the Senate decreed and placed the governor in a residence, the matter was an open question. We can assume with some confidence that the matter of the selection of the regional capital was self-selecting in that it was based on what was understood to already exist. But with the stunning growth of the Roman settlements, it was possible, if not inevitable, that a good case could be made for the relocation of the Governor and thus his administration. Perhaps at this point we should dwell for a short while on the issue of boundaries.

Where possible, maps were drawn and, although rudimentary by later standards, these guides did at least refer to geographical features that made natural boundaries. When a military outpost was selected this tended to firm up the creation of the border between Roman provinces or between Rome and her enemies. This is how the exterior boundaries of the provinces were set – by chance rather than design. We can sometimes fix these major administrative boundaries by a combination of good detective work, the statements of Roman scholars and letters, the existence of surviving granite markers and mileposts, coupled with sensible guesswork. However, within each province, there needed to also be a whole series of internal boundaries and these were far harder to fix and for us, they are far harder to identify.

As recently as 2016, historians and archaeologists grappled with this issue. It was and is the University of Zurich that took and continues to take the lead in trying to better understand how the internality of the empire worked.[82] The matter of Rome's Internal Frontiers was the central issue taken to Rome in 2016, and reinforced the Roman need for a subset of internal boundaries for tax collection purposes above all else. As we know from Cicero's representation of these men, these were a powerful elite of moneyed people who collected the lifeblood of the empire – gold and silver – from those that the empire protected (and exploited). The tax-collecting contracts that were auctioned in Rome, often annually, were highly sought after, especially in the more affluent and peaceable provinces, and were lucrative, but they needed clear internal boundaries to avoid duplication and conflict. Exactly how these boundaries were devised, designed and on what basis they were 'sold' remains one of the exciting new areas of research and requires a multi-disciplinary approach. It stands to reason that those vital issues of regional characteristics, population size, number of inhabitants and economic output must all have been evaluated in some way by the regional civil service, and the Roman treasury calculated what they could expect from each internal boundary and therefore the province as a whole. It was a far from random exercise. In the final report, authored by Professor Philippe Della Casa, the notion of a division of provinces based on each being able to either display an identifiable cultural identity or a clear 'entity unto itself' was a key conclusion, for example, looking at the regionality of pottery – '*different pots – different province?*' But there is much more work to be done across a range of research areas before we are able to come to some sort of conclusion about how these internal boundaries were decided and then codified by the central and the regional administrations. Like modern-day United Kingdom politics when there are constituency changes, a vast array of considerations need to be taken into account in order to satisfy both the local politics and the new tax collectors.

The Continuing Issue of Hispania …

The history and development of Gallia Narbonensis was, to a large extent, also affected by what happened in Spain. Almost always on the radar for discussions in the senate, Rome was acutely sensitive to matters in Spain because of the vital and huge deposits of gold and silver from the expansive mines across the region. Any would-be emperor needed Spain either under control or preferably on side to provide money for troops or campaigns, and any senate needed Spain under control to ensure economic stability across the empire as a whole. When rebels escaped from a battle, it was often to Spain that they ran – either through Gallia Narbonensis itself or by ship across the northern Mediterranean. If we are in any doubt about how some provinces could be nothing but problematic, we only have to go as far as the works of the mysterious Florus who, writing history in the mid-to-late second-century CE, gives a perfect example of why the Republican senate had always been so reluctant to create an empire:

> *'Plus est privinciam retinere quam facere, itaque per partes iam huc iam iiluc missi duces, qui ferocissmas et in id tempus liberus gentes ideoque impatientes iungi multo labore nec incruentis certaminibus sevuire docerunt': 'It is harder to hold onto a province than to create one. And so generals were sent throughout* [Spain], *now here, now there. With much toil and not without bloody conflict, they taught the fierce peoples – hitherto free and so defiant of the yoke – to be slaves.'*[83]

The contrast with Narbonensis could not be more striking. Could it really just be a matter of geography and cross-fertilisation that made Narbonensis a natural extension of Italy and not a land to be brutally conquered and enslaved? Perhaps it was the Provençal way of life that lent itself to relaxation rather than war.

Over the two main centuries of conflict between 100 BCE and 100 CE, Gallia Narbonensis functioned almost independently without any major rebellions against Rome. There were armies fighting elsewhere and, in the Year of the Four Emperors (69 CE), Narbonensis certainly did feature in various cities taking the wrong sides, but overall it was a peaceful province. Wars were able to wage all around it but luckily not in it. Battlefields littered the outer provinces as civil wars raged while life, very generally, went on and the eternal '*Provence*' of today simmered away quietly just as the '*Province*' of Roman times.

The revolt by Sertorius in Hispania (both parts) in 80 BCE lasted eight long years until 72 BCE, and while the Spanish tribes and kingdoms were fitted with the 'yoke' of enslavement (the imperial language of conquest often refers to the subjugation of foreign peoples as animals needing to be 'harnessed' or 'made to put on the yoke') the further development of Gallia Narbonensis as a province continued unaffected.[84]

Narbo Martius emerged as the de facto leading settlement in the province, but the question of where the capital was, was not high on the Senates' list of priorities. Instead, the province was a transit area for Republican armies and generals heading to and from Hispania in the civil war between those who supported the new dictator of Rome, Sulla, and the followers of the old Roman general Marius. It was during these long years that men such as Gnaeus Pompeius Magnus (Pompey the Great) passed through and rested at various locations along the mountains and coastal plains of southern France, noting their beauty and the vitality of the new province for the first time. Given command (*imperium*) far beyond his years, partly in desperation at recent losses, Pompey assembled and equipped an army of 30,000 men to take his chance of glory. Angry at the lack of support and resources provided by the senate, Pompey unleashed a scathing letter angry about wasting time having to send despatches. However, we must be thankful that he did indeed take the time to write and that they have partially survived, as they provide a valuable resource in our understanding of the history of the new province.

In his despatches Pompey revealed that he had in fact taken a different route through southern Gaul (Gallia Narbonensis) than that expected. This may have been to avoid or engage with certain tribes who chose this moment to revolt alongside Sertorius – they may have been encouraged to do so by bribes or simply been festering under the Roman presence in these early decades of Roman rule. Pompey writes:

> *'Recepi Galliam, Pyrenaeum, Lacetaniam, Indigetis et premum impetum Sertori victoris novis militibus et multo paucioribus sustinui hiememque castris inter saevissumos hostis, non per oppida neque ex ambtione mea egi.': I recovered Gaul, the Pyrenees, Lacetania, and the Indigetes; with raw soldiers and far inferior numbers I withstood the first onslaught of triumphant Sertorius; and I spent the winter in camp amid the most savage of foes, not in the towns or in adding to my own popularity.'*[85]

To have recovered Gaul one must assume that it, or at least parts of it, had been lost as part of the revolt by Sertorius, which would indicate that, no matter how entrenched *Romanitas* already was, there was still a strong lingering sense of national, or at least tribal, identity which Pompey had to once more erase. But this was small scale stuff, localised and far from being a provincial rising in any real sense. This attitude of Pompey together with the bombastic, militaristic phraseology used by Cicero displays a certain contempt for the provinces as opposed to the stated or preferred means of working with the subjugated, and therein is a certain paradox between the stated philosophy and actuality. In reality, by this period then it is possible to discern an openly imperialistic policy emanating from Rome and the caution of the earlier Republic seems to have changed. Certainly, success breeds success and the empire was expanding in all directions: there was an ever increasing demand for resources, coupled with the need for more young and ambitious Roman men to have their chance of military glory and start their climb on the *cursus honorum* – this is how late-first century Roman imperialism flourished, by constantly feeding the furnace of ambition with the consumption of more territory. When small insurrections did occur, they became magnified into full scale threats to Rome – just as Cicero was to boast when governor of Cilicia. The language of a small local difficulty was replaced with that of the national hero worthy of his Triumph. In reality, Gallia Narbonensis did not take sides. It was not unified enough for that in any case.

What Does Cicero's Speech *Pro Fonteio* Tell Us About the Reality of the Governance of Gallia Narbonensis in 70 BCE?

By 72, and with the civil war successfully concluded in the young Pompey's favour – for which he became the latest and perhaps best known of the new heroes of the age – Marcus Fonteius had already returned to Rome. We know from earlier in this chapter that Cicero was defending him against serious charges of bribery and extortion while he had been governor of the 'province' during the civil war between 76 and 73 BCE – during which he would undoubtedly have spent much time either with, supporting, or communicating with Pompey and his army when not in Hispania and instead stationed in his province. Cicero's defence – rather like the later account by Tacitus of Agricola in Britannia – pulls back the curtains on a great deal of information that otherwise would have been obscured. Cicero has already confirmed in his *Pro Fonteio* speech, that Narbo Martius was well populated and that the region needed subduing in the past few years during the civil war – no doubt Pompey and Fonteius could argue over who played the major part in this. Cicero also very cleverly tells the jury that the presence of Pompey's army provided large numbers of senior officers, legates and tribunes who would have interacted with Fonteius as governor, and yet the prosecution has not one of these present as witnesses to his supposed misconduct.[86]

Although generally accepted as not being one of the best of Cicero's speeches, he does make passing references to all sorts of other aspects of the governorship of Fonteius that provide very valuable clues as to the state of the province at this time – regardless of how critically history has evaluated the power of his rhetoric – and, although only part of the speech survives, we are still able to rely substantially on Cicero's evidence.

Apart from establishing for us that Massalia was the premier settlement in terms of size, loyalty to the Roman state (see above), and that it had been enlarged as a result of land grants, Cicero also outlines the extent of the tribes occupying the province – the Volcae, the Allobroges, the Ruteni and the Volcontii. The Helvii, although not mentioned specifically in *Pro Fonteio*, must have been part, or a former part of the province as it was some of their lands that were handed over to Massalia by Pompey – indicating that they were perhaps the tribe that most needed to be suppressed at this time and therefore had been 'erased' by the time of the speech by Cicero. These then were the major tribal groups that Roman administration had to learn to work with, alongside and around the existing *civitates*, still extant Iron Age settlements and *coloniae*. Cicero goes on to tell us that, as Governor, Fonteius was in post for three years, longer than the average by a year or more, and appointed two legates – C. Annius Bellinus and C. Fonteius. The latter is very likely a close family member – nepotism was a key component of maintaining the quality and stature of an aristocratic family and this was not questioned – and they were both tasked with overseeing the road building programme, as the governor was taken away by more pressing business.

The position of legate was therefore a vital part of the administrative structure in the provinces. In former days – that is prior to the military and political reforms of Marius – the *legatus* was a supreme military tribune drawn straight from the aristocratic families of Rome. The senate made the appointment and always tried to ensure that the chosen *legatus* could work in harmony with the governor – another reason for keeping things in the family. With the Marian reforms, multiple posts with the rank of *legatus* were added to each army, and each commended his own legion of around 5,000 men – this was the *legatus legionis*, while the *legatus pro praetore* was a civilian role in a province. Regardless of whether the job was given as a military or civilian one, the *legatus* was entitled to twelve *lictors* – these were the civilian men who accompanied senior ranked politicians and officers, partly to display their status as holding *imperium* (military power) or magistracy with the ability to dispense justice on behalf of the Senate and People of Rome – carrying their bundles of rods and axes, they symbolised the power to punish or execute.

The charges against Fonteius ranged from his making money out of excess taxes on imported Italian wine, profiting from road building by accepting substandard work with a higher price, and general extortion from the Gallic people. Cicero had in fact only recently prosecuted a former governor, Gaius Verres, for his time in Sicily, on almost exactly the same grounds – Cicero's speeches were devastating and confirmed his status as one of the new and foremost advocates in Rome. The resultant law or *lex* of 70 BCE, the *lex Aurelia*, changed the composition of Roman juries to allow *equites* back onto juries investigating extortion, corruption and misconduct in office: previously exclusive to senators, courts or *quaestio* were as often as corrupt as the men they tried. Cicero, in defending a man on the same charges he had so recently prosecuted another governor, was possibly acting as a friend to Pompey, given Pompey's friendship with Fonteio and Cicero's desire to bask on the glow of Pompey's influence.

In terms of the accusations of fraudulent taxation on wine, this interests us at this juncture very much, not just because it emphasises the scale of the wine trade in and out of Gallia Narbonensis, but also because Cicero made this comment in his speech:

> *'Referta Gallia negotiatorum est, plena civum Romanum. Nemo Gallorum sine cive Romano quicquid negotii gerit, nummus in Gallia nullus sine civium Romanorum tabulis commovetur': 'No Gaul ever does business independently of a citizen of Rome; not a penny changes hands in Gaul without the transaction being recorded in the books of Roman citizens.'*[87]

No doubt Cicero exaggerates, as all lawyers do, but his point is well made and reveals to us a sense of just how active economically commercial enterprise was in the new Roman province and the extent to which the Roman merchants – the people making the province – actually were. Cicero mocks the prosecution for their lack of credible witnesses, most of whom were Gauls who had suffered in some way under Fonteius, and the entire case does in fact reveal how quickly Gallia Narbonensis and its people became pawns in the Roman power game. In an article of 1968, Allen Ward examined Cicero's motivations for taking the case which, as mentioned earlier, were likely to be centred on his affection for Pompey.[88] The motivations of the Gauls, when they must have doubted their ability to bring down a sizable political figure like Marcus Fonteius, are more questionable, and Ward points to the Metelli family – great opponents of Pompey – as the true originators of this attempt to bring down an ally of Pompey as part of a political plan of subterfuge in the ongoing power struggles in the senate.

Cicero even goes as far as stating that he can understand the advantages of the Metelli in attacking Pompey, but he cannot fathom any advantage for the Gauls.

Cicero explains that no Roman has any complaint against Fonteius – the *negotiatores, coloni, publicani, aratores, pecuarii* – all are willing to act in defence of the former governor, as is the entire population, it seems, of Massalia. No doubt there were real grievances with the Romans in all sorts of ways; estates were being seized, commerce was being dominated, and the world was changing for the Gauls, and perhaps the attack on Fonteius was symbolic rather than specific and part of the general reaction to empire that was commonplace wherever the Romans arrived. The surviving texts do not tell us the result of the trial but, given the strength of Cicero's defence, it is likely that Fonteius had grounds to celebrate.

The next governor we can safely state was C. Calpurnius Piso who, as consul in 67, managed to obtain a proconsulate over both Cisalpine and Transalpine Gaul, and thus oversaw our emerging province too. Little is known of his actions – possibly because the area was so vast, he was hardly in evidence. However, there is a reference to his allowing Pompey to recruit Gauls into his army – Pompey having been granted a commission to eradicate the substantial pirate threat around the Mediterranean – another indicator of how important free flowing trade was to the growing empire. Piso is said to have needed to pacify the Allobroges – a euphemism for beating them back into submission – thus Pompey may have enforced some form of conscription to get the men he needed. We then know that L. Licinius Murena assumed office in Gaul in 64 BCE, but, as far as the current evidence suggests, his impact was limited although this did not stop the now usual charges of corruption on his return to Rome to campaign for the consulship of 62 BCE – the *lex Aurelia* became a password for political football, with opposing families using it to attack each other on return from a governorship. Once more it was Cicero who acted for the defence and immortalised Murena for posterity with his *pro Murena* defence and, again, we can glean details about events in the new province.

In all probability, political intrigue in Rome had been affecting citizens in Gaul from the earliest times – this was nothing new. What was new was the use that the new province could be put to in providing political ammunition and capital in the games of power politics at the centre. A prime example of this relates to the events surrounding what is usually referred to as the Catiline Conspiracy in 63 BCE, where an attempted coup by Lucius Sergius Catilina was thwarted by Cicero, now consul for that year, in what he liked to feel was his finest hour. Central to the unmasking of the plot was the presence of two envoys in Rome from the Allobroges tribe from the north-west region of Gallia Narbonensis, or Gaul as we can still refer to it – as separate from Cisalpine of Transalpine

Gaul – and as such represented the far northern border of the province as separate from the 'barbarians' of the northern Gallic tribes. The envoys were in Rome in 63 BCE to complain about the high level of taxes being exacted from their tribe. This was not the first time the Allobroges had sent a mission to complain – their chief Indutiomarus had tried once before in 69 BCE to no effect. The Allobroges were not alone in feeling the pain of what was a period of considerable economic hardship for Rome and her imperial possessions, with a debt crisis of staggering proportions – Catiline was arguing for the cancellation of debts and was potentially therefore a popular choice amongst certain sections of society, and his prolonged and vicious attacks on Cicero and the senate threatened to bring down the establishment. Supported as he was, although in the background, by the scheming Caesar and Crassus, he was a formidable foe. The accounts by Cicero and the reports by the contemporary Roman historian Sallust tell of how these envoys were approached by allies of Catiline to rise up against Rome: indeed they had these requests also in writing, but on their return were intercepted by allies of Cicero and this part of the plot was revealed by the envoys to C. Pomptinus – including the letters of conspiracy – for which, Cicero tells us in his *In Catiliniam,* the envoys received considerable rewards. The fact that interests us at this juncture is just how fragile Rome's hold on its new province was, and that rebellion by one or other of the great tribes could quickly spread across the region and Rome would be in serious difficulty.

Indeed, serious difficulty is exactly what followed when in 62 BCE a revolt did occur – and led by the Allobroges. Receiving his own reward for his support in the Catiline affair, Pomptinus was awarded the governorship of – who would believe – Gaul or Gallia Narbonensis. His thanks from Cicero were not reciprocated by the Allobroges, who pocketed their 'considerable rewards' and then followed exactly the advice they had been given by Catiline – to take on Rome itself. According to Rivet, the Allobroges were a real threat being 'the one tribe in Gaul that really mount war against the Roman people', which is no doubt why Catiline selected them in the first place.[89]

It is to Roman historian and senator Cassius Dio, writing in 165-235 CE, that we can turn for a more detailed account:

> *'The Allobroges were plundering Gallia Narbonensis and the governor C. Pomptinus, sent his legates against the enemy but established himself in a place convenient for observing what went on, so that he was able to give them useful advice and aid, as might from time to time be helpful to them. Manlius Lentius attacked the city of Ventia.'*

Later, Dio tells us:

> '*Lucius Marius* (who replaced Lentius) *and Servius Galba crossed the Rhône and after ravaging the possessions of the Allobroges finally reached the city of Solonium and occupied a strong position commanding it. They conquered their opponents in battle and also set fire to portions of the town, which was partly constructed of wood; they did not capture it, however, being prevented by the arrival of Catugnatus* (new Chief of the Allobroges). *Pomptinus, on learning of this, proceeded against the place with his entire army, besieged it, got possession of the defenders, with the exception of Catugnatus. After that he more easily subjugated the remaining districts.*'[90]

Historians have been unable to positively identify the 'city' of Solonium and estimates range through Saillens, St Marcellin, Salgnon and Solaie to name a few. What we do know is that after this crushing defeat and rape of their homeland, the Allobroges withdrew to an existing *oppidum* and a new capital – Vienne some 35km south of Lugdunum – but still well to the north of the new province, and their ability to potentially master Rome was, almost, at an end. Their valiant attempt to maintain some degree of independence, culture and traditions and distance themselves from their Roman masters did not last long however as, some fifteen years later, Vienne itself was taken by Julius Caesar in 47 BCE and turned into one of his many *coloniae*. The word 'almost' is used advisedly, because the Allobroges still had the desire for national independence and actually ejected the Romans from Vienne, forcing the Romans to found the new colony of Lugdunum – modern day Lyon and just over 33km to the north. But Vienne had only a brief period of independence and early in Augustan times the matter was addressed with force and once more the town became Roman property to then be called Vindobona, and it was to be Caligula who, as Emperor in 40 CE, made the city a full *colonia* again.

Vienne or Vindobona became a Roman provincial capital and played a significant part in the administration of the province as it emerged into the full light of *Romanitas* and Romanisation. The Allobroges gradually lost their identity although there are still visible signs of their existence with fragments of pottery, coins and sacrificial knives on display in the city museum – a sad commentary on how their existence was almost extinguished in a place that they had occupied since before the fifth century BCE.

It took the best part of ten years for the victorious Pomptinus to achieve permission for his triumph through the city of Rome for his suppression of the Allobroges – why so long we do not know, but the fact that he did not give

Vienne is a short train ride from Lyon and it is well worth the trip. Three museums contain large quantities of Roman artefacts, there are a number of sections of the huge Roman town wall and near the centre of the central park there is an excellent exposed and restored stretch of Roman road named the Voie Romaine – complete with cart ruts.

up agitating for this honour further illustrates just how vital the ritual was to the Roman elite.

Although Julius Caesar was granted the governorship, his life at this time was so dominated by his Gallic Wars in the rest of France that there is precious little we can learn from Caesar by way of the daily life of the governor of Gallia Narbonensis prior to his assassination in March (the Ides of the 15th) 44 BCE. It would seem that many of the governors of Narbonensis had bigger issues on their mind than running a province, so it is safe to assume that the day-to-day maintenance of some sort of administration was simply left to the various praetorian officials who worked with a civilian cohort of vital civil servants out of Narbo and the other emerging Roman centres of provincial control until a Governor arrived who really did want to run his fiefdom from the senate in Rome.

What we do know is that, in the war between Pompey the Great and Julius Caesar – or between the Republic and the would-be dictator between 49 and 45 BCE – Gallia Narbonensis, played its part in the overall events that led to Caesar's ultimate victory. Massalia was especially loyal to Caesar until the arrival of L. Domitius – newly-appointed governor of Gaul, recently freed enemy of Caesar after the Battle of Corfinium and ally of Pompey – who persuaded the city to close its gates to Caesar's troops. It is now that the first mention of Arelate (Arles) appears as it is here, with its prowess in shipbuilding and design, that Caesar ordered twelve warships to be built for an assault on Massalia from the sea. Caesar's armies camped across Gallia Narbonensis in winter quarters to rest and refit as they prepared to enter Spain, where further enemies of Caesar awaited him. Caesar himself stayed near Arelate and the unfortunate poet Lucan (39-65 CE) relates how a sacred grove was sacrilegiously cut down for timber for Caesar's ships – with Caesar striking the first blows and symbolically, for Lucan and perhaps Caesar's own soldiers, accepting that his fate will one day be sealed by the revenge of the Gods for his attack on a sacred *nemeton*. For an in depth look at this event, a 2006 article by Antony Augoustakis is especially useful.[91]

After his victories in Spain, Caesar eventually returned. Aware that the battles he had left in the hands of his lieutenants D. Brutus and C. Trebonius had not resulted in victory, Caesar personally defeated Massalia – though not perhaps as severely as he might – and left it as an independent city within the province. After a second hurried journey back through our province – this time to defeat the two sons of Pompey still holding out in Hispania – Caesar then left, probably along parts of the same route as our courier from the 140s, and returned to Rome to take his place in history – and with the Gods.

It was in 46 BCE that Caesar had also ordained that Arelate become a *colonia* for his retiring soldiers and, in the same year, he appointed A. Hirtius as governor of Gallia Narbonensis. Hirtius was quickly followed by another Caesarean appointment as proconsul of both Hispania Citerior and Narbonensis – that of M. Aemilius Lepidus.[92]

The period under Lepidus was that of the next bloody civil war in 43-42 BCE between the Second Triumvirate to avenge the assassination of Caesar, led by Mark Anthony and Augustus, against the *Liberatores*, Caesar's assassins led by Marcus Junius Brutus and Gaius Cassius Longinus. Although mostly fought on the mainland of Greece, there were outbreaks of loyalty and betrayal across the whole empire, depending on how generals and political leaders felt the wind was blowing. In Narbonensis, this meant another period where local officialdom had to make do and mend, running the province on behalf of their political superiors and taking instructions from senior civil servants in Rome. In Pliny's wonderful letters with the emperor Trajan, we know that the bureaucracy in Rome was scrupulous, and had been for hundreds of years, with its record keeping.[93] As Trajan wrote: *'The date of your arrival in Bithynia I have noted from your letter'* – the imperial archives would have required this to precisely date the start and finish of his period as governor.

For our purposes it is important to know that across Narbonensis, more Roman *coloniae* were being founded. Like the positioning of pawns on a chess board, the general who had rewarded his legion with land and funds for their retirement could count on their loyalty, both to ensure that the province did not rebel but also rearm in time of need and rally to their support. Such colonies were now founded in Valence, Vienne, Béziers, Lodève, Nîmes and, very importantly for the north of the province, Lyon, but it was not until 22 BCE that Narbonensis was officially returned to senatorial control and peaceful administration could resume, and by then Augustus was already also making his own provincial appointments as de facto dictator.

For the concluding years of the Republic, Narbonensis was governed by military men, such as Agrippa between 20-19 BCE, and, for three years between 16-13 BCE, Augustus himself seems to have been running the province, building substantial stone walls and monuments in Nîmes, repairing and extending the Via Julia Augusta through La Turbie and beyond, as well as dedicating monuments to his own glory and the new imperial cult.

Celebrating Imperial Power – La Turbie

The imperial monument at La Turbie is fascinating from a number of respects. On a misty day up on the mountainside where it sits, one looks over the metropolis of Monaco which in the time of Augustus was in the process of evolving into a busy little Roman port. On a day with the crystal-clear blue skies of the Mediterranean, one can see Italy to the east and Narbonensis right around to Nice (Cimiez), Antibes and St Tropez to the west – this was a site especially chosen to display the grandeur of Rome and the power of Augustus. The scene is so awe-inspiring that one often forgets to look behind, but if one does then the majesty of the Alps Maritimes spreads out to the north – some of the mountain tops still even retain their snow. The base of the Trophy of the Alpes (Tropaeum Alpium) was constructed by Roman engineers from 6 BCE onwards and tells the reader that it was built to celebrate the victory of Augustus over the forty-five tribes that populated the region of the Alps. These tribes had maintained their independence from Rome for hundreds of years, but their time had come and a military campaign was launched in 16 BCE, the moment Augustus arrived in Narbonensis as 'governor', which lasted through to 7 BCE. The stone came from a local Roman quarry only 600m away which was cut deep into a sloping hillside – the effort to drag the raw stone up the hillside onto the Via Julia Augusta, which passed through the small settlement and linked Vintmille to Cimiez, then to be shaped by masons and set in place, must have been immense – no doubt a good number of slaves were put to this task. On the base the following (restored) inscription can still be very clearly seen:

> *To the emperor Caesar Augustus, son of the deified* [Julius Caesar], *Pontifex Maximus, hailed as Imperator for the 14th time, in his 17th year of tribunician power, the Senate and People of Rome* [built this], *in commemoration that, under his leadership and auspices, all the Alpine peoples, from the Upper Sea to the Lower Sea, were submitted to the Imperium of the Roman People. Conquered Alpine peoples:*

Trumplini	*Vindelici*	*Lepontii*	*Brigiani*	*Ecdini*
Camunni	*Cosuanetes*	*Uberi*	*Sogionti*	*Vergunni*
Vennonetes	*Rucinates*	*Nantuates*	*Brodionti*	*Eguituri*
Venostes	*Licates*	*Seduni*	*Nemaloni*	*Nematuri*
Isarci	*Catenates*	*Veragri*	*Edenates*	*Oratelli*
Breuni	*Ambisontes*	*Salassi*	*Vesubiani*	*Nerusi*
Genaunes	*Rugusci*	*Acitauones*	*Veamini*	*Velauni*
Focunates	*Suanetes*	*Medulli*	*Gallitae*	*Suetri*
	Calucones	*Ucenni*	*Triullati*	
	Brixenetes	*Caturiges*		

This inscription reveals at least three aspects of Roman imperialism at this time. Firstly, the extent to which Rome had had a very slender grip on the province since the Punic Wars two hundred years before – large parts of what was to become Narbonensis remained in local hands throughout this period – it was the coastline that was the vital link to Spain: the time would come when the rest would be brought into line, and it had. Secondly, worth noting is that these smaller tribes did not vanish easily. *Romanitas* was an anathema to their own culture and way of life and it took a military campaign lasting nine years of, mostly summer, campaigning to bring them to heel. Lastly, when we recall how tentatively the Romans had embarked on imperial expansion, the concerns that second-century senators had about engaging in overseas wars, the costs and the potential for failure, we witness a total change of psychology and strategy. The tribes had been 'submitted to the Imperium of the Roman people' – they were not equals but barbarians to be defeated, punished, put into slavery and then taught the values of loyalty to the Roman state. Finally their names were to be displayed for all to see and read as they passed by to and from Narbonensis as people who had been 'conquered'.

La Turbie – The Trophy of the Alps
The Edward Tuck Museum can be found inside the monument and includes fragments, plaster moulds and photographs showing its once very parlous state and then reconstruction in the 1920s. A carved stone funeral lid for a soldier of one of the many legions that passed this way is also on display and there is a 1:20 scale model of the original trophy.

The Governor

In terms of hands-on governance of a *provincia*, it was the governor, when he was there, and his officials that played the major roles – this was increasingly the case in our emerging province of Narbonensis – and posterity is blessed to have at least three sources of primary evidence on which to base our knowledge of the life and responsibilities of a governor of a *provincia*. The first of these are Cicero's despatches to the senate while he was proconsular governor of Cilicia from 51-50 BCE, then the letters from Pliny the Younger as he fulfilled his role as governor in Bithynia from 110-112 CE, and finally there is the book by Tacitus on the character of Julius Agricola, who was governor of Britain from 77-83 CE. All three make substantial and invaluable contributions to our knowledge of how a Roman governor functioned, what his responsibilities were, how the relations with Rome changed over time and what the governors of Narbonensis would have experienced during their period in office.

One of numerous aspects that leap out as being a shared experience for all three, is the way in which the appointment was used to distance rivals, reward supporters and, only occasionally, to place the right person in the right place at the right time – in other words, there was no automatic choice of who and where. All manner of calculations would come into this judgement and none of them in their own hands. For example, in the case of Cicero, he clearly did not wish to go – nor did he wish to go to Cilicia. His record of achievements more than merited a post consular governorship – he had climbed the *cursus honorum* at every level, was recognised as the outstanding speaker and lawyer of his time, and he had been consul, but it was the political dynamics in Rome and his deteriorating popularity that played a key part in sending Cicero away at all and, as in the case of many similar appointments, the dark arts of senatorial politics played their part. He did not want to be away from the centre of events where Caesar and Pompey were heading for a seismic clash and Cicero saw an opportunity to play mediator and hero of the Republic – again. His beloved daughter Tullia needed a new husband, the selection of which he was keen to oversee and he was losing influence. Finally, nor did he want to be shipped off to such a poor province. His letters to Atticus tell of his longing for Rome and how his talents were wasted on Cilicia.

Before Agrippa was chosen by Augustus to deal with Britannia, we know from Dio that Julius Caesar used the provinces unscrupulously for his own ends. The sudden expansion of the empire left Rome facing multiple challenges on all fronts – the very thing that the senate had always wanted to avoid – but for Caesar in his short period as dictator, provincial allocations were like a game of chess and Dio says that:

> *'yet he (Caesar) declared that he would not govern all the provinces, and in the case of such provinces as he should govern he would not do so indefinitely; and he did, in fact, restore to the senate the weaker provinces, on the ground that they were peaceful and free from war, while he retained the more powerful, alleging that they were insecure and precarious and either had enemies on their borders or were able on their own account to begin a serious revolt.'*[94]

What is of interest here is not so much that Caesar used the provinces to his own advantage – he was after all dictator after winning at Pharsalus – but that the provinces were described in this way, as potentially in turmoil, rebellious in places, dangerous in others. This then is a snapshot of the state of the new Roman empire around 47-46 BCE.

Thirty years later and with Augustus and the selection of Agrippa as governor of Transalpine Gaul, the decision seems to have been based around more pragmatic needs – a successful military commander being needed to ensure stability. In the case of Pliny the Younger (his uncle Pliny the Elder having died near the beach in the eruption at Pompeii), he too more than merited the glory of a provincial governorship, having been a legionary tribune, quaestor, praetor, prefect of the treasury and senator.[95] Gaius Plinius Caecilius Secundus (the Younger) was trusted, literate, intelligent and able, but more importantly than all these qualities was the fact that he was well regarded by the emperor Trajan. So we can conclude that, over time, the decisions on the appointment of governors varied with the personalities and power of the individuals involved. They were largely sinecures for those who had completed their consulship, but equally they could be used to reward friendship, quell disturbances and were not always in the gift of the senate.

With the death of the Republic and the arrival of the imperial era, it was the emperor who selected his governors and not the senate – they made recommendations of course, trying to maintain some form of control over Buggins' turn, but emperors who could not outwit the senate would not last long. Just as a king selects his advisors, a president selects his secretaries of state, or a prime minister selects his cabinet, so the senate, or later the emperors, selected their governors based on considerations of loyalty, political expediency, satisfying a promise, or balancing power across the empire – the ability to perform the role may have been contemplated, but that was sometimes well down the list of concerns.

Governors of the *provinciae* were often selected from men who had been consuls – the senior elected magistrates of Rome who, after their year of office, looked forward to a period in the empire to either get away from Rome, hide from Rome, or profit from the empire to pay the debts of their election. Theirs were proconsular appointments. The second type of appointment to a province was a former praetor or chief justice of magistrates – this could be a former army commander or a civilian magistrate. These were *propraetorian* appointments. Sometimes a lower ranking government official could receive a smaller province – such as Judea – on special grounds, such as they were selected by the emperor during the imperial period or that they had special knowledge or reason to administer a certain area.

A second aspect that shows itself across all three collections of evidence is the initial journey to their allotted province. It was often a long way and often difficult, wide-ranging personal matters had to be attended to before departure, and families had to take the strain – or go with the new governor to his province with all that entailed. The journey could be hot, dangerous and exhausting, before they arrived to be greeted by officials who may have been in the province for many years and seen good, and bad, governors come and go.

The journey to Narbonensis was actually not so bad. The distances involved were shorter than average, a short sea journey, though dangerous, could cut the time in half, and all of the route, after 80 BCE at least, was on Roman soil with Italy, Cisalpine Gaul, Transalpine Gaul, Narbonensis and Hispania now all linked together. For the governor travelling to Narbo Martius, there were all the various *mansiones* en route that we saw being built in earlier chapters, and there would be numerous wealthy hosts eager to invite the new governor to stay and enjoy a business dinner along the entire length of the trip – even in Roman times there was no such thing as a free lunch.

For Cicero, the trip involved sea, difficult roads, frequent stops, the need for guides, and hot, dry, dusty travel on unmade roads before he reached his destination on the southern coast of Turkey. En route, he was able to constantly dictate letters to his retinue of scribes who accompanied him – and would no doubt be as miserable as he was about having to make the journey at all. Mind you, Cicero was also able to enjoy the proclamations of the people as his lengthy proconsular column of personally-attending lictors, slaves, wagons, mounted soldiers and possibly chariots passed through their towns. He wrote to Atticus: *'So far my journey through Greece has been the admiration of the country, and I must say that I have no complaint to make so far of any of my party.'*

Cicero was mindful of the almost constant concern of Atticus that it was not he as Governor that worried him, but the behaviour of his officials and Cicero tried to allay these fears when he wrote: *'Every day I think of how to fulfil your often-repeated exhortations* [which fell on willing ears] *to get through this abnormal duty with the strictest decency and propriety, and so I impress on my companions….'*[96]

One hundred years later and Pliny's journey was no easier – as *Legatus Augusti* (specifically selected by the emperor) he did not have all the proconsular baggage of Cicero in train with him – although he was still entitled to six lictors close by him, representing his authority from the emperor at all times, and he would have had something by way of his personal entourage. This was a new level of appointment. The period between 51 BCE and 111 CE, when we think Pliny took up his post, had seen enormous change in Roman governance, not least of which had been the fall of the Republic and the start of the reign of the emperors. In constitutional theory the emperor was the proconsul of all the *provinciae*, so there was no longer any such role, and with the emperors came a new sense of responsibility – and dread. Pliny travelled much the same route as Cicero, but this time heading for the northern shores of Turkey. Writing in his very personal style to the emperor Trajan he stated:

15. ***C. Plinius Traiano Imperatori***

> *'Quia confide, domine, ad curam tuam pertinere, nuntio tibi me Epheseum cum omnibus meis* [rounding Malea – the very southernmost tips of the Peloponnese] *nauigassequamuis contrariis uentis retentum. Nunc destino partim orariis nauvibus, partim uehiculis prouinciam petere. Nam sicut itineri graues aestus, ita continuae nauigationi etesiae reluctantur.'*

> *'Because I feel sure, sir, that you are interested, I am reporting to you that, together with all my people, I have reached Ephesus by sea, after 'rounding Malea', despite being held up by opposing winds. Now I intend to set out for the province, by coastal vessels part of the way, by carriages the rest. For, just as oppressive heat is an obstacle to travel by land, so are the Etesian winds to an unbroken voyage by sea.'*[97]

Another letter to Trajan, stating that he had suffered illness from the heat and fever, received a response from the emperor. Imagine the scene, Pliny dictating by lighted candle from within a tent oppressed by heat somewhere in the middle of a dusty and rugged northern Turkey to his equally hot, dusty scribe scratching away in ink at his parchment before scrolling, sealing with wax, stamping with Pliny's ring of office and then dispatching by courier in the morning – or that night. In contrast, the response was dictated by the emperor walking his marbled floor, surrounded by scribes each with a letter dictated by the emperor and going all over the empire – this one to Pliny returning by courier over the seas, roads, rivers and numerous nights on the roads to tell Pliny what was on his mind:

18. Traianus to Plinius

> *'(1) I could wish that you had been able to reach Bithynia without any complaint about your own physical condition or that of your people, and that your journey from Ephesus had been similar to your experience of the voyage as far as there. (2) The date of your arrival in Bithynia I learnt from your letter, my dearest Secundus. The provincials, I believe, will understand that I have taken thought for their interests. For you in turn will see to it that it is evident to them that you have been picked out to be sent to them in my place. (3) Moreover, you must above all examine the accounts of the communities: for it is established fact that they have been in confusion. I have scarcely enough surveyors for those works which are in progress at Rome or nearby; but men who can be trusted are to be found in every province, and therefore you will have no lack of them, if only you are willing to search for them diligently.'*[98]

A third shared aspect was the state that their province was in when they arrived. Certainly, for Cicero, Agricola and Pliny, their selection was partly based on needing someone trusted enough to reverse the maladministration of their predecessors. Bithynia had suffered from successive periods of extortion, before Pliny arrived to set matters straight, and Cilicia had in Cicero's words been 'permanently ruined', suffering from the 'appalling excesses as of some savage beast rather than a human being.' Finally, Tacitus wrote of the state of Britannia prior to the arrival of Agricola as governor, that 'Neither before nor since has Britannia ever been in a more uneasy or dangerous state: veterans butchered, colonies burned to the ground, armies isolated.'

There is little doubt that political appointments still occurred in the late Republic and throughout the Imperial age but, with a larger empire, greater threats and vastly quicker communications, the rogue provincial governor was becoming a remnant of a past age. In Narbonensis, the rogue governor could easily be found out and brought home – some like Marcus Fonteius were even put in trial – but further afield corrupted officials still operated, movements for independence and rebellion still occurred, and indigenous people needed pacifying – in the worst provinces it was sometimes a case of having to deal with all three. Thus, while we can applaud the successes of men such as Cicero, Pliny and Agricola, their careers were based on reversing the appalling maladministration of their predecessors which begs the question just how good was Roman administration in reality and how well was Narbonensis administered?

Just how effective was Roman administration?

The need to correct periods of corrupt and poor administration is not only evidenced by the surviving texts of Cicero's words, Pliny's letters or the books of Tacitus. The almost constant stream of court cases against provincial governors suggests a patchy level of control at the very least, and a number of questions continue to arise out of this aspect of Roman history. Were the treasury and archives in Rome kept informed of corruption separately to the senate? What evidence is there that Narbonensis suffered the same fate as Cilicia and Bithynia? What does chronology suggest about the scale of the problem – was corruption as rife under the Republic as it was in the early Principate? To what extent was Rome able to control her governors and, as importantly, what prevented governors from behaving like the worst kinds of emperors – for in their realms or *provincia* they were kings. Finally, was there anything provincial administrators could do to make up for or control their governors, or did they just have to see it through?

In a 1961 scholarly article on Roman administration of the *provinciae*, P.A. Brunt assessed how increasing legislation was needed to hold governors to account – this was because, despite earlier laws, provinces still reported cases of extortion, illegal punishments and bribery, sometimes on an epic scale.

The law of *repetundae* became one of the most frequently tried cases in the central and senatorial courts, and Caesar himself tried to grapple with the problem and settle matters once and for all with his own *lex Julia* when he was consul in 59 BCE. Running to 101 chapters, it was this law that stood the test of time and was the basis of practice in administration until the third century CE. Brunt comments 'The very length and complexity of the *lex Julia* suggest that it dealt fully with innumerable types of illegal enrichment.'[100] Cicero's predecessor in Cilicia and less than congenial associate in the senate, Appius Claudius, was not only charged for extortion but also under the *lex maiestatis* for treason against the state, and this shows just how serious the issues surrounding governance could become. However, whatever the charges brought by citizens or slaves against their governor, the result was all too easy to predict. There were exceptions, but if one saw the writing on the wall then a wealthy and influential former magistrate would simply opt for self-banishment to some part of the empire (probably not where they had been governor) and take their ill-gotten gains and family fortunes with them, after which they could reasonably expect the senate to move onto other more pressing concerns – the complainants simply having to accept that would never recover their losses.

In an article of 1939, John Hough uses the letters between Pliny and Trajan to investigate the levels of administration in Bithynia.[101] After reminding us that Pliny had actually defended the two previous governors of the province against charges under the *lex repetundae* – and then found himself appointed special legate for the emperor to go there and restore faith in the province. Hough makes a very valid point: that Bithynia was not one of the great provinces and thus may not have been equipped with the best administrative support. This is something well worth remembering, that in our assessment of how well a province was governed we should place this in the context of whether it was likely to have been given any sort of priority, or not, for effective civil service help. For example, were civil servants able to volunteer for a role or posting or ordered to go like a soldier in a legion? If the former, then the choice of Antibes in southern France versus Carlisle in northern Britain would seem to have been an easy one. In turn this would leave the lesser *provinciae*, such as Cilicia and Bithynia, very short of the numbers and the quality of administrators to either support or check the governor.

The challenge for the Republican senate and for the emperors under the Principate was how to find the right people for the right jobs – people who could do the job and would not exploit the obvious problems in managing an empire of gigantic size with limited administrative resources, when there were so many opportunities, and indeed expectations, for abuse. Despite being geographically much closer to Rome, the same problems affected Gallia Narbonensis – how to allow independent action by the governor and his officials but still monitor their performance. It is in the invaluable and fascinating letters from Pliny to Trajan we can see just how this could go awry.

It does seem that Pliny, for all his legal prowess, displayed his own levels of incompetence and fawning by his desire to find any opportunity to write to Trajan, and therein, flatter his leader. Occasionally the responses from Trajan show the expected and obvious irritations as if to say: *'I appointed you to deal with these matters, not to bother me with them!'* Pliny requests specialists from Rome to help build aqueducts, baths and gymnasiums, but Trajan replies, more than once, that he needs them himself and Pliny should source them locally. Pliny asks for clarification over the enlistment of slaves into the army – the practice was illegal but was widespread. The law was the law and as a lawyer surely Pliny knew what he should do, but instead the emperor is put on a spot that he does not wish to stand on. The matter of imperial passes is another case in point – Pliny wants to know when they expire, as if the emperor knows or should know when, in fact, Pliny, as Governor, has the power to extend or date his own.

Hough makes the point well – that the detail of the letters amplify and expose just how difficult it was for Rome to maintain any sort of continuity in administration. A good governor takes the province forward, a series of mediocre ones drag it back. A change of laws requires a change of interpretation, and some men can do it while others cannot. So, a very mixed picture emerges, and it is important to note that just because someone is sent to a province to sort out maladministration it does not mean that they themselves become a good governor.

The fact that Pliny had been personally selected for this role caused Trajan communication problems that he could not have foreseen. R. Fransworth in his 1996 article on the relationship between the two men, points out that the temporary suspension of the normal relationship of hierarchy caused Pliny to treat Trajan as a sort of confidante or special friend: they were, in Farnsworth's words 'liberated' from the normal etiquettes 'making them unique in the normal type of communications between provincial governors and emperor'.[102]

It was also normal practice for the governor to reward his own followers through the generosity of the emperor, and in one letter (LXXXVII) Pliny makes one of many such requests, which help us to further understand the power of the emotional relationship between these two men:

C. Plinivs a G Traiano Imperatori

(1) Nymphidium Lupum, domine, primipilarem commilitonem habui, cum ipse tribunus essem ille preafectus: inde familiariter diligere coepi. Creuit postea caritas ipsa mutuae uetustate amicitiae. (2) Itaque et quieti eius inieci manum et exegi, ut me in Bithynia consilio instrueret. Qoud ille amicissime et otii et senectutis ratione postposita et iam fecit et facturus est. (3) Quibus ex causis necessitudines eius inter meeas numero, filiam in primus, Nymphidium Lupum, iuuenem probum industriam et egegio patre dignissimum, suffecturnam indulgentiae tuae, sicut primus eius experimentis cognoscere potes, cum preafectus cohortis plenissium testimonium meruerit Iuli Ferocis et Fusci Salinatories clarissimorum uirorum. Meum gaudiam, domine, meamque gratulationem filii honore cumulabis.

C Plinius to Traianus Imperator

(1) 'I had Nymphidius Lupus, the former chief centurion, as a comrade in arms, sir, when I was tribune and he a prefect: then I began to feel a close affection for him. Later these feelings strengthened with the long duration of our mutual friendship. (2) Therefore, I made my claim on his retirement and required him to help me with his advice in Bithynia. This he in a most friendly way has already done and will continue to do, having set aside the usual consideration of leisure and old age. (3) For these reasons I count his relatives as my own, especially his son, Nymphidius Lupus, an upright, hard-working young man, and most worthy of an excellent father. He will be well qualified to receive your generosity, as you can learn from the first trials you have made of him, since he has earned as prefect of a cohort the fullest commendation of those most distinguished men Julius Ferox and Fuscus Salinator. You will crown my happiness and satisfaction, sir, by conferring an honour on the son.'[103]

Chapter 12

The Roman Civil Service

Unlike Bithynia, in Gallia Narbonensis there were to be a number of key administrative centres. Chief amongst these as we know was Narbo Martius, but in such a dispersed province covering such contrasting regions and mountains, it would be necessary to create new urban centres to dispense Roman government and justice.

To the north was not only the colony of Vienne (Vienna), Valence (Valentia) and Alba, but also the powerful metropolis of Lyon (Lugdunum), which was to become the capital of all of Gaul in a very short space of time under the Augustan period, as we have seen earlier. To the west, there was Narbonne (Narbo Martius), together with a long string of major cities and colonies along the main roads through the province – places such as Carcassonne (Caracasso), Toulouse (Tolosa) and Béziers (Baeterrae), while along the southern coastline we have Arles (Arelate), Nîmes (Nemausus), Marseilles (Massalia), Aix-en-Provence (Aquae Sextiae), Fréjus (Forum Julii) and finally Nice (Cemenellum) and Cimiez. These, together with the inland settlements of Orange (Arausio), Gap (Vapincum) and Cavaillon (Cabellio) formed the network of provincial communication centres for the entire province.

The scribes (*scribae*) are perhaps the heroes and villains of this aspect of governmental control over the provinces – like a collapse in the internet would be today, so nothing could function in the Roman empire without the tens of thousands of scribes working either for clients or for the government. In his invaluable book on the subject of Roman *scribae*, Benjamin Hartman delves deeply into the world of the scribes, their aspirations, the power they could wield, the influence they had and the necessity of having them.[104]

The scribes were the top level of four in what was called the *Apparitores* or civil servants. The number of literate Romans is difficult to determine as a per centage of the average population, but each of the regional centres needed a collection of administrators to service the needs of all the officials in their duties and to respond to the constant calls for information from the key government departments in central Rome. The governor would be in daily communication both with Rome and his provincial officers, the officers who oversaw all the various aspects of transport, the law, military matters, political issues, festivals and ceremonies, the calendar, personal issues, journeys needed to be coordinated with the fleet if going by sea and with the legions if security was an issue – all needed scribes to draft the requisite instructions or requests.

For scribes wishing to expand their horizons, then volunteering to travel to and work in the provincial administrations was probably the best route – second only to be chosen to work for an elite family or politician. Hartman has scoured the available evidence to present a picture of just how formidable and indispensable the scribe was in Rome, in society generally and certainly in the provinces. What happened in Rome was mirrored throughout the empire, and the scribes recording the critical records of debates and meetings of the senate would have had their regional and provincial equivalency in the various centres of administration – no doubt with copies sent to Rome as records of events and local decisions.

The *scribae* also had an accounting role. Many scribes were trained in financial auditing and record keeping and the best would have been employed on the *tabulae publicae* which was the public record office of the Roman state – their version of the National Archives in Kew – situated in a very large multi-storied building overlooking the forum. Data collected from the provinces was collected here too and a small army of *scribae* would work to create summaries of income and expenditure, revenues and taxation for the senate to ponder – this too would have been mirrored on a smaller scale across the provincial centres of government. The empire and the state needed men of talent, and Hartman tells us that '*these posts were a feasible opportunity for social advancement for the young and well-educated men of Italian cities.*' So, at a time when the empire was expanding, so too there was a need to expand the abilities and numbers of scribes to service the new demands. Although viewed always as a 'profession', and thus part of the working class of Roman society, in time the talents and intellect of a growing number of scribes came to be recognised as having a social status deserving of recognition, and under the Principate we see increasing numbers of scribes being listed by name on the imperial staff – not just as writers but also as advisors, given their rich experience.

Social standing was vital to the life of any Roman regardless of their class and movement between the classes was extremely difficult. Despite this, Hartman also tells us that he has identified thirty-five *scribae* that were accepted into the equestrian order – the second order of Roman society – what numbers of talented young men saw their abilities recognised in this way in Narbonensis is very difficult to identify but certainly they would have been there – perhaps even ending up in Rome on the staff of a returning governor. Not only were the scribes an essential tool in the machinery of Roman administration of the provinces, the role also offered advancement and prestige to those with the ability to grasp it and the luck to be noticed.

Of the thousands of Latin inscriptions listed for the province of Narbonensis, one concerns a completely unknown but equally valuable L. Pompeius Hermeros. Described by Hartman as a *scriba IIIvirum,* Hermeros practised his work in Aquae Sextiae and is listed in the *Inscriptions latines de Narbonnaise* (ILN) as one of the names preserved in stone for eternity. In what area he worked is beyond the current evidence but he represents to us another of the people who was helping to create the province of Narbonensis.

But the humble and obscure Hermeros is not alone, because T. Sammius Tertiolis is also recorded as working as a scribe in Cularo, a small Roman settlement to the extreme east of Narbonensis. Renamed Gratianopolis in 381 to honour the emperor Gratian, here was another Gallic city with a rich and ancient history. Today it is named Grenoble, but when it was the Roman settlement of Cularo one of the residents was a close friend of Cicero named Lucius Munatius Plancus – we know this from a cynical and cutting letter written from Plancus to Cicero, from Cularo, remarking on the sorts of people flocking to Caesar's camp during his civil war for control of the Republic.[105] Referring to them as 'ruffians' and 'wretched people bent on the ruin of the fatherland', Plancus has left us with a vivid description of the types of people arriving to enlist in Caesar's army to fight to bring down the republic. Like a MAGA crowd today in the United States of America, Plancus left us in no doubt of the sorts of people supporting Julius Caesar.[106]

Also resident in Cularo was the scribe Tertiolis and the inscription tells us that he was a *scriba aerarii* – an interesting description as it denotes, according to Mommsen, that Sammius Tertiolis was part of the *non-assidui* – a person who has seen a degradation of class, a non-holder of land and unable to vote or serve in the army. An alternative interpretation of *aerarii* that is not so punitive is that people in this class were residents of towns joined with Rome by a *hospitium publicum* – a particularly Roman arrangement where the divine right to be a guest was met by the divine right to be a host. In this latter sense then, Tertiolis may have been a resident of Cularo when it was seen as just such a settlement – not fully Roman citizens, but its residents were friends of Rome and Tertiolis was regarded as a friend of Rome who was also a scribe.

Alongside the variety of different *scribae* and also helping to keep the administration moving were the *lictores* or lictors. They functioned within the *apparitores* and, apart from guarding the senior magistrate everywhere he went – he would have a group of eleven in his entourage – they also arrested citizens and punished them, or acted as adjutants to the governor, for example in organising courts. But their roles were far wider than this when on a provincial tour of duty.

There were no job descriptions as such for any of these roles required in the service of Rome in her provinces and it is now accepted that much of Roman administration was 'for this' or ad hoc, and things got done because they needed to be done – 'you are needed … for this.'

The *viatores*, as their name suggests, travelled the roads of the empire. Not military couriers who moved from legion to legion, but civilian messengers, these were also central to the metabolism of Rome as they were the blood cells carrying messages around the empire. Nameless and invisible now, they were a vital part of the civil service structure and, like all posts in the civil service, they were paid from the public treasury whether in Rome or the various provincial centres.

Overseeing the work of the whole administration whether in Rome or in a province was the *commentariensis* – the chief clerk or registrar. In the army, the *commentarienses* (*pl.*) maintained the lists of active and sick soldiers, while in the civil service he was responsible for all public records and returns of the province and put together the various registers to construct literate control and order over the province – and so guided and informed the consuls and emperors with statistics as best they could and ensured the best quality work of the scribes. This vast array of personnel and all their associated baggage, tools and records was replicated throughout the empire and would have been working somewhere in all of the administrative centres of Narbonensis – we just do not know exactly where, although near or next door to the forum of each site would be normal.

Each province also had a *procurator*, whose tasks were to manage the imperial properties and estates, if they existed, as well as deal with all affairs regarding taxation and money. If there was to be corruption at the highest levels in a province, then the procurator would have to be involved, either as a willing participant or a bribed, bullied or intimidated member of the *apparitores*. Of course, the same could be true in reverse, where a Cicero or Pliny arrived as a new governor, determined to enforce good service to the Roman state and people, only to discover that the corruption and rot began in the office of the procurator. This is not to suggest that the procurators were a corrupt lot – far from it. This was a senior and important role and selection for the office in the first place depended on high levels of experience and probity.

In his work on Roman provincial administration, John Rogan cites the ladder to be climbed by Titus Haterius Nepos – ultimately prefect of all Egypt, but at one time a procurator who served two emperors in his lifetime – Augustus and Trajan – which makes him a contemporary of Pliny. Any achievement of public position in Rome depended on climbing the appropriate ladder, and history is fortunate to have a detailed description of his life preserved from Fulginiae in Umbria. Although the tablet does not show his earliest start, Nepos was from an equestrian background and, as a member of the *equites* class, he already had a good start in life if he wanted to take it. He first appears as the prefect of an *ala* or auxiliary cohort in a legion, and then as a *censor* or census official in Roman Britain – a letter to Flavius Genialis, prefect of a cohort stationed at Vindolanda has been identified as being written by some named Haterius Nepos dated between 97-120 CE. Promotion to military tribune followed – a significant rank on its own. Still serving in the military, Nepos became a prefect of cavalry in Britain, and it was then that he left the army and took on the role of procurator of Greater Armenia, so it is probable that this was a likely route for many men moving from long and successful military service into a senior role in the civil service. and there would be men similar to Nepos that would serve in similar roles in Narbonensis.

In the case of Sextus Varius Marcellus, who was procurator of the aqueducts, we also know from an inscription that he was paid a salary of 100,000 sesterces before becoming procurator of Britain, with his salary doubled before becoming vice prefect of the Praetorian Guard and city of Rome. Marcellus in fact went further – becoming a senator, prefect of the military treasury (paymaster for the army), commander of a legion (Legio II Augusta) and governor of Numidia. Impressive to say the least – but this does show the importance of a good marriage in Rome, both under the Republic and the Principate – given that Marcellus was married to a niece of the empress Julia Domna, wife of Emperor Severus 193-211 CE.

There were supervisors of areas, *civitates*, the *coloniae*, and public works, all of which needed to inform and make decisions on the development of each *municipum* – red tape and jobs-worths are far from new, and we can thank the Romans for many things, including the often-frustrating officialdom of local administration.

The *cursus publicus* or the 'public way' was the courier and transportation system of each province and therefore the empire. More accurately known as the *cursus vehicularis*, we know of only one such official in the historical records – Lucius Volisius Maecianus who held office under the great emperor Hadrian. His role was to supervise – using a chain of similar roles in the provinces – the operation of the network system of stables and rest stations, to ensure that the road system was maintained and not abused, and to ensure the safety of public messages. These pivotal cogs in the complex wheels of Roman governance tended to be recruited from former army officers or retired senior centurions who had been *speculatores* or reconnaissance troops and who were not frightened of travelling the vast and often dangerous roads of the empire, perhaps in places that they knew well, to check on standards. In Narbonensis, such men would have served in the legions that were now invested in new lives and homes in the *colonia*, but it was in everyone's interest that the postal system and therefore the *cursus publicus* worked well. Journey times, and therefore life or death, could depend on the effectiveness of the *mansiones* and the horse relay stations, so it was an important role. With bad news travelling much faster than good, eager officials travelled fast – and Plutarch describes the speed of couriers bringing news of the death of Emperor Nero and Tacitus talks of the mutiny of troops under Galba. A laurel crown could be attached to a horse or spear carrying good news of a victory as the rider charged along the roads to Rome or a feather in the case of bad news.

Equally vital to each province in terms of good governance was the army. As we have seen, the early days of the creation of Narbonensis were marked by local conflict and the need for small legionary forts in strategic areas. Over time, some of these were selected for growth into major and permanent encampments and barracks that could house an entire legion of five thousand troops, plus a large number of camp administrators and officials. These camps, as we can see at Vindolanda on Hadrian's Wall, developed their own towns outside the walls, and these in turn developed into large municipal areas or were then named as permanent *coloniae* for retired veterans. Not only was the army the guardian of security and the ultimate enforcer of Roman power, but it was also a huge resource of skills and labour within the province. The legions did not just sit in camp, they were active in all sorts of ways and in Narbonensis, there are numerous examples of sites of very sizeable military forces that came and went over the centuries and under the many new emperors.

Chapter 13
Oligarchic Collaboration

It is difficult to assess the impact of positive support from the local population on the speed of the Romanisation of any individual province. The degrees of welcome or resistance could vary wildly from one part of the empire to another and factors such as distance from Rome, the history of relationships between principalities and kingdoms within a province and levels of cultural exchange and trade all affected the speed at which the Roman conquest of an area developed into Romanisation. Another crucial element was the attitude of local elites and the degree to which homage to their new rulers was just superficial or an indication of immediate acceptance. Influential families and individuals across the cities and regions of Narbonensis were therefore crucial in shaping the behaviour and attitude of the population. Oligarchical control existed before the arrival of the Romans and, in many ways, the Romans wished to keep these interest and power groups in place and simply buy them or bend them to their will. Depending on the idiosyncrasies of the domestic and local political scene, provincial elites could be used to Roman advantage while they could pretend to resist passively, but in reality, the commonest reaction was to quickly see that resistance was futile and working with the conqueror could open up new avenues for wealth, success and status.

Up until the reforms of Caracalla in 212 CE, where the *Constitutio Antoninia* or Edict of Caracalla granted full Roman citizenship to all free men in the Roman Empire, Roman citizenship was the most prized possession for any family or ambitious individual. Both during the centuries of the Republic and for some time after the Augustan period, the Romans used this lure extensively to both bribe opponents and reward supplicants. From across the empire increasing numbers of *extranei* or outsiders arrived in Rome, many as proud new citizens, expecting their world to change. While the senate and Roman establishment had been battling for survival for centuries, with reasonable levels of success, the civil war waged by Augustus robbed Rome of a generation of young heirs. This decapitation was not total, but it did herald a new era for the provincial elites to attempt to fill this partial power vacuum that had been created – and Augustus was not against this drift.

The wholescale destruction of family fortunes and generations of political power led by Augustus was a revolution in Roman society and led the way towards a new power base of adherents and enablers who saw the death of the Republic as a personal opportunity for themselves, rather than the nation.

True continuity of power and political strength does not lie in constitutions but in the ability of the governing class, the oligarchies, to stay in control of events and in power. The United Kingdom is perhaps the best example in the world where unelected but powerful figures control the lives and the future of the people. There is no constitution and yet the influence of an unelected monarchy, an unelected House of Lords and a self-selected City of London combine to lurk behind the surface of a simulation of democracy: so too in Rome, the reality was that Augustus was a tyrant hiding in plain sight. For Augustus, the future lay in the empire and the imperial ability to seek out and promote men and families who were not tied to or tainted by the historical ties to one faction or another and whose loyalty was owed directly to him and his successors.

Of all the major historical works on this theme in Narbonensis, it is those by Sir Ronald Syme (1903-1989) that still maintain a strong influence on our understanding of how one oligarchy was replaced by another in the transition from Republic to Principate. His view that the noble and aristocratic families of ancient and Republican Rome were unable to adapt to modern times, new tactics and new morals still carry great weight. The graffiti was on the wall well before Caesar came on the scene, and Cicero prophesised the collapse in Roman values throughout his career from the 80s until his death in December 43 BCE. The plutocratic values that were to now completely dominate Augustan and imperial politics into the first century CE meant that there was no longer room for history, ancestry or lineage as prerequisites for office – those families that did not change, perished. Instead, argue Syme and Peter Burgers in 1997, '*the people who began as clients of the Caesars ended up supplanting them.*'[107]

It is against this backdrop that we must now view the development of our province of Narbonensis. While Narbonensis developed during the last years of the Republic, so Julius Caesar was carving out history in conquering the rest of Gaul to the north and east of Provence, and naturally his victories shone a light on what the future would hold. Caesar's Gallic Wars between 58 and 50 BCE gave impetus for Narbonensis to forge ahead, and men with ambition did exactly that to create an advantage in a race for influence in Rome. By the time Augustus was in power, so Rome was already 'living on foreign talent' and much of it was arriving from Gallia Narbonensis – the creation of a new province created a new Rome.

The fact that we can identify six full military colonies in Narbonensis by 14 CE suggests that generals knew that the province would be popular with their men as a place to retire and that it was Italy over the mountains – they felt at home in the climate, in the soil and were close by if needed. The fact that the legions recruited local men meant that it was local men that could rise through the ranks and emerge as being of use to the empire. Finally, the fact that some of the most impressive Roman structures in evidence today are to be found in southern France, in Narbonensis, tells us just how important that province was becoming.

> *'In the quickly Romanised province of Narbonensis a new local elite developed, consisting of the more successful Roman and Italic settlers and the indigenous elite, of which many members had acquired Roman citizenship at an early age. The citizenship, according to Brunt "symbolised, rewarded and fortified the loyalty of the magnates" and "also prepared the way for the final step in Romanisation: their admission to a share in imperial government, which removed the distinction between rulers and subjects".'*[108]

The first consul to be appointed from Narbonensis was Valerius Asiaticus who was from Vienna (Vienne), and this was the result of a consistently sustained effort by the influential men of the city to push for representation in the senate in Rome. This must have been celebrated in style back in his home *civitas* and was the first of what was now to become an influx of successful examples of enhanced social mobility from Narbonensis. Tacitus had cause to note this when his father-in-law, Cn. Julius Agricola rose to fame and fortune; from his own childhood in Fréjus he was not alone and the province grew in stature and importance in its relationship with Rome. In the Julio-Claudian period alone, that of the first five emperors, which lasted 95 years from 27 BCE until 68 CE when the line ended with the suicide of Nero, Narbonensis provided thirty-eight knights, which was the largest of all the provinces in the empire.

Numerous personalities emerged from within the province – either having moved there after the occupation, helping to make the province what it now was during the first century BCE, or having been established Romano-Gallic families even earlier than 120 BCE – and went on to reach the very highest levels.

> Fréjus was the first naval base in southern France, and nearby are remains of a large boat building area. The ruins in the town include the walled fortifications and a large amphitheatre. It is well positioned on the Côte d'Azur, and the towns of Cannes, Nice and St Tropez are all under an hour away. Finally, the Roman aqueduct dates to the first century and the Musée des Troupes de Marine provides a wonderful exploration of naval warfare in the Roman period.

Some years after the death of Augustus, what was to be the last of the Julio-Claudian line became Emperor. The fascinating and truly Roman story of his life is not our concern here but the role that his infamous mother, Agrippina, played is certainly pertinent. Amongst her fears was that her son would never reign and that he would be murdered – she was partially correct of course, but not until Nero had marked out his place in Roman history as one of the most barbaric and cruel of all the emperors, ruling between 54 and 68 CE.

Sextus Afranius Burrus – a man from Narbonensis

It was as guardians and guides to the young Nero that Seneca, a statesman, Stoic philosopher and post-Augustan-age poet, and Sextus Afranius Burrus, commander of the now-very-powerful Praetorian Guard in Rome, were central to the protection of the new emperor. Burrus has been referred to as 'the most influential Narbonensian of the first century'. Born in 1 CE, Burrus grew up in Vasio Julia Vocontiorum (Vaison-la-Romaine) in the Alpes/Côte d'Azur region of France. Although not one of the earlier *coloniae* or *civitates* of Narbonensis, Vasio soon blossomed as a Roman settlement and Burrus must have entered the army at a young age and shown himself to be courageous, intelligent and lucky as a commander in order to have risen to the top of the Praetorian Guard. His military career would have seen him serve under the emperors Tiberius, Gaius and Claudius and, although perhaps not immediately astonishing when one considers that this prime post would have been the target of many noble Roman families for their sons and heirs, Burrus was clearly exceptional – being from one of the provinces clearly did not stand against him.

> Vaison-la-Romaine is a gem of the Côte d'Azur. It has a wealth of Roman ruins and at one point was the centre of the Vocontii tribe and remains of a large *oppidum* can be found nearby. It became one of the richest towns in Gallia Narbonensis and even boasted of pavements made of mosaic. The statue, the Vaison Diadumenos, is of Tiberius and can be seen in the British Museum.

But the importance of Burrus to Gallia Narbonensis does not end there. In order to shore up the levels of protection for both the manipulative and devious Agrippina, as well as protect the emperor from plots and rebellions, Burrus looked to other men from the province – instead of the families of Rome – and a Narbonensian enclave was built around Nero. Pompeius Paulinus, from Arles, was given command of four powerful legions in Germania Inferior – on the orders of Nero and, no doubt, the advice of Burrus, while Cn.Domitius Corbulo, also from Narbonensis, was given command of the armies of the east. These are only the ones we can identify from the evidence, but this does not mean that there were not others too. The fall from grace that befell Burrus did not mean a decline in the reputation of men from Narbonensis – he had helped push the door further open, and the province and Rome were now indivisible. On the back of this influx of Narbonensian influence, other families also established their position in Rome, purchasing the very best houses and attending the very best social gatherings. One can imagine the Narbonensian elite forming their own very powerful and fashionable power base in the best parts of the city. One such family was to rise to the purple itself. Born Titus Aurelius Fulvus Boionius Antoninus, he was actually born in Lanuvium in Italy, but his father and his family were a branch of the Aurelian family who had moved to and settled in Nemausus (Nîmes), which made them all one of the many new families emanating from the flourishing new city within the thriving province of Gallia Narbonensis.

The massively developing economic activity of Narbonensis, coupled with the network of carefully arranged familial arrangements and marriages within the province, created the new Narbonensian oligarchy of the province itself. The natural extension for this group was to reach beyond provincial politics and to immerse themselves in the politics, society and culture of Rome.

Augustus was determined that peace and prosperity should now rule the empire and it was therefore a perfect time for new blood and new ideas on managing the empire to emerge. Augustus himself was positive about the involvement of provincial talent and Rome became awash with new contacts between the competing oligarchic groups where old money and politics met substantial 'new money', forcing the established noble families in Rome to associate themselves with the new wealthy families of the empire – in the hope that they could prove beneficial one day.

This invitation to 'infect' what had been hundreds of years of solely Latin dominance, had been refuted as a strategy many times in the past. Cicero had often talked of the mixing of metals, the alloys that corrupted the strength of true Latin blood – referencing how only true success and longevity for Rome rested on herself and not the empire. The genius of the speeches of Cicero was now, however, long forgotten and the young Augustus had blossomed into the mature Augustus and change was the fashion. New money from the provinces could be lavished on new homes not just in Rome but at the playgrounds of Baiae on the coast or the mountain top villages once home to the great aristocratic families of Republican Rome – even the homes of the great Roman names of history; Marius, Sulla, Pompey, Caesar, Cicero and Mark Anthony – were up for grabs.

If they had not been destroyed then they needed upgrading, modernising in the latest fashions, and the Narbonensian elite had the money – they just needed the status to go with it. Property prices in the most sought-after areas became ludicrously high, but if one wanted status then displays of wealth were vital and so those houses and last remaining plots of land that were both near the forum and could be seen by the public fetched the highest amounts: *'And Cicero learned early in his career that one could not always count on one's accomplishments being spread by rumours. Being seen by the public was the only guarantee, and this was one of the chief advantages that he sought when he purchased his* domus *on the Palatine.'*

Even rents became beyond the reach of all but the wealthiest merchants and families. To compete therefore, Narbonensis must have been creating vast levels of wealth for some individual families across a number of commercial enterprises.

Titus Aurelius Fulvus, the grandfather of Antoninus, had already had a successful career both in Narbonensis and in Rome, and was in fact consul in 85-86 CE and was part of the first substantial wave of new men from Narbonensis that swept into Rome in the mid-first century CE during the Julio-Claudian period. It was his son, also named Titus Aurelius Fulvus, who also rose to the rank of senator and was consul in 89 – he married the daughter of Gn.Arrius Antoninus – a close friend of Pliny the Younger, our governor of Bithynia.

Our record of exactly how many *novi homines* from Narbonensis rose to the rank of senator in the first century CE is incomplete, and Rivet (85-6) explains that this is because the province was a relatively quiet one and thus the traffic and records of events is that much diminished compared to elsewhere. The records may be incomplete and the volume of traceable evidence smaller, but we are still able to identify a wide range of individuals for whom the first century CE, in the new post-Augustan world, was indeed just as positive for them as Augustus had intended. In his exhaustive work *Les Fastes de la Province de Narbonnaise,* H.-G. Pflaum was able to calibrate the rise and the range of the men from Narbonensis.

The list of *dignatio vironum* or worthy men from Narbonensis is impressive and especially strong characters emerge during the mid-to-late first century CE. These would have been the same men who were key members of the Narbonensian oligarchy who already controlled the province – alongside each governor naturally. A roll call of names contains the following:

D. Valerius Asiaticus *cos* in 53 was originally from Vienne
Cn. Domitius Afer was a praetor in 25, *cos* in 39, was from Nemausus
Pompeius Paullinus, who was a nephew of Seneca, *cos* in 53, was from Arles
L. Duvius Avitus, *cos* in 56, was from Vaison
P. Marcus Celsus, *cos* in both 62 and 69, was most likely from Nemausus

M.Vestinus Atticus, *cos* in 65, and L. Pompeius Vopiscus, *cos* in 69, were both from Vienne

The great and well-known Cn. Julius Agricola, *cos* in 77, came from Fréjus and T. Aurelius Fulvus, who was the grandfather of the future emperor Antoninus Pius and mentioned earlier, was *cos* in 85 and no doubt one of the most influential men in Rome, and possibly led the Narbonensian elite group in the senate. How far these families and their familial connections worked together within the province or acted independently with connections in Rome is an interesting question. Roman politics was based on factions and compromises, so just how unified was the Narbonensian elite in their approach to Rome?

The degree to which Narbonensis therefore profited from assimilation into the Roman empire can be partially assessed by this influx of men into the highest positions of power in Rome. Indeed, in social and political thought, Narbonensis probably ceased to be seen as a province very quickly after the reign of Augustus and instead became just an extension of Italy. There would no doubt always linger in the air the conceited and aloof disdain from the 'blue blood' families in the senate for the impostors from the provinces, but Rome had come a very long way from the times when men like Cataline regarded Cicero as an 'outsider' in the senate merely because he was born north of Rome in Arpinum, and not inside the *Pomerium*.

It is worth noting at this stage that becoming a senator was a substantial achievement, but staying one was perhaps even harder. The costs of sustaining a senatorial lifestyle, both in the ability to entertain but also create the display so essential to the *dignitas* of office, meant that time, education, money and connections were all needed in abundant supply. Naturally these requirements excluded many men of talent in the equestrian order – men whose lineage was proud and strong but whose fortunes did not exist. Thus, it follows that the Narbonensian elite that managed both the affairs of their province, with the Roman governor naturally, and carved out careers and status in Rome, were men of substantial means perhaps inherited or more likely created from the massive expansion of the Narbonensian economy since occupation and annexation in 118 BCE.

The reforms of Augustus made the obligations of becoming a member of the *ordo senatorius* harder and were designed to achieve many changes and to underpin the stability of the Empire after his days. Debate continues as to exactly what these obligations were – for example Augustus tried to make aspects of senatorial rank hereditary – hopeful that he would be securing a steady stream of young heirs into the leadership of the state and thus create a new senatorial class for the future. The qualification rose from 400,000 sesterces to a million under Augustus, which was clearly an attempt to restrict the office to a select few throughout the empire. But this did not mean that young male heirs were *obliged* to take on a life in politics – many decided on the complete opposite, it was just that the door was now open for them to walk through. There is plenty of evidence that many regarded a non-political career as appealing in its own way.

Augustus was acutely aware of the need for passing on a legacy – he was without his own heir and even those he adopted died before they could take office. When young men who were descendants of senators – *libris senatorum* – reached maturity, Augustus had decreed that they could wear the toga with a broad purple stripe, they could join the legions just as in the old days of the Republic, and serve as junior tribunes and, as Suetonius explained, they could even attend meetings of the senate in order to teach them the arts of political debate and instil in them a desire to serve.[109] Such a process and availability would not have been possible for the men from Narbonensis who made up the first wave of provincial appointments to the senate, but their sons and grandsons may well have been encouraged in some ways – overtly or covertly – to maintain the family line and expectations in Rome. The Via Domitia and the Via Aurelia, the main Roman roads that led to and from the province, would have been in constant use – none more so than by the great families of Narbonensis as they made their political futures in Rome.

Part IV

The Evolution of the Province from the Principate to the Severan Period 27 BCE–235 CE

Chapter 14

Urban Expansion in the Early Principate – a Case Study of Glanum

'Agorum cultu,viorum morumque dignatone, amplitudine opum, nulli provincarium postferenda breviterque Italia verius quam provincial'

'Its agriculture, the high repute of its men and manners and the vastness of its wealth make it the equal of any other province: it is, in a word, not so much a province as a part of Italy.'[110]

At some point during the writing of his mammoth *Naturalis Historia* (Natural History), Gaius Plinius Secundus, author, naturalist, naval and army commander and friend to the emperor Vespasian, turned his attention to describing southern Gaul. Pliny the Elder was uncle to Pliny the Younger, our prolific letter writer to the emperor Trajan, and opens for us a beautiful window into our province of Narbonensis – before his tragic death in the catastrophe at Pompeii on 24 August, 79 CE.[111]

With so much rich land to cultivate, rivers to communicate, and wealth to accumulate, Gallia Narbonensis became exactly as Pliny the Elder saw it, an extension of the homeland and thus it was very attractive to Roman men and women and to the rest of the empire, and typical of the development of the early Republican town was Glanum.

The site of an ancient water cult and Celtic-Ligurian *oppidum*, Glanum was founded by members of the Salyes tribe, partly because of its strategic position at the base of a valley, where it lay on a crossroads making their way around the peaks of the Alpilles and the site of the supposedly magical waters of the God Glan that flowed down the steep hillsides overlooking what was to become the northern end of the settlement.

Archaeology suggests that the *oppidum* began to accommodate Greek style houses and villas well before the arrival of the Romans in the 120s BCE, and that it was already a sought-after stop over to ascend the steep steps up onto the hillside and drink or bathe in the healing waters as part of one's journey to Hispania.

With the revolts of the 120s and again in the 90s we might recall that Flaccus and Calvinus both defeated the Salyes in a brutal battle in this area. Calvinus based his army around Glanum, and then cleared the entire area of potential rebellion – which in effect meant killing any young men that they found in any settlement and destroying it when they left. Much of the small ancient and Hellenistic site on the southern slope was therefore burnt to the ground leaving it open to the arrival, settlement and redesign by the Latins. With the gradual Romanisation of southern Gaul and the formation of the province of Narbonensis, Glanum slowly recovered into a thriving town and was given the status of *Oppidum Latinum*, giving the citizens the status, if not the rights, of Roman citizens. The peace and prosperity offered by Augustus in fact lasted over 200 years and it was not until 260 CE that the town was overrun as part of an invasion by the tribes of the upper Rhine, the Alamanni, and with large parts destroyed, Glanum was abandoned for a nearby settlement which developed into what we now know as Saint-Remy-de Provence. However, the misfortune of the people of third century Glanum became a fortune for prosperity. Lying desolate, the town was picked over for much of its stone and some of the roofing tiles – while, over time, other roofs collapsed inwards sealing the contents and floors below. This, along with a series of floods down the hillsides over hundreds of years, sealed parts of the town deep in silt and this has left archaeologists a veritable tomb to explore in the twenty-first century.

Those familiar with Van Gogh's painting 'Olive Trees' from 1889 may know that he painted at least fifteen such images in a series and all-around Saint-Remy-de-Provence – at least one of which was looking through the Olive trees that had grown directly over the ruins of Glanum and onto the mountains behind. This scene, while on his journey to voluntarily enter himself into the nearby asylum of St Paul, he aptly named Olive Trees, and with the Alpilles in the background; a sign can be seen on the site today indicating where he stood for his view. Van Gogh would have been aware of the Roman remains in front of him, with the protruding mausoleum and the top of the crumbling arch – both of which have now been revealed in all their glory.

Excavations began in 1921 and from 1928 Henri Rolland (1887-1970) began working in the Vallon de Notre-Dame de Laval for most of his life, and it is to him and his team that we owe the site we see today. Divided into three distinct phases of development, we can better understand how an Iron Age holy site and settlement became Romanised from the second century BCE and continued to develop well into the third century CE.

The oldest settlement is referred to as 'Glanum I' and was at the end of the cramped gorge – the houses then expanded southwards down from the hillsides and out into the alluvial plain created by the silt and wash coming down from the hills all around. Glanum I is the smallest part of the settlement and ends with a destruction layer associated with the arrival of the Roman troops in the late 120s – and again in the 90s.

Slowly the Celtic and Latin survivors returned to rebuild and repopulate the site with domestic life and began rebuilding over Glanum I, and this is referred to as Glanum II. During the last century of the Roman Republic, when we see a huge and sustained flow of immigration into the province in what was described earlier in Chapter 9 as 'people making the province, not policies' – so Glanum II becomes the largest phase. As the settlement grew, the buildings spread ever southwards and the roughly constructed buildings on an irregular pattern are replaced by a more thoughtful and high specification range of houses – some with rich mosaic floors and painted walls. These buildings fit with the themes of a rapidly growing population, a thriving and diversifying economy, and peace across the province. There was a *mansio* within the town for travellers on their journeys between the Rhône and Italy – the Via Domitia passed just to the south of the town – and the *mansio* later moved to Saint Remy just 2km north of the town. In Glanum III one moves into the late-Augustan and imperial period where significant public buildings are erected; Roman temples sit alongside the surviving Greek ones and monuments are dedicated to the emperors. Later, an aqueduct bringing water to the expanding, busy and energised Roman town completes the development alongside a triumphal arch over the entrance route to Glanum.

Approaching the town from the south, one can visualise the red roofing tiles and white walls of a thriving Roman town, smoke rising from workshops and houses, carts and people moving around and the taller roofs of some quite significant buildings. It may all just seem like a pile of grey stone now, but Romans loved colour and many reds, blues and yellow hues would create a Mediterranean scene, blessed by sunshine and happy travellers arriving and leaving – even an emperor. Rather than a single item separated from its environment in a museum or a lone building exposed on a hillside or a villa in a field, the size and shape of this town, the width of the streets and the dimension of the buildings allow one to imagine the streets full of people, children and animals as they led their ordinary lives in an ordinary town. Like Pompeii, we are transported back through the ages and the only limit on the experience is the vibrancy of our imagination.

The Triumphal Arch

The Triumphal Arch is considered by many to be one of the best preserved of its type – although not as large as that at Orange, it is thought to have been the first Triumphal Arch to have been built in the whole of the province and set an imposing southern gateway from the Via Domitia, some 250m in advance of the Augustan phase of the town. Perhaps fixed there as indicative of the start of the towns' *pomerium,* it is decorated with reliefs showing captured Gallic prisoners and is dated to between 10 BCE and 20 CE marking it as another part of the Augustan celebration of final dominance over the Gauls of this region – although this time there are no lists of conquered tribes (unlike Lugdunum and the Trophy of the Alps at La Turbie).

> Triumphal Arches can be found in many places in southern France but the most notable examples are those of Orange and St Rémy (Glanum). The twin arches at either end of Le Pont Flavien in St Chamas are also remarkable, as they remain very much as they looked to travellers throughout the Roman era, while the theatre remains in Arles contain numerous impressively built arches – although these are not part of a formal triumphal arch. North east of Montelimar stands the town of Die. Often forgotten in any tour of southern France as it is so far inland, one of the two main Roman gates, built in the second century CE, is formed of a massive Roman Arch and is still in use today – named Porte St Michel.

As with the construction of any triumphal arch, the design would have been agreed with the town dignitaries, perhaps the benefactor and the master craftsmen employed or brought to the town from elsewhere, perhaps even Rome, to complete the work. Travelling bands of masons could tour an area moving from job to job before returning to Italy. What can be seen from the remnants of the four main reliefs display a common theme of the dominance of Rome, the end of military opposition – with the Goddess Dea Roma sitting on a pile of military weapons – coupled with a toga-clad man, surely a Roman, with his hand on the shoulder of a Gaul representing reconciliation. If Augustus and his propaganda machine did in fact sent out requests for *Pax Romana* to be enshrined in this way, this would explain the surge in the building of triumphal arches in this period – at Orange, Carpentras and the two arches at Pont Flavien.

The Monument

Just to one side of the arch is what may be a mausoleum or in fact a monument – the debate continues – but what is not in doubt is its scale and beauty. Possibly a tribute from the town to the sons of Augustus, the more convincing argument in Bromwich is that it was erected by a local family who had claimed fame and fortune in their support for Caesar in the civil war of the 50s and also Augustus in the more recent 30s. Sharing in the imperial family names the inscription reads:

SEX.L.M. IULEI. C.F. PARENTUS. SUEIUS

'Sextus, Lucius, Marcus, sons of Caius, of the Julian family to their parents'

Again, the reliefs are of the highest quality and on the four sides of the base there is a mixture of scenes, including the east relief, which has a striking scene of a winged creature reading from a scroll over the death of one person while another is dying of his wounds. These could be contemporary images of the deaths of the children of Augustus, but more likely they are representations of past family members. The other reliefs are a mixture of battle scenes and mythology – especially Greek – and would have been well known legends at the time.

Further into the site and visitors can view the vast array of houses built for the various residents and families of Glanum over 200 years. Some of these have been identified with individual occupants, which has left their names captured for posterity, while others await further excavation. The site widens out on the approach to the water sanctuary which is protected by a wall and tower creating the suspense and divinity that one would expect with healing waters where Nymphs and Gods appear.

The two forums

In the wider section of Glanum are the remains of an earlier and then much larger later forum, with the Basilica to the south much like on the model of the forum in Rome itself, although on a much-reduced scale. The practice of replicating the mother city in terms of layout was very common across all Roman cities and the space needed to erect these two spaces – one on top of the other and with the second larger forum – meant that the older Greek-style buildings needed to be flattened. The second forum was built in around 10 CE, and again was part of the Augustan boom in building and town confidence that we see across the province.

The *Curia*

The council house or *curia* is another representation of Rome and one can imagine the number of important meetings held here, discussing town business, relaying news of the visit of Agrippa or the emperor and how the town would receive them, taxation and how to collect it, elections, court cases, civic celebrations and public announcements of all kinds. Together with the forum, these two places were the vocal mouthpieces of any Roman community.

Temples

Closer to the sanctuary wall and to the right of the *curia* were a collection of temples. A pair named as the Gemini temples were of classic Roman design with high platforms reached by wide staircases, a foyer or *pronaos* each with six Corinthian columns and a *cella* at the rear. Rolland, in his earlier excavations, was convinced that the temples were built at the same time and dedicated to the adopted sons of the emperor Lucius and Gaius, and a statue of a headless young man found between them may be a clue that he was correct. However, the 1980s' excavations led by Gros suggests that the two temples were built at different times – maybe 30 years apart – and they started out as being dedicated to Hercules and Sylvanus. Gros feels they were then changed into temples for the imperial cult to practise its work and appointed new priests from within the town. This interpretation fits with the visit of Agrippa to Glanum, and probably more than once. A limestone cut architrave bears his name:

(VAL) ETVDINI . M (arcus). AGRIPPA

Restored to good health. Marcus Agrippa

Simple and straightforward, it has been suggested that this simplistic style was what Agrippa liked to see – pragmatic, modest and keen on urban improvement, but not keen to be seen as the all-important provider. There is little majesty with inscriptions for Agrippa and these may mirror his personality – gratitude yes, fawning no.

> Glanum remains a Roman time capsule just outside Saint-Remy-de-Provence. This extraordinary archaeological site disappeared around 280 CE as a result of the very first barbarian incursions. Excavations continue periodically, and the entire site feels like a living city with evidence of the many individuals that lived and died here in the Roman period.

The Two 'Imperial Princesses'

Some of the many archaeological finds of Glanum were found at the bottom of a well – at some point in history, damaged sculptures seemed of no value and were simply thrown away adjacent to one of the temples. Two of the items recovered in 1951 were finely carved busts of Roman women. That their hair is in the imperial style and the carving of real quality in white marble has led some to postulate that these are more than just important local women but in fact imperial portraits of Octavia – sister of Augustus and married in 40 BCE to Mark Anthony – and Livia, wife of Augustus from 38 BCE. The notion that the imperial cult took over the temples in Glanum would fit the presence of these heads as part of the display of reverence to the divinity of Augustus – Livia herself becoming adopted into the Julian family after her husband's death and taking the name Julia Augusta with cults of her own for the remaining years of her life. There is no current evidence for the presence of a *flamen* or high priest but it is very likely that there was a succession of them just as elsewhere.

The hotel de Sade in Saint-Remy-de-Provence is a place of history for the local area and where many of the finds from Glanum can be seen. Once home to a member of the Sade family – though not to the infamous Marquis himself – the building is beautifully laid and positioned, with rooms dedicated to the excavations at Glanum and is well worth a visit.

The Baths

In the early part of the first century BCE, the town of Glanum decided they wanted their own public baths. In order to locate them centrally, again this required demolishing earlier Greek-style housing which has subsequently been identified by excavation. The baths suited an up-and-coming Roman town, especially with increasing numbers of hot and dusty travellers stopping by from the Via Domitia, and were surrounded by underfloor heating which can be seen as part of the remains on the site today. In the Augustan period, and with their new status as *Oppidum Latinum*, the baths were redesigned and enlarged to suit the town's prestigious benefactors, including the Mask Fountain which provided water to the exercise area of the baths.

The thermal baths are especially important, and the waters had been used for healing purposes for hundreds of years by the Phoenicians, Greeks, the Celts who dedicated the springs to their god Glanis, and then the Romans. The survival of the baths was due to hundreds of years of alluvial silt descending from the hills surrounding the town. The fountain of the sacred spring was, and still is, the symbol of Glanum.

One of the most notable aspects of Glanum is that it seems dominated by public buildings, and the homes of the average citizen, some of whom were more than averagely wealthy by Roman standards, are there but merely the walls and foundations of their lives. This should not be unexpected given that the public buildings were more substantially made, nor should this minor observation detract from what is a gem in a sea of Roman remains across Provence.

Of course, Gallia Narbonensis was and still is littered with examples of Roman architecture, but the risk of creating an encyclopaedia mitigates against a definitive list in a book such as this one that tries to describe the development of the province in all its facets – social, political, cultural and economic. Even the outstanding examination of the development of the urban centres of the province, A.L.F. Rivet's book, is short of material on the major sites and memorials, while J.C. Anderson's *Roman Architecture in Provence* (2013), although a heroic attempt to rectify this deficiency, becomes closer to a catalogue of sites rather than a contextual analysis.[112]

What is clear is that, as sites such as Glanum, Arelate, Baeterrae, Lugdunum, Nemausus, Narbo Martius, Orange, Apta Julia, Aquae Sextiae and Massalia developed in their own unique ways, they were all equally susceptible to the fashions from Rome and to civic competition – this is why they all developed in the same way and with bigger, better and more expensive developments.

When an arch went up in Nîmes, others went up elsewhere. When new baths were created in Narbonne, so Glanum and other towns and cities wanted the same. As artists created mosaics in Béziers, so they received commissions across the province from similar clients, and when an emperor was planning his visit, communities vied with each other to create the most attractive receptions. We should also guard against seeing these phases as just something associated with the earlier imperial period. The second and third centuries also saw generous civic schemes with their own chronology that overlaid what had been fashionable in the past, taking down, redesigning or destroying what was seen as outdated, inconvenient and reminiscent of an age long forgotten. Just as urban regeneration does today, it was hard for Romans to decide on what was culturally vital to protect – when it was in the way of a new extension to the facilities they wanted.

The Further Commercial Expansion of the Province in the Augustan Period

The Potteries of Narbonensis

Wine was produced in ever-increasing quantities from Gallia Narbonensis and, to service the demand, larger numbers of amphorae and ships arrived into and departed from the enlarged ports of the Mediterranean coast. The main family of wines or *conditium* were spiced and intoxicating with their pungency and very different from those we understand today. Our term 'condiments' has its etymological derivation in this phrase, and one can easily see why when pepper, honey, saffron, laurel and dates could be added to the fermentation process to create either *Conditium viatorum* – or wine for the traveller on the roads – or *conditium paradoxum* – a surprise wine usually drunk in the home or *domus*. Indeed, having a specific type of wine just for travelling illustrates what a major part of the lives of Roman citizens was spent in travel between destinations.

> Although today Golfe-Juan Vallauris is a typical tourist destination in the south of France, in the Roman period it was known as the 'valley of one hundred potters'. Vallauria in Provencal means 'the golden valley'. This whole area specialised, and still does, in culinary pottery – which allows food to cook without losing any fat, something that was important to the Roman palette.

To service the wine and other trades, pottery amphorae were manufactured in abundance across numerous towns and cities and traded all over the empire – in the United Kingdom, pottery manufactured in southern Gaul has been discovered as far north as Vindolanda on Hadrian's Wall and as far south as the ethereal Fishbourne Palace in Sussex. Stamped with a maker's mark and sealed with a description of the contents, amphorae remain the outstanding image of Roman land and seaborne trade.

The unknown manufacturers of the classic red Roman roof and floor tiles – the *imbrices* and *tegulae* will also have made huge fortunes out of the demands for construction materials as each provincial settlement expanded. For example, in Vienna, Austria in 2023, a site was being prepared for new building and further remains of part of the Roman garrison camp were discovered. Situated in Michaelerplatz right next to the Hofburg Palace, of special interest were the red floor tiles each stamped '*legio X SPQR*', indicating that either a local tradesman received the commission or perhaps the legion carried its own pottery makers with it.[113]

The pottery of Vallauris which is so sought after today began life amongst the huge clay deposits around Golf-Juan Vallauris. But for one of the greatest varieties of potteries and the mines that went with them one should travel to Forum Iulii (Fréjus).

Situated at the eastern end of the province, the settlement was called the market of Caesar and was at the crossroads between the Via Julia Augusta coming from Italy and the start of the Via Domitia, with Tacitus naming the port at Forum Iulii, *claustra maris* – gateway to the sea – indicating that, geographically, Forum Iulii was perfectly situated. It is thought that the foundation of the new Roman settlement was 49 BCE and it was here that Augustus repatriated the galleys taken from Mark Anthony at the conclusive Battle of Actium – later the area became a colony for his veterans of the VIII Legion and it could claim to have been the nominal capital of the new province in these early years. Surrounding the town are the large clay deposits of the Massif de l'Esterel, and it is this Mediterranean coastal mountain range with its red Rhyolite tuffs that was attractive, not just because of the clay but also the building blocks of reddish Rhyolite stone. In and around Fréjus there are numerous examples of Roman kilns, reminding us that pottery production was huge in this region, and A.L.F. Rivet in his excellent map of the area has pottery kilns surrounding Fréjus:

> *'Further pottery kilns have also been found in Ste-Croix and la Madelaine, at Bellevue, at St-Lambert and, in the west, at les Escaravatiers (just south of le Puget) showing that Fréjus was well able to produce much of its own pottery from its especially useful clay.'*[114]

But even the activity at Fréjus was not on the industrial scale of that surrounding Tolosa (Toulouse). Here the entire area for 40km surrounding the *civitas* was covered in a complex patchwork of pottery kilns, mines, quarries, and especially tile kilns, all feeding into the two rivers that serve Toulouse – the Aude and the Garonne. The demand for roof and floor tiles would have been immense and Tolosa responded to that call.

Although not elevated to the status of *colonia*, the very large number of villa sites surrounding the town, the presence of a substantial theatre and forum, and the fact that there were two aqueducts providing water to the settlement and the estimated plan of the early town indicates that it was a thriving community – not least because it also served as the western boundary town of the province of Narbonensis. The road system running to and from Tolosa was also impressive, and the current roads that join to Carcassonne and Narbonne are littered with the remains of Roman buildings, such as *mansiones* and numerous villas, for example those at Coulieu, Bordier, Pinsaguel, Clermont, Grepiac, Auterive, Cintegabelle and Sana have been excavated and are open to the public.

The Watermills at Barbegal

Even hard-working potters have to eat, and another commercial activity vital to the health of the province was the production of wheat for flour and bread.

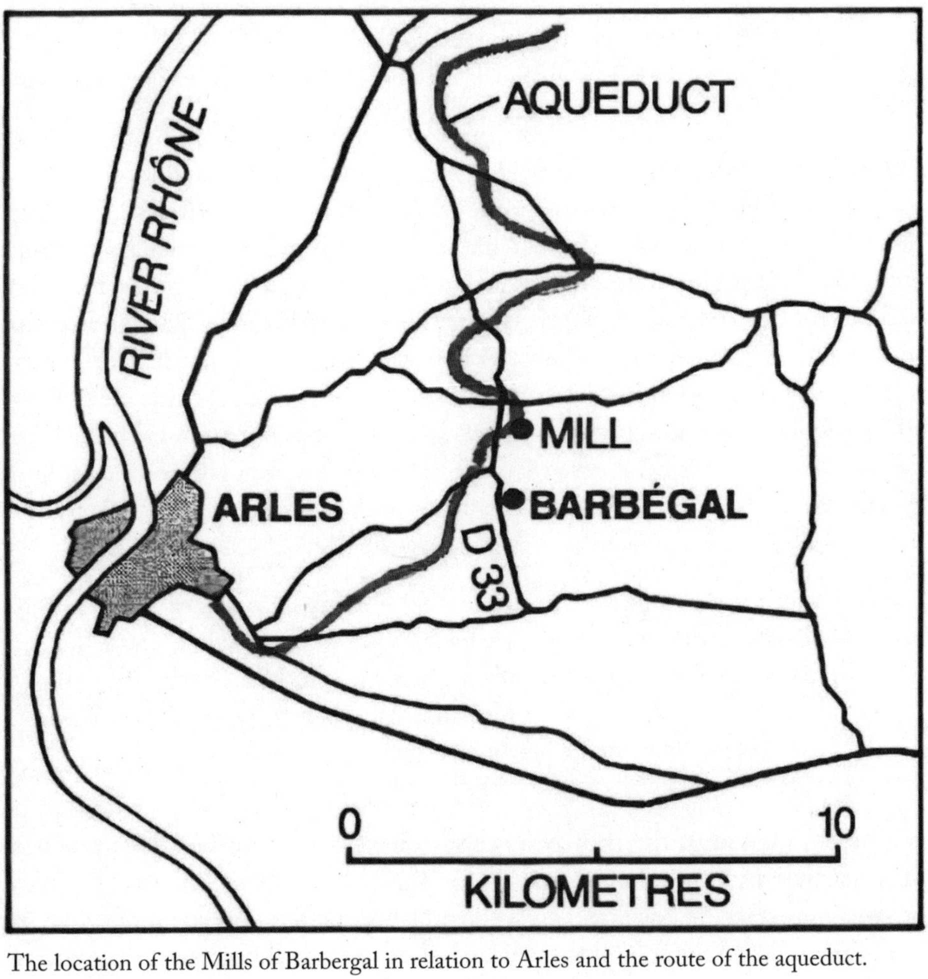

The location of the Mills of Barbergal in relation to Arles and the route of the aqueduct.

An artistic impression of the Roman watermills at Barbegal – the largest grain producing centre in the south of France.

Across modern day Provence, the fields are given over to all manner of agricultural production, and the mixture of vines on sloping hillsides mixed with the large flat fields of corn are part of what makes inland Provence so charming and attractive. It was the same under Roman rule, although far more of the land was given over to dense, dark green forested areas through which the Roman surveyors had to plan their routes. When it came to flour production, every settlement had its own bakers and ovens, each with their own small milling ability, which was enough to produce a small number of leaves each day. We have a rare example of the type of small bakery in the funeral monument and epitaph in the form of a poem on the tombstone of a baker found in Narbo.

The Baker's tombstone was found in the 1973 excavations of Le clos de la Lombarde, where houses and a bathhouse were revealed, along with hundreds of artefacts including the mosaics in the House of the Genius (see page 81) and the baker's tombstone. All of these can now be seen in the Musée Archéologique in Narbonne.

As the population of the province grew, so mass production of flour was not only a necessity but an opportunity for the commercially-minded Roman businessman. Across Narbonensis watermills were built, perhaps more than in any other area of France, and there is no better testament both to the ingenuity of Roman engineering coupled with a commercial eye than can be seen at the complex works at Barbegal, Bouches-du-Rhône near Arles. This complex of Roman buildings has been called '*the greatest known concentration of mechanical power in the ancient world.*'[115]

Situated 12km east northeast of Arles near Fontvielle, a steep escarpment rises up near the old Roman aqueduct revealing the site of sixteen water wheels set in two parallel rows of eight on each side. The mills were built one above the other, descending the steep slope with staircases and water channels, accommodation and ancillary buildings. Although there may have been a mill on the site in earlier centuries, this huge factory for milling grain into flour was built and operated during the second and third centuries CE, and estimates suggest that the mill could produce twenty tons of flour per day, or enough for the 30,000 or so people that now lived in Arelate by that time. To power the mills, two aqueducts were built with a sluice to divert water into the mills, and into the two at the same time. Stacking mills down a steep slope was not an uncommon occurrence in Roman times and they can be seen in various places such as Byzantium and in the Moselle.

The Imperial Mint in Lyon

Iron, copper, lead and silver were being mined near Narbonne, Béziers, Nîmes and Fréjus, and all of these materials were in great demand and fetched increasingly high prices with the expansion of building projects in Narbonensis throughout the first and second centuries CE. But the most exciting development of all in terms of the mining and use of precious metals came with the decision to establish an imperial mint in Lugdunum or Lyon to the north. By 15 BCE, it seems that Lugdunum had eclipsed Rome itself as the main mint for the whole of the empire, and although it sat just outside our province, it did mean that coinage in staggeringly large numbers, marked with the mintmark of LD for Lugdunum, was available to flood into the province of Gallia Narbonensis. The Celtic tribes had had their own coinage from around the sixth century BCE onwards, but the quantities of copper, silver and gold in circulation were small and the designs and uses were localised. As the Romans overwhelmed their societies, so Roman coinage too was a symbol of power and control. Roman numerals, Latin lettering and images of emperors and gods all served to communicate to the users that the Romans controlled commerce. In the early coinage of the new province, cross-cultural influences can be seen in Celtic-Roman coins – for example where the carnyx was found on early Roman coins minted in Lugdunum to represent both a Roman victory but also recognise an aspect of cultural identity amongst the Celtic population that was being Romanised.

Eventually Celtic mints and designs went out of use altogether and the metals were melted down and remade into Roman coins. Lugdunum was to lose its special place as an imperial mint under Nero, but much later, in 328 CE, Arelate also became a mint with the mark AR.

Public and Private Baths

The Roman baths that typify modern reflections on what Roman life was like for the ordinary people were naturally a key part of every urban development across the empire. The richness of the average *domus,* still preserved in so many towns of Provence, all had their own luxurious bath complex and these can be seen in all the major towns and cities, but the communal baths were a great deal more important than just places for the people to keep clean.

The communal aspect of bathing not only helped to keep the poorer classes clean, controlling the smells that would permeate the average town, but also allowed for social interaction between classes in a way that was just not possible anywhere else. A trip to the baths for a massage, a spa treatment or a good wash was also a place to discuss business, meet old friends, for men to have sex with willing male partners and, as Mary Beard comments, to leave either clean or with the clap or perhaps both. Thus, every town or city needed, as a priority, to build its baths, and they could be modest or on a very grand scale. Even the emperor might be found in the communal baths – Hadrian was known to have mixed with his people in the hurly-burly of the busy baths – maybe to look at the young men or even meet them.

Baths could be crammed on busy hot days, so walkways were needed around a number of pools with changing areas, toilets and private rooms. Some of the best preserved in Narbonensis can be found in Fréjus, where five sets of Roman baths have been identified, as well as, of course, those we have discussed in Glanum.

Mining – the Roman contribution to climate change

With the commercialisation of the province came all sorts of demands – transportation needed to be faster and better, safety and security needed to be dependable, investment and money was essential, status and wealth demanded the ability to be ostentatious, and access to Rome's political theatre needed to be granted. But the Romans also needed raw materials. Across the empire, the acquisition of territory afforded vast new opportunities to seek out, seize by force or open new mines for the raw materials of the Roman economy – silver, lead, gold, copper, tin, mercury, iron – all of these were needed and most of them could be found in Gallia Narbonensis – especially towards the western end as the Pyrenees rose up dividing the territory from Spain.

Our contemporary concerns with mapping and quantifying climate change have also led to increased focus on historical change. In a March 2023 research article by Noemi Silva-Sanchez and Xose-Lois Armada, it is clear that the rapid increase in Roman mining in very distinct periods and in identifiable areas, contributed surprising amounts towards hemispherical pollution which remains today. The evidence comes in a range of places that have been accessed and analysed – lake sediments, human and animal bones from distinct periods, and even mussel shells dated to the Roman period. However, it is in the Arctic that 81 out of 89 cores tell us very clearly about the levels and extent of Roman mining pollution and when it was most harmful.[116] The late Republican period saw low levels of pollution showing in the arctic cores – probably due to the disruption of the civil wars between Pompey and Caesar. This period was followed by the turmoil of further conflict between Augustus and the *Liberatores* between 44 and 43 BCE and the lasting disruption that followed, but in the era of *Pax Romana* and on into the first and second centuries CE – the main periods of explosive urban population and provincial growth – the cores show a four-fold increase in pollution levels. For comparison, later periods of plague across the empire also showed a decline, with manpower in short supply and commercial activity in a slump.

In Narbonensis, during the pre-Roman Celtic Iron Age, there had been mining and smelting of iron ore in most regions of southern France, but this was both small scale and very localised, whereas the Romans industrialised raw material extraction and added substantial Roman mines in places such as Etang-Mort at the southern end of the Pyrenees – to the far west of Carcassonne and Aulus-les-Bains in the central-northern part of the province. The demand for lead for pipework in Rome, in the villas of the wealthiest citizens, and across the empire was such that the Roman mines worked their slaves twenty-four hours a day to extract lead ores, which were then smelted across the landscape in large quantities. Slag heaps built up and earth turned black in what was a Roman-era industrial revolution, with smoke from the smelting process hanging high over the countryside where the mines were located. The fact that lead in drinking water in Rome has been evaluated at over one hundred times greater than spring water is testament to the effective lead supply generated from these mines.

To the east of the province, new research published in 2017 evaluated levels of pollution emerging from the deepest ice on Mont Blanc. With global warming causing ice levels to recede, scientists are able to examine cores in the French Alps – part of which edged into Narbonensis – and again the results are revealing. The new study shows that the levels of air toxicity from lead pollution and mining emissions was far higher than thought:

> *'Our very first study of pollution during antiquity inferred from an alpine ice core allows us to better evaluate the impact of Roman emissions at the scale of Europe and to compare this old pollution to the recent use of leaded gasoline in Europe between 1950 and 1985. The Alpine ice shows that the lead emissions during antiquity enhanced the natural level lead by a factor of ten … over several centuries.'*[117]

Such research has completely altered the standard assumption that air quality was 'natural' prior to the industrial revolution and pollution levels measured from those base lines. In fact, air pollution began on a large scale with the Romans and pre-Roman air quality was far purer than we think: *'All standards of pollution that rely on this assumption of a pre-modern, pre industrial baseline, are wrong.'*[118]

So in fact one hitherto under-estimated negative impact of Roman imperialism that has most recently been revealed is that the new Roman provinces containing precious metals became highly polluted – the UK was especially heavily mined, although research has not yet been completed to show how heavily it has been polluted by the toxicity of lead and other metal mining and smelting over the period of the Roman occupation.

> *'The findings show the Romans impacted air quality beyond simple lead pollution and their effect on the European atmosphere was longer-lived than previously thought.'*[119]

Lead toxicity infiltrated the Roman *domus* in more ways than just lead piping of water. The production of painted pottery was vast, and lead was used both to add weight and colour to clay as well as make it stronger and more durable. Glazes too had lead added to the paint – as well as arsenic and antimony – making these pots, often used for cooking, a heady mix of poisons in the average Roman home. The worst of all was 'white lead', which was very popular in Rome in such items as marbled ware and graffito ware. When one considers the range of often-quoted illnesses that were common in urban centres, where lead would be in the highest quantities, then lead use is the obvious assassin. Developmental delay in children, low IQs, ADHD, sterility, paralysis, vomiting, hearing loss, miscarriages and fatigue are all symptoms of lead poisoning and would have been major and widespread problems in urban settings where lead was so commonly used.

But it was not just toxic metal mining that was in large scale production and, as mentioned earlier, the area around Fréjus, with its large red Rhyolite mountains, was also heavily mined for clay but also the red Rhyolite tuffs (volcanic ash from a vent that solidifies into a soft, grainy red rock) was extensively used in building construction across ancient Rome. There are the remnants of Roman Rhyolite mining all over the north and east of Fréjus – consequently the mining and of clay and blocks of Rhyolite was a major export from the port and on to Rome and the entire Mediterranean.

In a 2005 article published in *Archaeometry* we are reminded that Roman builders and engineers were highly competent and skilled in knowing which areas provided the best building materials, and this knowledge, as with almost all wisdom in ancient Rome, was passed down by word of mouth and experience to the next generation of builders.

Pyroclastic deposits were mined from at least seven different locations within Italy itself, but with the addition of new provinces to the empire, so the Roman equivalent of the modern-day geologist was able to scan new areas for new sources of stone and set the miners working. It seems clear from samples taken from different periods of Roman buildings that tougher materials were sourced as the decades and centuries passed, and Rhyolite stone, despite being a great material to work with, was not very durable and needed to be covered with stucco, travertine and, for the most expensive buildings such as villas and temples, marble cladding to protect them from decay.[120]

The huge, long-term discharges of smoke and dust particles from the hundreds of potteries, quarries and mines across Gaul, Britannia, Hispania and elsewhere created an industrial landscape of their own well before the 'Dark Satanic Mills' of the hymn *Jerusalem* – enough pollution certainly to cause widespread illness and death amongst the thousands of slaves and officials working in these new mining areas, and the Roman pollution footprint in history has now been more precisely revealed.

Granite shafts

But not all Roman materials were subject to decay over time. Until the last century BCE, Rome itself was mostly a city of red bricks and red roof tiles, and it was only with the creation of the empire that more 'imperial' architectural designs required better-quality building materials, and Rome turned white.

Facing with white marble changed Rome from red to gleaming white – floors, walls and even ceilings were faced in white marble garnered and transported from all over the eastern empire. But marble was brittle and not strong enough to support the more monumental designs of the Caesarean and later years – for this the Romans needed granite.

When we visit the remains of a Roman city or settlement, we are mainly looking at the remnants of materials that have survived both time and place – the time is currently at around 2,000 years and the place is what is left after hundreds of years of pillaging of materials for use elsewhere. The medieval world was ruthless in the exploitation of Roman stone, sculptures and anything else that could be moved to the palaces and homes of the wealthy or into churches, abbeys, monasteries and baptisteries across Europe, so it is remarkable that there is anything left to admire, let alone research.

Granite however was harder to move and harder to weather down by time, and additionally granite shafts – single units of granite carved directly out of a mine – are often able to be identified in terms of where they came from. This detective work allows archaeologists to not only study the remaining granite in Roman settings, but also to look at granite that has been plundered and now rests in a post-Roman, medieval or later building and still be able to identify where it originated from. The tremendous effort to cut a granite shaft by hand, then extract it from a mine, perhaps polish the surfaces, again by hand, and then transport over hundreds if not thousands of miles, made such pieces highly valuable and they occur all over the great cites of Europe.

In Gallia Narbonensis, research shows that, currently, 276 shafts of granite still exist taken from twenty-one identified mine sources. The largest concentrations of granite shafts are in Aix, Arles, Die and Riaz, which between them account for just over 50 per cent of the total. Grey, speckled and pink granite are mixed amongst what remains and some items are still huge – fortunate given how often the granite column might be cut again into smaller pieces in later centuries.

The mechanical integrity of granite made it a highly sought after rock and the foundation of Roman architecture, able to hold up the heaviest of weights and to be transported without the concerns over cracking and brittleness such as found in marble. The ability to polish the silica in granite creating a glass-like surface also made it a highly attractive material, with grey or pink columns contrasted against the white marble slabs fronting over the red brickwork walls. Finally, granite does not fade with age unlike white marble, where the rain and time tends to turn the white to grey.

Research carried out in recent years by French archaeologists supports what we know already about the wide-ranging building projects in the province during the Augustan and later period, but also that the granite shafts used came mostly from Turkey and the island of Elba – which meant that granite shafts were probably being hauled across the sea routes and into Narbonensis.

The areas of greatest use concentration have been found to be Arles and Riaz, but this may mean that, for whatever reasons, these two communities were able to hold on to their granite. Smaller concentrations are located in Fréjus, Orange, Antibes, Marseilles, Narbonne and Vienne, and these were probably stripped of their granite in later years. Interestingly, no traces are found in Glanum at all nor in Nîmes, Béziers or Toulouse, which is most likely the result of intense spoliation and stripping, although, as secondary settlements, it may also be that their use of granite was minimal – it is challenging to come to a conclusion. Archaeology suggests that 65 per cent of the original granite shafts used in the Roman period has been removed and used in other medieval building projects, such as a 27cm diameter Troad shaft in the porch of Saint Trophine Church in Arles.

> The church of Saint Trophine in Arles is designated as a UNESCO World Heritage site and is a former Roman Catholic cathedral. Arles became a pilgrimage centre on the route of Santiago de Compostela. Numerous parts of the church building are composed of what were originally Roman carvings and pillars, which gives the church its Romanesque style.

The widespread import of pink and grey cut shafts of granite from Turkey and Elba are exactly what one could have expected in the Augustan period of new imperial architecture, where the finances of the province, and individuals within it, were such that Narbonensis continued to develop as a second Italy and its settlements as smaller versions of Rome itself. Fixed judgements on actual use are impossible at this stage, and it is possible that some of the granite was even imported from the same mines during the medieval period – although the tremendous effort and skill required tends to mitigate against that when slave labour was so abundantly used in these monumental building tasks in the Roman period.

Further Construction – Villas, homes and mosaics

Taken as a whole, the province of Narbonensis became a vast site for not just commercial activity and making money but one of urban and rural expansion. The number of already-thriving centres of population at the end of the Republic meant that, under the Principate and imperial periods, there were dozens of zones demanding building materials and communications. The construction of roads became a priority with the Via Domitia, now long since completed, so the branch lines of the road system also needed to be upgraded, more mines were needed to quarry the stone, more slaves needed to cut the channels for the roads, and more surveyors to map out the routes. In the towns and colonies, a frenetic pace was set where rival communities vied to build the best forum or create new baths, Temple sites were selected and marble ordered from Italy – paid for by the patrons and benefactors of the towns looking for electoral support in their political careers – a microcosm of that in Rome. But it was in the plains between the beautiful coastline of Narbonensis and the mountains to the north that the most luxurious new building developed.

New town houses sprang up in every Roman *civitas* or *colonia* and, just like in the modern world, their new owners wanted the latest in fashionable decorations and style. Almost every town and city in southern France today can boast a Roman villa or town house to visit, restored or partially restored, such as that at the Maison à Portques at Clos de la Lombarde, a suburb of Narbo Martius (Narbonne). A central panel has been photographed and put on social media thousands of times, but it still is more remarkable to stand in front of and gaze at the winged Victory alongside a half-naked genius holding a cornucopia – an increasingly-common theme for artists of frescos and mosaics during the second century. In fact, it is probable that there were artists who marketed the same themes to new customers – offering a small range of the same pictures to save on new designs and colours of tesserae – and so it is not uncommon to see very similar designs within the same region and even as far as Pompeii.

The first item to greet a visitor to Narbo Via (Narbonne Road Museum) is a milestone with Domitius Ahenobarbus' name inscribed upon it, along with XX indicating that it is twenty Roman miles to Narbo Martius. But it is the 'wall of stone' that makes this museum special. The demolition of the old city walls in 1868 revealed hundreds of carved stones, probably taken from crumbling funeral monuments outside the town walls, and now 760 of them form a 76m-long collection. Many are Bulls Head friezes, which would link with the settlement of the Tenth Legion here under Caesar as this was their legionary motif. Amongst the thousands of other objects testifying to the vibrancy and importance of Narbo Martius is a white marble altar dedicated to the *Pax* or Peace of Augustus by Titus Domitius Romulus, with an intricate laurel leaf motif alluding to the laurels given by the Roman senate to Augustus in 29 BCE for ending the civil wars.

Narbonne is also home to a remarkable and 'must-see' museum in the new Narbo Via Museum, which was opened in May 2021 and contains thousands of Gallo-Roman artefacts beautifully displayed, including more mosaics.

Vaison-la-Romaine is another centre with a concentration of urban Roman housing. Once the home of the *Vocontii* and named Ovasion – 'the town on the Ouveze River' – it is thought that this town may have become something of a holiday resort for Romans escaping the capital. We know from earlier sections in this book that Sextus Burrus began life here, but the town also produced Trogus Pompeius who became a senator and consul of Rome in 56 CE – it has also been suggested that this was the home town of Tacitus himself. Apart from the personalities that developed here, there is the opulence and the volume of the impressive housing, and the presence of a magnificent theatre cut into a hillside that could seat 7,000 people. In addition, Vaison does not lie on or near any main road system to anywhere substantial and so it does scream out as a place off the beaten track for the wealthy Roman middle classes to congregate away from the hot summers in Rome.

In all, some seventy sites have been identified as the *domus* of a wealthy owner, containing a large number of rooms and also still-extant mosaics. The House of the Dolphin is just one particularly important example. Taking its name from a white marble fountainhead of a cupid riding a dolphin, the house was developed by the same family or a number of different owners over some 250 years. Starting as a farmhouse of 1,400m^2 in 30 BCE, the site became absorbed into the expanding Roman town and then had numerous new rooms added, along with lead piping, thermal baths and staircases to upper floors.

> Although the layout of the street patterns in Vaison do not conform to a 'new town' under the Romans, it is an important site as it displays how haphazardly some communities accepted Romanisation and *Romanitas*. Rather than relocating to a better site, existing roughly built housing, such as the Dolphin House, was transformed over time with the Iron Age Street pattern retained. The Romans squeezed what they could into these existing spaces, converting as they went, with new Roman suburbs constructed in later periods. Vaison has a rich variety of Roman ruins other than the Dolphin and other houses, including the theatre, Nymphaeum, temple and shops, and is served by a lovely museum.

It is estimated that more than 1,000 sites of Roman villas exist across the southern coastal plains of Narbonensis – each site carefully selected by its new owner, fresh with newly-minted gold and silver from their commercial activities, and designed along the most fashionable lines of the time. In later years, new owners added to the complex, and demand for surveyors, architects, workmen and slaves, building stone, marble pillars and columns, carpenters and masons, painters and plasterers all went up exponentially. One craft that saw a massive explosion in demand were the artists who designed and created the hundreds of mosaic floors and wall frescos across the cities, towns and villas of Narbonensis. These tremendously skilled men, and probably women, were in short supply, could charge high prices, and left us numerous examples of their work to admire and cherish. Clues to their workmanship continue to be uncovered, with excavations at Pompeii and Herculaneum revealing a seemingly endless display of Roman colour in homes, shops and larger houses across the city, which would have been replicated in Narbo, Baeterrae, Nemausus, Arelate, Massilia, Forum Julii, Vienna, Genava, Glanum and Aquae Sextiae.

The Mosaic business

The first mosaics in Roman antiquity seem to have arrived from Greece during the third century BCE, and it was in Hellenistic-Greek Sicily that the first such examples can be found – the ancient port of Syracuse being the link between the two cultures. For the next 600 years, a central part of Roman life was the purchase and provision of mosaics wherever Roman feet walked. Polychrome and monochrome mosaic floors decorated commercial and social buildings, private and public thoroughfares, sacred and secular temples, and palaces, but it is in the villa that we see the most imaginative and creative styles. Gods were immortalised, theatrical scenes played out, mythical legends given shape and human form, famous gladiators were celebrated, emperors praised, beasts, fish, horses and all manner of the natural world became shaped by tens of millions of small, square *tesserae* with shards of pottery and glass mixed in. The ideas of the mind were created in imagery, religious belief was given a human form – the mosaic craftsmen and women were artists and no doubt highly paid as a result.

Across the province of Narbonensis then, we are able to see numerous examples of mosaic work preserved perhaps under a ploughed field where the foundations of rubble from a villa have deterred farmers from digging too deep, or perhaps under the roof timbers of a collapsed building in the post-Roman era. Looting and pillaging Roman sites for building material was responsible for most of the destruction of Roman remains, wherever they were situated, but it was not easy to lift an entire floor – certainly not piece by piece – and it would make one really difficult jigsaw to recompose. But there have been notable exceptions, and the Getty Museum in New York contains two mosaics looted from Narbonensis many years ago and which were saved from a quite incredible journey to now be safely seen and preserved. But the majority of mosaics tend to stay where they were laid – hoping by chance to survive and be discovered and preserved for eternity.

Uzés is a beautiful small town between Arles, Nîmes and Avignon. Often bypassed because of its more illustrious neighbours, it is well worth the time to visit. Elegant and gentle, the many mediaeval remains sit alongside the valley of the Eure River, where you can see the ruins of the draining basin for the Roman aqueduct that supplied water to the city of Nîmes in the distance.

One such new discovery came in Uzés in 2017. Originally named Ucetia, this smaller community was once a Gallo-Roman *oppidum* and must have had some regional administrative role given its proximity to Nîmes. It was mentioned on inscriptions in Nîmes, but was rediscovered thanks to the discovery of a large public building during excavations for an extension to a boarding school. The large monochrome and polychrome mosaic floors were of exceptional quality, across rooms large enough to house many people at the same time, with the most substantial covering 650 square feet, making it one of the largest so far discovered in southern France.

Given the administrative and cultural dominance that Nîmes had over this part of Narbonensis, we should not be surprised that the Musée de la Romanité is replete with Gallo-Roman artefacts charting the changeover between the two cultures, and it is one of the most visited museums in the Gard and Occitanie region of France. Intricate and expensively-produced mosaics however appear across Narbonensis, supporting the fact that this was and developed into one of the richest provinces in the entire Roman empire.

The Musée de la Romanité in Nîmes is one of the new generation of interactive museums seen throughout France, uses multimedia devices throughout – wonderful for adults and children alike – and provides new windows into the imagination on how the Gallo-Roman period felt for those that lived through it. It contains some stunning mosaics too. The glass covering of the Museum is wavy in design and looks and feels like a mosaic and there is a stunning view over Nîmes from the 360-degree rooftop platform.

Arelate (Arles) also deserves great praise for the wide breadth and quality of its Roman remains, and their collection of Roman mosaics are some of the best preserved anywhere in the world. Trinquetville was a small unassuming neighbourhood on the other side of the river from the main town where a number of luxury houses and villas were constructed in the late-Republican and early-Augustan age. Just close enough to reach the town easily and be protected by it, but also just far enough away to avoid the noise and smells of a busy port, Trinquetville has yielded numerous wonderful mosaics, including Aion, the passing of time, or Annus, the passing of the year, and again these are similar images to those found in other notable settlements around the empire. Antioch and Carthage were recognised centres of excellence in the making of mosaics in antiquity, and their figures could have been made and exported to then be surrounded by the far easier skill of the borders – equally detailed drawings could have been circulated or traded between workshops in order to produce the finest proportions and shading on the more complex designs.

Finally, in any account of the mosaics of southern France, it would be difficult not to, once again, mention Vaison-la-Romaine, which became one of the richest settlements in the whole of Gallia Narbonensis. Apart from the House of the Dolphin which we looked at earlier, and the House of the Laurelled Apollo, there is also the Villa du Paon. In the House of the Peacock one of the best sets of mosaics were discovered across five different rooms, including the famous peacock mosaic – a magnificent bird surrounded by partridges, parrots and ducks – a splendid sight which must have been the envy of many a Roman visitor during the Flavian period (69-96) when it was constructed.

The Expansion of Construction Across the Province

Apart from the busy rural scene of post Republican villas being erected across southern Narbonensis with local roads crammed with carts and wagons of building materials, wooden posts and beams, bricks and roof tiles, there were the real monumental, large-scale building projects – the aqueducts. In these monsters of engineering, the Romans were the undoubted masters of the mathematics and construction, and their masterpieces litter the remains of southern France. The first-century BC Greek historian Diodorus Siculus once wrote that it had been recorded that there were seven wonders of the ancient world. One could argue that the list should in fact be eight when one takes in the complexity and genius of the building of the Roman aqueduct. In his scholarly article on the water supply of ancient Rome, David Denning most poignantly cites Pliny the Elder, again from his Natural History:

> *'If we only take into consideration the abundant supply of water to the public, for baths, ponds, canals, household purposes, gardens, places in the suburbs, and country houses; and then reflect upon the distances that are traversed, the arches that have been constructed, the mountains that have been pierced, the valleys*

that have been levelled, we must of necessity admit that there is nothing to be found more worthy of our admiration throughout the whole universe.'[122]

Further impetus to the building programme in the province came during the reign of Augustus, and it was his right-hand man Marcus Agrippa who did more for luxurious living in Gallia Narbonensis than any other figure in this post-Republican period. Recognising that there was much work still to do across Gaul – left undone by Caesar's conquest with no follow up – Agrippa decided to base himself in Nemausus (Nîmes). There were revolts to crush to the north and west of Gaul and the army needed a plan of action to control such a vast territory – so vast that it was still in fact divided into three strategic areas, but more on the army later.

With the arrival of such a luminary as Agrippa in Nemausus, a consequential rash of new buildings followed – Agrippa redesigned the street plan of Nemausus, erected a new city wall with impressive gates, and ordered the construction of civic amenities. It was Agrippa who also ordered the construction of a new Corinthian-style temple, today called the Maison Carrée (the 'Square House') dedicating this in 15 or 16 CE. How far around the province Agrippa travelled is difficult to ascertain, but the impact of his presence was enough to spur on a new era of rivalry between the *civitates*.

The Maison Carrée can be found in the centre of Nîmes and is one of the best preserved Roman temples in the former Roman empire. Originally this was a temple of the Imperial cult and was therefore know as a *caesareum*. The inscription, which originally dated to c.4-7 CE, was plundered in medieval times but fortunately we can still read what the bronze letters told us. The temple is in the Tuscan style but with Corinthians pillars, and overlooked the forum of the city of Nemausus. The interior is original but no Roman decoration remains.

In fact, Agrippa seems to have had more than a professional interest in Nemausus, as there is a definite sense of paternal interest in the smallest comforts of the *civitas*, and possibly Agrippa saw Nemausus as his 'Rome' and Gallia Narbonensis as his empire, away from the majesty and power of the charismatic Augustus and where he could be himself. The temple was of classical proportions – in hexastyle, with six Corinthian columns under the pediment and twenty along the *cella* or inner chamber – but as importantly, it was very similar in style to the Pantheon in Rome, which Agrippa had also overseen – and the size of the *pronaos* or outer portico was almost a third of the entire length of the building.

Above the *pronaos* of the temple of Nîmes was the following dedication – originally in bright bronze lettering that would have glinted in the sunlight, but now identified by the fixing holes:

M AGRIPPA L F COS III IMP TRIBVN
POTEST III COL AVG NEM DAT

Marcus Agrippa, son of Lucius, Consul three times, Imperator, holder of the tribunician power three times, gave (this building) to Colonia Nemausus.

Colonia Nemausus had been minting coins for some time – mostly bronze small change – with the city's emblem of a palm tree and crocodile stamped on one side and the heads of Agrippa and/or Augustus wearing his laurels on the other. These, together with the baths which were also dedicated by Agrippa, show his special affinity with the *civitas* and the population must have basked in his affection and generosity – no doubt there were numerous social and political ceremonies where Agrippa walked the streets that we walk today, embroiled in the festivities, listening to the cheering crowds and receiving glowing tributes – feeling much like an emperor himself.

It was however water that fascinated and took a lot of the attention of Agrippa and it is possible that he began the exploratory investigations of the surrounding area as to how best to build an aqueduct for Nemausus – again just like he had and was doing in Rome.

Aqueducts and Water Supply

The aqueduct was an essential part of Roman life, as the provision of running water directly into an urban site marked their civilisation out from others by their sheer size and numbers. Greeks had used the same water supply technology, but not on the same scale as the Romans. Water supplied to a Roman area was not just for drinking – fresh and clean drinking water would have been in steady supply for the settlement long before the arrival of the Romans – instead the *aquaeductus* supplied the Roman passion for bathing with a constant supply of changing water, taking away the impurities that filled the baths every day from the thousands of bathers cleaning their bodies and socialising amongst the pools of pleasure. The numerous fountains and troughs found in Roman cities were just another source of drinking water in each *civitas* where the public could come and draw the water that they needed for free every day.

The decision to build an aqueduct was not taken lightly, and apart from all the physical and engineering considerations to be taken into account, there was the cost, and as we can see by more of the letters between Pliny and his emperor Trajan, the state was not going to step in easily:

C. Plinius to Traianus Imperator

(1) The people of Sinope, sir, are short of water; this, it appears, both good and plentiful, can be brought to them from the sixteenth milestone. However, there is ground which is suspect and soft, just by the source, a little more than a mile away. In the meantime, I have given orders for it to be investigated, at little expense, to see whether it can take and support a structure. (2) Money, collected under our supervision, will not be wanting if you, sir, permit this kind of building which will contribute both to the health and the attractiveness of a very thirsty colony.'[123]

Traianus to Plinius

'Investigate thoroughly, dearest Secundus, just as you have begun to do, whether the ground which you consider suspect can support the structure of an aqueduct. And I do not think there should be any hesitation about bringing water to the colony of Sinope, provided only that it can in fact carry the work through out of its own resources, seeing that this project will contribute very greatly both to its health and its pleasure.'[124]

In this exchange of letters, we can see something of the relationship between need and the economics required to bring such projects to fruition. Depending on the personality and values of the particular emperor concerned, the patrons of the project would need to use either flattery or practicalities to elicit the support of the omnipotent leader of the empire. Flattery in the case, for example, of Nero whose need to attract adoration trumped his desire for frugality – not that he could ever be accused of the latter. On the other hand, the imperial treasury would be easily drained, especially as opportunities for plunder dried up, if every project received state funding – hence Pliny's clear assurance to Trajan, that the money could be found locally if Trajan were to give his permission – the clinching factor.

In Narbonensis, many such large-scale projects were only completed because of the fantastic wealth of men like Agrippa – who paid for his own temple and a few viaducts along the way – and the vision of men who saw that the Roman *coloniae* could not expand without planning ahead for an increase in the water supply. The practicalities, however, were immense and could also include a military need with garrisons on or in the centre cities with thousands of men and animals to water, and that might be enough to tap some or all the funds needed from the tons of imperial gold and silver stored in the state treasury – the *aerarium* in Rome. If not, then it would have to be pressure groups, petitions or senatorial patronage that paved the way for the agreement to build an aqueduct to any one particular site.

Fighting the state officials in a nation's Treasury is not a new phenomenon. but Augustus demonstrated a novel way of getting around the problem of over-protective state officials. Augustus was so frustrated at the processes required to obtain finances for his reforms and projects so, showing the mark of a true leader, he simply opened another treasury and ordained that a per centage of funds were diverted there for him to dispense – and who would argue? This opened the way for many new aqueduct building schemes to go ahead in Narbonensis during the mid- to late-first century CE, such as at Pont du Gard near Nîmes and at Fréjus.

Of the emperors, it was Hadrian who built most across the provinces and who also travelled the most. Followed by Augustus, Trajan and Tiberius, these were the 'good emperors' who spent wisely but also freely in order to upgrade the facilities of the provinces. Sometimes the emperor, or his close advisors, could be creative with taxation – diverting the taxes due from a province back into a building project so in fact the tax payers were paying for the work themselves – creative accounting in the state treasury is not just a practice limited to the modern world, nor is the political spin that could be put on this state investment into a region.

The Aqueduct at Fréjus was fed from captured water from both La Foux at Montauroux and also from La Siagnole in Mons. Starting at an altitude of 515m, the water flowed along a 42km route, built by the hands of slaves and overseen by the surveyors and foremen of the various building companies. This construction required thirty-six aqueduct bridges with twenty-eight for the Reyran valley alone. One of the best ways to see the remains of this colossal structure is to try to drive north out of Fréjus heading along the route of le Reyran, through Boson, and you will be able to see the many towers of brick and stone standing erect in the fields the entire length right up to the source at Signole.

However, it is not just an aqueduct's monumental arches and the cost with their huge cut stones and use of hydraulic concrete that should fascinate us. The structures that we recognise as an aqueduct are often the final stages of a long story of bringing water from a fresh mountain spring many miles away to a community, and was composed of a series of trenches, shafts, substructures and tunnels, some many miles long, before actually arriving at the aqueduct.

The gentle but consistent flow of water, which could be a drop of only 1: 20,000 (that is a few inches only per mile) required perfect mathematics and skill. To persuade Pliny, the governor in Bithynia, that the ground and the engineering would work, Roman engineers would need to dig deep excavation shafts, prepare recommendations and rely on the *dioptra* and *chorobates* – just as we witnessed in the earlier road building for the Via Domitia. All that was needed after these men had made their calculations, was a decision to go ahead, a large supply of slaves, and money.

Once a constant flowing source of spring water was located (Romans often avoided lakes, believing the water to be impure) surveyors dug deep pits to ascertain where the shafts would be placed for the columns and then decided where to dig their tunnels through the mountains. Although the water level would rarely rise above the knee, in order to dig effectively and to provide maintenance, tunnels had to be tall enough for slaves and workers to walk through. Tons of waterproof cement then lined the tunnels to minimise leakage and depressions and valleys were bridged by one, two or even three tiers of arches.

The Aqueduct at Pont du Gard is one of the classic Roman bridges of Europe. The span is 275 metres, with a 6.5 metre width. There were originally 47 arches, structured in 3 layers. Coins dating from 19 to the mid-50s CE have been found in various parts of the stone work, indicating that this was the period during which it was built. Much of the stone work was plundered in medieval times, but it remains in very good repair and is a UNESCO World Heritage site. It is a technical and artistic masterpiece.

It was in our province of Narbonensis that one of the world's most impressive Roman constructions still stands as testament to the skill, ingenuity and vision of Roman politicians, surveyors and engineers – but also her slaves and their concrete.

The Pont du Gard outside Nîmes is a three-tiered aqueduct that once relayed water over a distance of 50km to service the increasing needs of the Roman city of Nemausus. In places over 50m high, the arches cross the River Gardon near the town of Vers-Pont-du-Gard and were built with limestone so precisely cut that no mortar was used. Where a valley was too deep or wide, the Romans built inverted siphons – with a tank system on each side, and a lead pipe between them – as long as the receiving tank was slightly lower than the sending tank then pressure would take the water up the slope on the far side. When hills or mountains got in the way, then tunnels were used again – with shafts coming down from the top and slaves going down to dig towards each other at a precise depth measured by the engineers. Finally, the water arrived in huge distribution tanks called *castella* which, when full, overflowed into the lead or terracotta piping system and on into the public baths, homes, shops, factories and fountains, so that Nîmes really was able to develop as a power house of both Roman civilisation, but also economic output. Sometimes a settlement tank could be used where water was diverted to stand for a period of time before being sent on its way again into the main or multi-*castellum* – this was especially helpful after large storms, which could wash tons of silt into the water and deposit it along the length of the system and eventually into a Roman kitchen. It is estimated that the colossal construction would have cost in the region of thirty-million sesterces and was so precisely built that there is a drop of 1cm in 182.4m – a remarkable feat that even today, with the help of AI and computer-aided design, construction companies would find hard to match. The entire structure is a UNESCO World Heritage site.

Despite a slowdown in building generally during the civil war between Augustus and the *Liberatores* between 44 and 43 BCE, and the years of reconstruction needed afterwards, the supply of water to most communities was usually plentiful. In Pompeii it is estimated that there was a fountain or drinking trough for every 150 inhabitants – they were everywhere. As public baths grew in size and complexity, some even had their own dedicated aqueduct to feed them. In Rome, and built much later in 212 CE, the Baths of Caracalla for example had 32 *castella* just to maintain the water supply, with a capacity of 2,000,000 gallons, and the outflow of dirty water was so large that it powered watermills outside the city – the size of Rome as recorded in the Augustan census of 28 BCE was just over four million people, giving some idea of the scale of the challenge to provide constant water and sanitation supply.

For the wealthiest in the elite sections of Roman society, an appeal directly to the emperor could enable you to have your own extension from the pipe work to feed your own garden fountains and private baths. But, if you were not lucky enough to have a direct line to the imperial palace, then you could steal the water. Cato the Elder – our senator with the single *ficus* – was appointed *censor*, which made him responsible for the civic amenities in Rome, and he apparently cut off the water supply to numerous private buildings as it had been linked up without authority. Theft of water happened everywhere, and no doubt in Narbonensis too as Sextus Julius Frontinus, the first-century CE engineer, author, senator and soldier, tells us when he was carrying out his most detailed audit of the capacities of the water supplies. In his *De Aquaeducta Urbis Romae* he stated:

> *'Our measurement is, however, all the more reliable because at the settling-tank near the seventh milestone from the City (seven miles from Rome), where the gauges leave matters in no doubt, we found 3312 quinariae (approximately 4.2 cm2 = one quinaria). This is more than the records show by 457 quinariae, although prior to the settling tank it makes deliveries according to official grants and we detected a good deal being stolen; the quantity of the tank is less, therefore, than it ought to be by 1295 quinariae. Also, in respect of delivery there is clearly fraud, the delivery figures agree neither with the amount of supply recorded, nor with the measurements we made at the intake …'*[125]

It is apposite to record at this point that Frontinus was in fact probably from Narbonensis himself – another product of the province reaching the very highest echelons of Roman society, despite coming from a province and of equestrian background. If the reader is in any doubt as to the levels of efficiency that Roman administration could reach, then all they have to do is read the entire report that Frontinus prepared, which is a systematic examination of pipe widths, water flow, capacity and how to control fraud or water theft. The figures and calculations would impress any present-day sanitation engineer and provides history with a wonderful resource with which to analyse the utilities needed for the city of Rome to function.

Remains of Roman aqueducts can be found all over the province, such as the Caperon and Eygalieres aqueducts of Barbegal (Bouches-du-Rhône). Not only did engineers therefore build the 16-wheel watermill system for flour milling, but also the aqueducts to supply the water. These two structures bring water from 9km and 35km respectively to Barbegal, and both run the 320m distance over the Vallon des Arcs – the valley of the arches – where both led on to Barbegal, and the Eygalieres carries on south westerly down the valley to Arles and the River Rhône.

Recognising the necessity of maintaining the structures that supplied the water, Roman communities appointed their own *curator aquarium* – water superintendent – to ensure that the much-needed maintenance of the supply was completed and that water was not stolen – excavations suggest that some were evidently more concerned than others about the importance of this public role.

A perfect illustration of the power house that was Lugdunum in the first century CE is not only the presence of the imperial mint and the importance of Lyon as the main administrative centre for the 'Three Gauls', but also that it was served by four aqueducts. These massive building schemes were financed as much from Rome as by local magnates, and two stand out above the others as worthy of a visit. The Aqueduct of the Gier is the longest and best-preserved of the four and drew its water from a small tributary south west of Lyon and is thought to be the longest of all aqueducts, as it transferred water from the Massif du Pilat in the department of the Loire, over into the department of the Rhône and terminated in Lyon. The slope is again staggering in its meticulous accuracy dropping 0.1 per cent – or a metre every kilometre – one might think how small an object could be to actually block the transit of water to a whole city. This construction would have taken decades to complete and could not have functioned until the whole was finished. Germain de Montauzon, in his *Les aquaducs antiques de Lyon* (1909) refers to a Hadrianic inscription at Chagnon (CIL XII 2494) which was in effect a no trespassing notice to local farmers to stop them stealing the water to supply their own fields.[126] From this he infers that it may have been completed in the reign of Hadrian – possibly even for his visit in 121 CE, although this does seem to stretch credulity in terms of even Roman planning and imagination.

The Aqueduct of the Gier can be viewed in numerous places, but one of the best places to view it is in Mornant. Various stretches of raised walls and arches cross the valleys and are dated to the reign of Hadrian – Bromwich suggests that the earliest foundations were laid well before the second century CE.

At the other end of the water supply, however, were the less attractive but just as essential sewers and drains taking away the waste water of empire and every Roman settlement. Roman communities needed to dispense with water that had arrived pure but left highly contaminated with dirt, oil, sweat and numerous diseases from faecal matter that found its way into the baths. Romans were affected by fleas and head lice, pubic lice, bed bugs, whipworm and roundworm, and all of these were washed into the public and private baths. Discharge straight into the street for smaller baths was common, and not many communities could afford a structure such as the Cloaca Maxima – the enormous main drain out of Rome. But what happened in Rome did not always stay in Rome, and disease could spread very quickly. Dunning tells us that:

> *'In Pompeii, human waste was usually disposed of by dumping it in cesspits, simple holes in the ground located in rooms about a metre square. No latrines were flushed by water. When the cesspit reached a certain degree of fullness, the contents were evidently sold to manure merchants (sterocarii) who in turn peddled faeces as agricultural fertilizer … And, (quoting Scobie, 1986, 417) "there is abundant evidence showing that many people relieved themselves in streets, doorways, tombs and even behind statues".'*

The public latrines in Vaison are well worth a visit, and this extensive construction provides a unique insight into the daily life of a busy Roman city with its communal bathing and defecation. Unlike modern-day French toilets, the latrines at Vaison would still work perfectly if they were put back into use, although a rather chilly experience.

While preparing for or clearing up after the typical Roman party takes on a whole new meaning, for those interested in the Roman sewerage system, an excellent example of a Roman drain can be found in Fourviere, a district of Lyon, where an almost intact Roman sewer, complete with lined brickwork, emerges from the rocks – a wonderful Roman theatre in the same district makes the journey more than worthwhile. For the start of the process, the public latrines in Vaison are impressive.

The Roman Ports of Narbonensis

To drive along the coastal roads of the south of France is both a pleasure and a danger to life and limb – as Princess Grace of Monaco found out in her tragic accident near Monaco. On the one side are bays, coves, beautiful scenes of small happy settlements, but while you observe the beauty, the roads wind left and right, up and down and there is always traffic. In places the roads narrow so tightly that only one vehicle can pass, sometimes the roads suddenly veer off into a chicane before you can resume your journey. These roads were not the fault of the Romans – they had the same experience too. Then, every so often, along the 500 mile coastline, a port comes into view and this is what made the coastline of southern Gaul so very attractive.

To the Roman, the entire western coastline of their own country was a challenge. Other than Rome, it was a journey south to Antium (Anzio) but this was too small for large scale commercial traffic, or Centumcellae which was expanded by the emperor Trajan and was praised by Pliny the Younger, in his usual sycophantic style, for the elaborate and imaginative design. The Romans had a vision of linking trade between their ports all around the Mediterranean Sea, and they hit a bullseye when it came to the coastline of southern Gaul. This is not to say the acquisition of Narbonensis for its ports was a cause of imperial growth, but it certainly had positive consequences for the Roman economy.

All along the French Riviera therefore, are signs of large-scale Roman port development – for those with the eyes or the interest to see them. Arelate, Forum Iulii, Masillia, Narbo Martius and Telo Martius stood out as areas for investment by Roman businessmen keen to expand the capacity of their docks, warehousing and communications inland.

Chapter 15

The Changing Role of the Army in Gallia Narbonensis 27 BCE–235 CE

Not surprisingly, the role of the Army in any one province changed according to the chronology of internal development and the political and strategic needs at any particular time. The army was not immune from change, and developed in tandem with modernising trends in every part of Roman society as history, technology, communications and politics developed. From the earliest days, the military was a militia force, raised to deal with immediate threats and wars and then disbanded, but from these origins, the Roman army became professionalised and permanent. Retaining experience and creating legends became the focus of a state that needed an army that was capable of reacting quickly, dealing death and control anywhere on the frontiers of an expanding empire, and one that was, as far as possible, loyal to the emperor of the time.

When Q. Fabius and M. Livius were on their way home from their 'unsuccessful' meeting in Carthage in 218 BCE, they would have been escorted by a body of troops ordered to make the journey with them. No doubt a considerable number of men for such a noble party of senators, accompanied by trusted centurions and probably a tribune or *legatus* or two to give the military presence some gravitas. However, when they eventually arrived back in Rome, tired but safe, the military escort had completed their mission and were discharged not long after back to their homes or farms, and their military service was over. This was the way of things – in the late-third century BCE, citizens presented themselves for service on the Capitol and waited to see if they were chosen. If they were, then they hoped to only be away for a few months and then return to their farms, hopefully richer for the experience and financially secure. By the late Republic, 200 years later, those days were long gone. By 100 BCE, recruits to the legions were expected to complete six- and later sixteen-years' service – much of which was to be spent outside Italy as the function and role of the armed forces changed with the expansion of empire.

In the aftermath of the Sullan proscriptions and Marian reforms, the Roman Army had already undergone a fundamental set of changes well beyond anything that had gone before. Apart from introducing the new standard heavy armed infantryman as the main component of the legion, complete with the standard equipment that we all recognise, Marius introduced the *aquila* or eagle standard to each legion, suggesting a harmony and unity in a standing force as opposed to the indiscriminate creation and dispersal of conscripted legions of the past. Marius added to this by allowing volunteers to join his legions – sometimes referred to as a proletarianization of the army where the poor and dispossessed could now see a future as a professional soldier – as opposed to only selecting men who were property owners and on the census. This paved the way for Latins living outside Italy to volunteer for the legions, and by the time Julius Caesar was recruiting for new legions in Gaul in the mid-50s BCE, it is clear that his legions were composed of Italians in the older more established legions but also Transalpines and many native Gauls – many of whom had never seen Italy, let alone Rome.

Thus, a picture emerges of a number of almost ethnically-pure Roman units and occasionally legions moving through and sometimes being based in early Republican Narbonensis. Garrisons would be made up of units of men recruited in Rome or Italy, constructing forts and defensive positions and massing to defeat the Cimbri and Teutones in the Battle of Aquae Sextiae in 102 BCE.

As the last century of the Republic unfolded, both Caesar, Brutus, Cassius, Pompey and Mark Antony created standing legions which were a mix of obviously foreign auxiliary units, legions of volunteers drawn from the provinces, and the 'pure', almost Aryan Italian Legions, recognised by their long service and experience, began to take in provincial volunteers based on their merit. Just like the Nazis were forced to do during the Second World War with the SS, the Romans had long since had to compromise on ethnic requirement and the provincial legion had been born well before the end of the Republic.

Other than the changes brought in by Marius and the provincialization of the legions, Augustus, in his reforms, sought to end the practice of rewarding legions with land as well as money. During the three civil wars between Marius and Sulla, and then Caesar and Pompey, and indeed Augustus and the *Liberatores*, generals had needed not only to recruit the numbers they needed but also to encourage their men with inducements to kill and win for them as individuals – they were not fighting for Rome. What were in effect private armies – with the exception of the Republican mass that stood behind Pompey – came to expect the offer of land and money come retirement or disbandment, and mutinies could occur if these did not materialise.

The *colonia* founded throughout Narbonensis were created in this very period, and the former soldiers who arrived in Narbo Martius, Nemausus and Aquae Sextiae, for example, were looking forward to their new social standing as landowners after long service to their warlord. Augustus, seeing the need to end this practice lest other competitors for the throne come along, decreed that service would be for sixteen years, with four in the reserve, at the end of which case a sum would be given of 12,000 sesterces (20,000 for the Praetorian Guard to ensure their devotion). These reforms did not go down well, but became the norm, and the drain on public finances could be severe, with discharge gratuities being delayed for months and even years – eventually requiring a new tax across Italy. The unpopularity of the Augustan military reforms is well illustrated with the various revolts that broke out after news of the emperor's death reached the legions on the Rhine and in Illyricum.

Tiberius too faced similar problems but, more seriously, potential recruits in Italy also lacked interest and enthusiasm to join for long service in the legions. The conditions on the far-flung frontiers were hardly attractive, and men sent to rot on behalf of Rome were not appealing recruiting poster material – there were few new campaigns to fight, only insurrections to put down in dangerous territory with little scope for plunder. Accordingly, in 23 CE, Tiberius announced that he would visit the area and Plutarch relates how it was as much a recruiting drive amongst the provincials as to release veterans who had completed their service.

The Army in Narbonensis under Augustus

The army in Narbonensis was an ever-present sight after the end of the Republic. The *coloniae* were developing at a quickening pace, but they still maintained a military presence while the older army garrison forts of previous centuries either fell into disrepair and were plundered for their stone, or were redesigned and became smaller settlements in their own right. It is important to remember that the majority of Roman forts tended to develop their own small *vicus* or village outside the walls and gates. These accommodated traders and workmen as well as families, girlfriends, shrines and potteries, all living from the wages of the legionaries and officers. Over time, these settlements developed paved roads, better buildings and a street plan all of their own and often, when the garrison was removed, the two became one and they merged into each other.

By the time of the Principate, the main military camps in the province were to be found in Narbo Martius (Narbonne), Cemelum (Cimiez), Nemausus (Nîmes), Aquae Sextiae (Aix-en-Provence), and, to the northern edge of the province, Lugdunum (Lyon). There were smaller garrisons all over Narbonensis but these had served their usefulness by the end of the Republic. Military command over the area still went to any general with *imperium* dispatched to or riding through the province, but on a day-to-day basis most military communiques were issued either from Lugdunum or Rome itself, with Lugdunum becoming the military

One of the best-preserved legionary camps in the south of France is to be found as part of the ongoing excavations in Sainte-Colombe, a suburb of Vienne near Lyon. The 60,000 sq. foot site has revealed early foundations of a Roman army camp as well as an entire neighbourhood and market square with shops, stores and a temple.

capital for the three parts of Gaul identified by Augustus – excluding Narbonensis which was, by now, seen as an extension of cosmopolitan Italy.

According to Tacitus, there were twenty-five legions established under Augustus – he having reduced by half the numbers that had been recruited to fight in the civil wars on both sides. This gave a standing army of 200-300,000 men when one adds in all the ancillary officers and logistical supply units – a substantial cost for the state. But the legions provided for much more than just security. When in camp, there were multifarious tasks that certain members of the legion could be seconded to. Rogan, in Ch. 9 of his 2011 work on Roman administration states:

> *'Within a legion of 5,000 a number of skills were to be found; agrimensores (surveyors), plumbarii (leadsmiths), specularii (glassworkers), aerarii (bronze smiths), carpentarii (carpenters), scandularii (roof makers), ferrarii (blacksmiths), lapidarii (stonemasons), aquilices (hydraulic engineers), fabri (brickmakers), architectus (master builder) and polliones (millers). All of these were, of course, primarily military roles, but they were also useful in civil enterprises. Such skilled soldiers were likely to be immunes, excused routine army fatigues and with the status of principales.'*[128]

So, the legion, which could be called to arms very quickly when needed, was a mobile market place for those entrepreneurs following the camp, a manpower and skills resource for the local governor or his officials, a security detail for road building, and a supreme military force for attack and defence. Some of the more experienced centurions could become *frumentarii* – diplomatic envoys or confidential couriers, or even sometimes spies, who were trusted to take communications between the governor and the emperor or to carry out special missions on their behalf.

While there was peace in Narbonensis, all around her borders conflicts were raging. To the north east, the Gauls of Germanica were a never-ending problem, and constant conflict marked service with the legions there. To the west, there were again a series of wars with the tribes of Hispania and between

36 and 26 BCE, no less than six triumphs were awarded to Roman generals to parade through Rome to the forum having, supposedly, put down the Spanish problem for good. It would be left to Augustus to do this, but we can see the importance of being able to rely on the people and cities of Narbonensis as a strategic partner – just as Romans had envisioned 300 years earlier with the Carthaginian threats.

If we recall the Narbonensian, Sextus Burrus, and his leadership of the Praetorian Guard and how other members of elite Narbonensian society joined him in his all-round defensive posture for the young Nero, then we ought to also look at the scholarly work of Patrice Faure. In and amongst a mass of research articles published by the *Archaelogie des Gaules* periodical, one in particular refers to the number of fellow Narbonensian citizens who also joined the legions at lower levels – and especially into the Praetorian Guard. It would seem that Burrus was very clearly intent on surrounding himself, in the same way as the emperor, with men he could trust. By the end of the first and into the second century CE, Narbonensis had become much more than a province and somewhere that looked and felt like Italy, it was an extension of Italy. The evidence for this comes in two parts – who these men were, and the political importance of the Praetorians. Taking the second point first, historians now agree that the Praetorian Guard grew from being a small personal bodyguard for Augustus, separate from the army and owing their loyalty directly to one person, into a much larger force that defended Rome and whose political influence grew during the first- to third-centuries CE to make it one of, if not the most important, power brokers for the role of emperor.

By the Severan period (193-234 CE), the leadership of the Praetorian Guard could make or bring down emperors. Patrice Faure examines their recruitment strategy, and, in a 2016 article, leans on the evidence of the numerous funerary monuments dedicated mostly to centurions who originated from Narbonensis.

The centurionate were the NCOs of the British Army Regiment – the backbone of any unit, charged with overseeing discipline, standards of performance and morale within the unit. So, the centurionate was the collection of centurions in any one legion who controlled *disciplinia* and who were the tactical and strategic pivot around which the legion performed in battle, and was also the mouthpiece or shop-stewards of the legion, the body with oversight of the *sacramentum* – the oath of loyalty to the emperor – and *fides* – their loyalty and honour upon which the morale and esprit de corps of the legion would depend.

In his research, Faure has been able to identify a large number of centurions serving in the legions who were recruited from Narbonensis, giving the province a high-status role in the officer and warrant officer corps of the Roman army. For this to have developed as it did, there must have been an accepted and identifiable structure for going out and recruiting the right sort of men to join the legions, men who were marked out for future positions of leadership and who had local Narbonensian connections at plebeian or equestrian levels in order to have the support and patronage needed for promotion quickly through the ranks to the most senior positions within the Guard. This privileged status amongst the provinces illustrates well how Narbonensis had quickly became an extension of Rome. Faure's anthropological approach has identified men such as T. Lucconius Quartinus from Riez, C. Valerius Pualinus from Fréjus, and T. Julius Ustus from Vienne.[129]

We have seen how people make provinces earlier in this book with commerce, religion and immigration, but also the rapid development of the Romanisation of Narbonensis can be also attributed to the role of the legions. The army had a good start, with five large colonies of retired troops being established roughly 100km apart across the province – Narbo Martius, Arelate, Baeterrae, Orange and Fréjus, and it must be said that the presence of the army in such active and retired numbers encouraged the rate at which Narbonensis experienced *Romanitas* and developed a strong sense of military service to the Roman state. Even though the actual numbers retiring to these colonies were probably quite small – hundreds rather than thousands – who knows how many sons of retired legionaries went on to join the army as their fathers had done. The Roman state or the emperor himself provided not only land but bricks, wood and building materials for new homes which became new towns and then suburbs of cities – the army therefore offered a catalyst through which the transition from Gallic forebears into full Roman citizenship and loyalty could be developed and *Romanitas* established. With Faure's work on the numbers of Narbonensian senior officers in the Praetorian Guard by the second century, it is also clear that Narbonensis was by that stage no longer a province but seen as an integral and reliable part of Rome itself.

Service in the imperial army was very different to that of their forbears in the army of the Republic. Now a full-time and professional force, it was possible to make a name and fortune before retirement, and even to forge a political career. By staying in the army, a man could make links, build a reputation, create a network of useful contacts and rise up the ladder of ranks. None of this had been possible in the early days of the republic and this more permanent career as a soldier ultimately created soldier emperors.

The power of the army to influence events therefore grew exponentially, culminating early on in the imperial period in the promotion of Titus Flavius Vespasianus or General Vespasian as Emperor in 69 BCE. The new levels of self-awareness amongst the legions, that they could make or break political rulers, was a dramatic development and partly stemmed from the new political power

The entire area around Alba-la-Romaine to the north of Nîmes is worth a visit or local stay as it contains numerous archeologically splendid locations from the first and second centuries CE. The Roman legions were based in and around Alba both to control the local tribes and to protect Narbonensis from incursions from the north. The legions also recruited from this area and in the Jewish cemetery in Bonn, Germany, the following inscription can be found on a Roman tombstone:

> *Here lies Publius Clodius, son of Publius, the region Voltina, born in Alba, the 1st Legion soldier, aged 48, died after 25 years of service.*

invested in the Praetorian Guard in Rome. No longer a volunteer army, the new legions were effective fighting, social, engineering and political entities, each with a character of its own and able to influence political events in Rome in ways that the democratic founding fathers had never envisioned.

While the legions developed their own individual characteristics, the life of a soldier was pretty much the same wherever one went on the frontier. Narbonensis, mostly due to the climate and generally peaceful environment, was a good posting for the soldier intent on rest, security and safety. But there were other, less hospitable and far more dangerous postings that one could receive and we have an amazing window in to exactly what composed the day-to-day existence of a Roman soldier stationed on the frontier with the ongoing excavations at Vindolanda in Northumberland.

The Vindolanda Tablets – letters from the frontier.

> *'It is hard to overemphasise the value of a dated body of material of such variety which comes from a part of the Roman world hitherto unrepresented in our evidence and at the opposite pole from the area which has given us most, namely Egypt.'*[130]

With the scattering of small wooden tablets rescued from the site of the auxiliary fort on Hadrian's Wall, we, and future generations, are able to read about everyday life in a Roman fort right at the edge of empire. Wrapped in the mud and water of 2,000 years of history, experts have been able to decipher words and phrases that build relationships between real people of the period, and we are able to construct a breathtakingly accurate understanding of who these people were and what life was like in a Roman province. What happened in Vindolanda would have been replicated in the forts of Narbonne, Arles, Glanum and across Gallia Narbonensis.

Prior to the discovery of the large quantities of tablets at Vindolanda, it had been assumed by most scholars that it was papyrus sheets that were the predominant form of writing and recording communications, and these were in plentiful supply in Egypt where writing 'paper' had been used for centuries. Given that levels of language and literacy were already strong in the eastern Mediterranean through the Greek, Egyptian, Phoenician and Roman civilisations, northern Europe seemed very quiet – and a shortage of papyrus would logically indicate that writing materials were in short supply. The first reference to using wooden slivers came with the helpful comments of the historian Herodian, who referred to thin leaves of lime-wood which were written on the inside and then folded with an address. Although limes were not native to northern Britain, birch and alder was and these provided the wood for the manufacture of these small wooden notelets. Not that they were rare – the flow of such communications into and out of Vindolanda suggests that this was a mode of writing that covered the northern part of the empire.

It is not unreasonable to say that the discovery, in 1973, and interpretation of these tablets revolutionised our understanding of the conversations between the average Roman family and friends with those on the frontiers of the empire, far away from loved ones, and gives an impression of what they knew.

The conversations that have been preserved range from requests for cash from family back in their homes in Italy, through to payments for boots, tallow and pepper. There are birthday invitations from the wives of officers to their friends, and requests for orders from soldiers and for their supplies of beer to be re-stocked. Originally written on a postcard-sized sliver of wood, no doubt dried and part of a stack of such cards, the text was usually in two columns – left and right – the first two lines of the left being the all-important opening address.

Chapter 16

Imperial Visits 14 BCE–123 BCE

It was inevitable that Augustus, once he had assumed the title of Augustus and begun the cult of his divinity, would wish to visit his realms, and Narbonensis became a favourite destination during his lifetime as emperor. The occasion of an imperial visit was no small event – the first and only time that the vast majority of the plebeian population would see their divine emperor and an opportunity for the equestrian and senatorial classes to try to get closer to the man who could change their lives with a single word. The imperial visit was the ultimate propaganda opportunity for Augustus, whose advisors had already planned to flood the empire with a more consistent image of the emperor through coins, statues, and religious imaginary. Such uniform messaging places Augustus and his closest advisors ahead of the field of history in terms of understanding how important the visual message was to the people – and as importantly, ensuring that the image was unchanging, no matter how old the emperor became or where his image was seen. This messaging also had a reverberation in the management of the administration of the provinces. In her most recent book on the emperors of Rome, Mary Beard reinforces our modern understanding of how the early Roman empire functioned – less on political theory and strategy and more on taking advantage when one could, seeking a balance between what could be done and what could not, experimentation rather than precedent and, often, complete ambiguity.[131] We have seen in the case of Roman law and religion how Roman ideas were drip fed into the new provinces rather than imposed, and the importance the Romans placed on the practicalities of change.

But Augustus and his closest agents of change such as Agrippa also needed to build more than just permanent granite or marble edifices to ensure the survival of Rome in the future. They also had short-term needs to maintain their survival after a period of bloodthirsty civil war where Augustus still faced as many enemies as those he had murdered. The pretence of a return to democracy after the revenge taken over the assassins of his uncle needed to be accepted by the senate and the wealthy nouveau-riche of the empire – the neo liberalism that Augustus preached needed to be backed up with benefits, so that his popularity on the surface matched what happened to the bank balances of the influential. Just as Trump in the USA has shown himself not to be a politician but a ruthless showman – although these two descriptions are not mutually exclusive – so Augustus needed his own 'shows' and performances: it was not all about the largesse of giving to settlements in the provinces, his image needed to be backed up by substance. The promise of jam and cream at the same time – peace and prosperity – had to be delivered to mask the reality of the new dictatorship. Future emperors were not quite as careful and paid the price for rubbing dictatorship in the faces of the people instead of playing the game of charades which Putin has done so well for so long in Russia.

Before Augustus could even begin to think about the power he had inherited or visualise the scale and challenges of the empire he now ruled, with his crucial victory at Actium in 31 BCE and the suicide of Mark Anthony in 30, he needed to negotiate and agree his 'settlement' with the Senate – and *ipso facto* the people of Rome. Part of the Augustan Settlement of 27 BCE decreed that Augustus was to directly govern the following provinces for ten years – all of Spain, all of Gaul, Syria, Cilicia, Cyprus and Egypt. Just as a passing note, it is interesting that, of all the smaller provinces that Augustus chose to directly administer, one was Cyprus where Cato the Younger had once been governor until his suicide in north Africa – a highly notable Roman who had lost his life trying to save the Republic from Augustus' uncle and then from Augustus himself. Was this a defiant act of revenge by Augustus over the sour memory of their clash? Whatever his thinking, Augustus would learn very quickly just how inconsistently his empire was managed, which no doubt fed into his belief that he needed to see it all for himself.

* * *

With the long-term planning required for the visitation of an emperor it was possible to complete building projects before his arrival so that he could bask in the radiance of his own benevolence. Augustus first travelled into Narbonensis at the age of forty-seven in 16 BCE and Dio tells us that this was partly because:

> *'For he had become disliked by any as a result of his long stay in the capital, and now was offending many who committed some act contrary to his decrees by the punishments he was inflicting, and at the same time by sparing many others, was being compelled to transgress his own enactments ...'*[132]

So, there was clearly an element of needing to be seen by the empire over which he ruled, but also a sense in which he could standardise his judgements and make clear, through his own words, how justice should work and what he expected of his subjects. Augustus had visited the lands over the Alps before when he took personal command over the armies in Spain between 26 and 23 BCE – soon after he had received the new *imperium* from the senate and they had given him the title of Augustus. The arrival of Augustus in Tarraco in north-western Spain, just south of Narbo Martius, might suggest the he either travelled by sea to meet with the army there or he travelled through Narbonensis along the coast and the Via Domitia. The fact that the old Via Herculia – the Spanish coastal road – was renamed in his honour as the Via Augusta may suggest that his was a road trip all the way, in which case the geography of Narbonensis would be known to him, but either way, it was to be ten years before he returned to Gaul.

After a tour of the eastern provinces between 22 and 19 BCE, Augustus focussed the next three years of his life on Rome, political battles and his personal life – which was complicated. He also needed to sort out the matter of his succession in this new era where elections were of secondary importance to political power. Hence Dio was probably right, that Rome had absorbed Augustus too much and he needed to be seen in the provinces again and Gaul needed to be settled.

The preliminaries for Augustus prior to departure from Rome in 16 BCE for between two and three years, were to dedicate a temple in Rome, followed by dispatching his trusted friend Agrippa to the east and then appointing his loyal general Titus Statilius Taurus as *praefectus urbi* (Prefect of the City of Rome) and governor of Italy. Augustus took his second wife Livia and her adopted son, Tiberius, with him, planning to visit and placate both Gaul – that is the areas to the north and west which were still in occasional serious revolt against Roman rule and which he planned to administer as three provinces – and then travel west through Narbonensis, no doubt through Narbo Martius, and on into Hispania before returning to Rome. Waiting for them in Gaul was the brother of Tiberius and a second stepson to Augustus, Nero Claudius Drusus, devoted and loyal to the family.

A slimmed down but nevertheless comprehensive mobile administration travelled with him, and we can only imagine the size of the imperial retinue or how many civil servants, scribes, couriers and wagons followed in order to keep the apparatus of state near Augustus. Equally, we might wonder where the entire column, probably the size of a legion, quartered itself each night. Possibly the camp was separate from the imperial family, who may have been welcomed into the villas of the Narbonensian elites – now that would be a name to drop at dinner parties. We do not know the route but it is again possible that Augustus took the Via Julia and then joined the Via Domitia as the first emperor to ever travel these roads along the southern coast as our military courier had done over 130 years previously – possibly even agreeing the site for his own Trophie of the Alps in La Turbie as he looked down over the small village of Monaco and, on a clear day, back to the Italian coastline that he had just left.

Between 16 and 13 BCE, meetings, councils, dedications and ceremonies would have marked the entire outward and return journeys – exhausting and no doubt managed carefully by his retinue of household staff and closest advisors. News of his movement through the province would travel fast and loud – it is not often that a God moved amongst men, even though Jesus would be born only a few years later in 6 or 5 BCE just as the Trophie of the Alps was dedicated to Augustus in La Turbie. Augustus spent many weeks and months dealing with issues, holding courts and meeting local elites, probably based in the best quarters available in Lugdunum, which Augustus had decided would be the administrative centre for the Three Gauls he wished to create. Drusus joined him in late 15 CE and was appointed *legatus Augusti pro praetore* over the three Gaulish provinces, and immediately began a vast building programme of his own, dedicated largely to Augustus.

The Altar of the Three Gauls

Between 14 and 12 BCE Drusus established Lugdunum as his headquarters and copied the same political structure as nearby Narbonensis with a *Concilium Galliarum* or Council of the Gaulish provinces, and began building the Altar of the Three Gauls on the hill named today as La Croix-Rousse in Lyon. Again, copying and reinforcing the same message as in Narbonensis, the altar was part of the new imperial cult that Augustus wished to see established across the empire. Many sources attest to the existence of this currently 'lost' monument to Augustus, with Dio stating that it came about under pressure when the armies under Drusus' command in the north were involved in a difficult campaign in the Rhineland and then the census in Gaul created a backlash with a rebellion in Gallia Comata or 'long-haired Gaul'. Drusus needed to deal with both problems and called a council in Lugdunum where representatives of the Three Gauls met and resolved their differences – or at least resolved not to take their differences further at this time.

Drusus then wished to seize this moment to erect a tribute to their good sense and his stepfather's glory. The images on coins of the time suggest a sanctuary and an altar – a 50m-wide marble base, flanked on each end with two red porphyry columns with gold capitals on top and winged victories holding palms and crowns. The dates of dedication are estimated at 12 BCE, after Augustus had returned to Rome, and a re-dedication in 10 BCE when Augustus was in Gaul for the last visit of his lifetime. Strabo, the Greek geographer and historian who was a contemporary of Augustus, described the altar as 'remarkable', but there are currently only five finds confirmed as being part of the original structure – a 15m section of wall discovered in 1990 which was part of the paved upward-sloping ramp on which one progressed to the altar, a fragment of a gold crown from one of the winged victories, the bronze leg of a horse, and marble fragments all within the same area. The fifth and perhaps most interesting item is a fragment of a bronze inscription found in 1528, not in Lyon but at the Croix-Rousse and the area of the Altar of Augustus. This was part of a speech by emperor Claudius in 48 CE given to the senate to clarify his support for an increased number of magistracies being given to candidates from Gaul, and therefore a greater number of senators from the Three Gauls. It is assumed by historians that this may have hung on part of the Altar of the Three Gauls or very near to it. For our study of the growth of Narbonensis, the original speech is further compelling evidence of the successful Romanisation of the province, as Claudius makes reference to Narbonese families who were granted citizenship very early in the absorption of the province and who went on to become faithful servants of Rome in a period of 'continuous and loyal peace'.

The Amphitheatre of the Three Gauls in Lyon

Sitting at the foot of the La Croix-Rousse hill in Lyon, the Roman Amphitheatre would have dominated the town. At least 60 tribes were represented at the celebrated gathering in the amphitheatre to agree on the future governance of the region – at that time the amphitheatre would only be able to seat 1,800 people and would have been quite personal. Later expansions took the capacity to over 20,000, to view such events as the martyrdom of Saint Blandina – a Christian martyr – who was burnt and thrown to wild bulls to be eaten during the reign of the philosopher emperor Marcus Aurelius in 177 CE. There is a post in the middle of the arena to commemorate this event.

The sanctuary of the great altar was dedicated with an inscription of the sixty Gallic tribes who gathered at Lugdunum to meet with Drusus. This directly corresponds to a large inscription of the forty tribes on the base of the Trophy of the Alps in La Turbie above Monaco. The most plausible reason for this correlation is the consistency of messaging and propaganda required by Augustus – not only the numbers of tribes that have bowed down to Roman sovereignty but also a sense of unanimity in monument design.

Part of the role of the powerful and influential priests of the imperial cult was to organise ceremonies to celebrate the life and success of the emperor and so, next to the sanctuary in Lugdunum, a wonderfully impressive amphitheatre was designed, built and opened in 19 CE – five years after the death of Augustus and ten years after the death of Drusus – and dedicated to the new emperor Tiberius, the second stepson of Augustus. The arena and associated buildings were constructed from funds donated, not from the state treasury or even the provincial treasury, but from the private riches of C. Julius Rufus – an old Gallic family from Saintes on the west coast of France and capital of Roman Aquitaine. The reason for this enormous expenditure can only be surmised, but if one wanted to be noticed by the emperor, then Lugdunum was the place and not Saintes – plus if you had imperial ambitions for your sons then this was the sort of gesture that would help. Along with the dedication, the names of the local tribes were also inscribed on the stones of the amphitheatre – the Avernii, the Tricasses and the Bituriges.

Augustus' final visit to Gaul began in 10 BCE and he returned to Rome in 7 BCE never to see this part of his empire again, and one wonders what he thought as he took his last look backwards at Narbonensis, either from his imperial trireme sailing eastwards back to Ostia and Rome or through the curtains over his window from an imperial carriage heading along the Via Domitia. Whichever it was, the view would have been as wonderful as it is today. Sixteen years later, Drusus would tragically die, but the memorials he created in Narbonensis to his stepfather live on with us today.

Agrippa's Visits to Narbonensis

No book that purports to examine the late Republican period should or would ignore the presence of Marcus Vipsanius Agrippa. He is present alongside the emperor Augustus throughout the whole dramatic takeover of power – the brutality of the civil wars and the reshaping of Roman history begun by Augustus.

Agrippa seems to be one of those rare Romans that later history has deemed to shine a light of approval and admiration upon – he was by all accounts what Pliny called 'the ideal Roman'. In her assessment of Pliny's appreciation of Agrippa as one of the greatest Romans, Mary Ann Burns points to how Pliny extolled the virtues of this great man, called early at the age of 51, who nevertheless was the architect of the Roman world, a practical but stern man whose life had been beset with tragedy, who was born feet first (from the point of view of augury, a disastrous start) and yet who still maintained his levels of happiness.[133]

Far more than just a successful military commander, Agrippa was also a scholar and a statesman, able to see Rome in context, where his place fitted into the grand scheme of life in the empire, and he was very sensitive to his relationship and positioning with Augustus. For the purposes of this book, however, it is the vision that Agrippa had for the empire and the people of the provinces that makes him stand out in these early years of the new province.

If Augustus was the catalyst of change, then Agrippa was his agent and enforcer. Both men undoubtedly realised that the empire needed to be managed better and that their messaging needed to be synchronised and consistent. Travelling the length and breadth of the empire, Agrippa ensured his journeys took him to as many settlements and cities as possible, bringing the glory and majesty of the power of Rome with his presence but also articulating exactly what the glory of Rome actually was.

The messages of Augustus through the buildings he sponsored and those of Agrippa that he unveiled were the same – the glory of Rome rested in the honesty and vibrancy of its people and their dedication to the state. It was no longer the senate that mattered but the regional senates and the new age of replica Romes that were now scattered throughout the provinces – each with their forums, their temples, their aqueducts and their loyalty to the imperial cult. But it was also a time where a consistent message was needed in administration. It was no longer good enough to muddle through with local or personal interpretations of Roman law, and what happened in the emperor's name was now far more acutely important than that of the senate. Thus, we should see the building programme in Narbonensis during the Augustan age as far more than just benevolence on the part of wealthy and powerful men. The altars, temples, aqueducts, forums, baths and theatres were all part of the same resonating requirement of duty and loyalty to Rome.

Although the evidence is scant, there is enough to establish that Nemausus, Arelate, Narbo Martius, Lugdunum, Glanum, Massalia and many others were visited by Agrippa: and what an arrival it must have been – as grand as that of the emperor himself, but completed with a clear air of dignity and modesty. Inscriptions that have thus far been found that directly state that Agrippa unveiled or ordered their construction can be found in Nîmes and Glanum but there were undoubtedly more that have not survived.

Apart from the tribute to better health which we saw earlier in this chapter in Glanum, there are similar modest and straightforward tributes in at least twelve locations across the empire – we cannot be certain he was present at each, but as Mary Boatwright states 'it is likely he was', and it is a testament to the time spent on the roads, rivers, seas and cities of the Augustan empire.[134]

If there was one Roman that recognised the importance of water on this scale more than any other, then it was Marcus Agrippa, and his time spent in Nemausus was not wasted, as he possibly sponsored and took part in the early surveys for the Pont du Gard before it was left to others to build under emperor Claudius around 40 CE – Agrippa having died two years prior to Augustus in 12 BCE. But Agrippa remained the face of a new Rome that was emerging through those that he inspired in his lifetime. The effort to leave behind the stigma of a corrupt Rome whose emissaries bullied, exploited and crucified their subjects would be made a lot easier by the dedication to the gods of gleaming white marble constructions that told of the glory, and not the gory, side of Rome.

In his time in Gallia Narbonensis, Agrippa was able to push forward the new, effective and efficient face of the province alongside the building, expansion and economic vibrancy of a once totally divided province. Agrippa helped to stimulate cosmopolitan Narbonensis where everyone could enjoy the benefits that Rome could bring. As Lindsay Powell states in his excellent biography of Marcus Agrippa;

> *'In his actions Agrippa displayed a belief that Roman civilisation had a deeper purpose. He was a man of principle, what modern commentators would call a conviction politician. Dio writes that he "had used the friendship of Augustus with a view to the greatest advantage both of the emperor himself and the Res Publica". His urban development programme was not limited to the city within the pomerium of Rome. The great project of forging a universal empire, a commonwealth of disparate nations, required its self-governing constituent communities to operate under Roman law in order to receive the benefits of peace and prosperity. He actively promoted those benefits. Whether it was building roads in Gaul, or paying for large buildings in Baetica, Lusitania or Narbonensis … Agrippa understood the value of direct assistance in fostering goodwill to Rome, using his own wealth to do so.'*[135]

Trajan and his impact on Gallia Narbonensis

Although the role and impact of a wave of new emperors provides us with anything but stability in Rome, in the provinces – or specifically Gallia Narbonensis – the decades passed largely without terrible disruption. In the intervening years between the passing of Augustus and the visits of the Emperor Hadrian in 121 and 123 CE, it is with some certainty that we can say that the 'Augustan Age' very much continued – despite the convulsions caused by reigns of unconventional emperors.

Earlier sections in this book testify to the continuing economic growth of the province of Narbonensis, the expansion of building projects, and an explosion in the value of exports and imports and the general levels of wealth displayed by the urban classes. The buildings of the *civitates* testify to ambitious local families keen to play their part on the central stage in Rome, and contemporary commentators were already well aware of the glitzy destinations for travellers to visit in Vienne, Avignon, Nîmes, Toulouse, Arles and Béziers. Pliny the Elder leaves us in no doubt that Gallia Narbonensis is a sparkling gem amongst the provinces of the Roman empire.

Alongside the rise of political stars from Gallia Narbonensis who were promoted into either the Praetorian Guard or the Senate, such as Agricola, the general and later governor of Britannia, were a number of new families who sought to provide their children with the best opportunities for advancement. There were also those for whom the provinces provided the chance of cultural following and identity.

Massalia (Marseilles)

Marseilles thrived throughout the Roman era. The location, depth and naturally very wide dimensions of the port of Marseilles ensured that it would always be one of the main gateways into Gaul, and consequently wealth flowed into the Greek and then Roman town. Although much of the Roman remains have been lost to development, there are still valuable indicators of just how busy, indeed frenetic, life must have been in this port.

> *'In spite of its wealth, power and progress in civilisation, the ancient city has left no remains of buildings, nor any traces of its existence beyond inscriptions (some in Greek), sarcophagi and a few fragments of sculpture.'*[136]

For the Roman enthusiast or scholar, much of the old buildings have now been revealed and placed into a garden setting, called the Jardin des Vestiges with reconstructed walls and pathways from differing chronologies. Excavations in the 1960s revealed a massive wall, and it is thought that this might be part of the huge wall built around Marseilles by the celebrity doctor Crinas, and Pliny the Elder has left us a snapshot of this darling of the wealthy upper classes:

> *'During the reign of the emperor Nero (54–68 CE), the destinies of the medical art passed in to the hands of Thessalus … he was at last eclipsed in credit by Crinas, a native of Massalia, who (…) united in himself the pursuit of two sciences, and prescribed diets to his patients in accordance with the movement of the heavenly bodies, as indicated by the almanacs of the mathematicians, taking observations himself of the various times and seasons. It was but recently that he died leaving ten millions of sesterces, after having expended hardly a less sum upon building the walls of his native place and of other towns.'*[137]

To have spent at least ten million sesterces on the walls around Masallia and other local towns, Crinas must have been a physician to the wealthiest of clients, although very little is actually known about him. Perhaps his tomb lays somewhere under the shopping centres of Marseilles waiting to be discovered by future generations.

But as a melting pot of wealth, cultural exchange and civilisation, the communities of first- and second-century CE Narbonensis were no stranger to producing numerous celebrity personalities to enliven and enlighten Roman society. Seneca recorded the rhetoricians Agroitas, Pactus and Charmis as all emanating from Masallia.

The Jardin des Vestiges can be found in the centre of Marseilles and also leads onto the Wall of Crinas which can be seen protruding all around the length of the garden. Discovered in 1913 near the Bourse, Crinas is lauded for either building the wall from scratch or for its restoration.

The Museum of the History of Marseilles can be located very near the old port and contains a very impressive large-scale diorama of what the port would have looked like in its Roman heyday. Completely renovated in 2013, the museum hoists a permanent exhibition on its Roman past and the hull of a second-century wooden plank-built dredger.

Across the province of Narbonensis, there was new fame too for orators such as L. Statius Ursulus from Toulouse and Votienus Montanus from Narbo Martius. There would have been many others whose names are now lost to time, but one perhaps still worthy of mention is C. Cornelius Gallus. Debate continues about his exact place of birth. It was the great scholar of Roman history, Ronald Syme, who considered Fréjus as the most likely home of Gallus and his birth around 70 BCE but others, such as Jean-Paul Boucher freely state it could have been one of at least five other locations. Although almost nothing survives of his work, we know from Ovid and other sources that Gallus was one of the major elegiac poets of his time and became a rising star amongst the courtesans of the Augustan court, to the point where the patronage of Augustus fell on him and he was appointed *praefectus* of Egypt – a considerable position of power and influence.

Gaius Cornelius Gallus – the price of a loose tongue

The story of Gallus however does not start and end in poetry, but in the fragility of grace and power within the Roman court. At one end of the scale we read of any number of great men who rose up the *cursus honorum* to go on to achieve great success and legendary status. This is what drove Romans forward, the engine room of power was achievement and new laurels for the Roman state. Gallus is a good example of this route to stardom. From a humble equestrian background, he supported and fought for Augustus in the Civil War and showed himself to be an able military commander, as well as a poet and philosopher. Augustus was clearly attracted to Gallus and enjoyed his company and selected him above many senators as the first prefect of Egypt after the deaths of Anthony and Cleopatra. In 29 BCE, Gallus led successful military campaigns south into the desert, and received missions from Ethiopia and it may have been the manner in which Gallus recorded his triumphs with statues, arches and displays lauding his own abilities that first alerted Augustus that all was not well in Egypt.

In essence all power was insecure and Augustus knew this better than anyone, given the murder of his uncle and benefactor Julius Caesar. Reputations could be made or broken within hours, and Gallus is a reminder to us all of the fragility of fame in Rome and even more so if one was close to an emperor. Having basked in the aura and glorious sunshine of the favour of Augustus, Gallus lost his way. Perhaps it was an intoxication of his own rise or a misguided self-belief in his invincibility and talent that led him astray. More likely it was just the splendour and luxury of governing Egypt and feeling like an equal to Augustus himself that saw him, in an unguarded moment, talk disrespectfully of Augustus. Ovid records his demise and Suetonius spoke of his 'ungrateful and envious spirit'. That was all it took. A few moments of disrespect and news was sent to Rome.

When the gossip reached Augustus' ears, he was furious and recalled Gallus to Rome. In what must have been an explosive meeting, Augustus banished Gallus from his home and the provinces. Once he was indicted by the senate, Gallus saw no way out and committed suicide in either 27 or 26 BCE. Augustus was distraught and clearly felt betrayed in a very personal way, but such was the lure of power for those unable to manage it and Augustus determined that Egypt was simply too overwhelming a province to risk being given to anyone in his court. If Egypt could turn the head of Gallus, then it could turn a friend into a rival. Instead, Octavian, or Augustus, retained full control over Egypt and even senators were not allowed to visit without permission – indeed they were not even allowed to visit the provinces without Augustus being made aware, such was his feeling of insecurity.

But it was in those families who sought political power, rather than just popularity, that advancement was essential to their future prosperity. By the time Trajan became emperor, Spain had become much more than just a potential haven for rebels – it was also now a producer of emperors. Both Traianus (Trajan) and Hadrianus (Hadrian) were born in the Spanish city of Italica, and the increasing ability of once-distant Roman families to influence events in Rome is best illustrated by these two men. Related through their fathers, both were sons to senators from outside Rome whose family connections and wealth had brought them to the epicentre of power and politics. Both young men were schooled in the arts of war and peace and received the very best that education could provide. Neither were wedded to Rome as their homeland, but both respected their Roman heritage as well as their provincial roots – in other words, both understood the responsibilities of and towards empire.

Both Trajan and Hadrian came to prominence through their family connections and their determination to create alliances with the strongest and most influential families in their provinces. Trajan, for example, despite his predilection for young men, would marry Pompeia Plotina, a talented and devoted young woman, probably from Nemausus in Gallia Narbonensis, while Hadrian sought out, or was introduced to Vibia Sabina – Trajan's grandniece by the same Plotina. Hadrian's parents died when he was very young, and Plotina became the matriarchal figure in his life, guiding him and pushing him into the right relationships. The relationship between Hadrian and Trajan was a complex personal one, not least because they both shared Plotina, though in different ways, but both also inevitably moved in similar and sometimes conflicting political orbits. The eventual transfer of power from one to the other, orchestrated by Plotina, was riddled with intrigue and suspicion. Nevertheless, the period between 98 – 117 and then 117 – 138 CE gave Rome and the empire a period of relative calm and tremendous consolidation under the leadership of these two men from the provinces.

Both Trajan and Hadrian were more than competent administrators – both were also enthusiastic about codifying and identifying what the empire actually was and how well it needed to be run. The degree to which both men dedicated themselves to structures, processes and probity throughout the administration of the empire links them back to Augustus, when the needs of the empire were paramount and trumped the individual vices of the intervening catastrophes that were Nero and Caligula.

Both Hadrian and Trajan spent much of their lives on horseback or in huge imperial wagon trains as they travelled the new imperial roads built by their predecessors and sought to understand the size and shape of the empire. The matter of defining – especially so in the case of Hadrian – where the boundaries lay, what was defensible and what lay on the other side was now a crucial task given the expense and strategic challenges allotted to a fixed number of legions. The campaigns led by Trajan are captured on his wondrous 'Column' in Rome. They were fought and recorded with a pace and energy that defies understanding in a world where life was hard and short for even the most luxurious of lifestyles and testament to the determination, ambition and vision of Trajan in his lifetime.

With the extensive correspondence created by Trajan, and which has survived in the letters to Pliny, we are able to almost be a fly on the wall in his imperial palaces as he dictated dozens of letters, probably daily, to ranks of *scribae* surrounding him, destined to fly in the leather satchels and bags of imperial couriers to all parts of the empire. The range of subjects and emotions Trajan dealt with in his correspondence with Pliny the Younger demonstrates as much about his personality as they do about his elasticity to cope with the multifarious subjects that Pliny placed before him. The tenth volume of Pliny's *Letters* remains, alongside Cicero's speeches, orations and letters, one of the most valuable resources for scholars of this period.

Trajan was above all a military commander, and arguably the most successful, depending on the parameters, of all the emperors of Rome. However, Trajan's focus was most often directed at the eastern parts of the empire and, despite being a prolific builder of monuments, arches, columns, bridges and buildings, there is little evidence that he had much time or interest for Narbonensis or even his homeland in Spain. Often worthy of the adulatory praise heaped upon his memory by contemporary and later writers, Trajan remains elusive in Narbonensis. He would have travelled in his imperial columns through the province to the north but save for a fountain in Narbo which he is said to have donated to the city – although even this may have been erected in his honour – there is little material evidence of anything more substantial.[138]

Where exactly was Gallia Narbonensis and how was it divided?

Helpfully, on the macro scale, our first-century Greek geographer Strabo described the ultimate shape of Gallia Narbonensis in this way:

> *'The configuration of this country resembles a parallelogram, the western side of which is traced by the Pyrenees, the north by the Cévennes; as for the other two sides, the south is bounded by the sea between the Pyrenees and Marseilles, and the east partly by the Alps'.*[139]

These natural boundaries fixed the shape of the province and, helpfully, there were no boundary disputes on any of these major borders. However, there were plenty to make up for this as far as the interior was concerned.

In the earlier years of the Roman occupation, we have only a sparse range of evidence concerning land ownership and how land was divided, even more problematic we have little evidence as to how regions were divided and agreed upon or whether they followed what the Gauls and Celts would have regarded as tribal boundaries. The survival of Cadastra A to C provides valuable evidence on a local scale, but what of the regional division of lands? With the rule of Hadrian, the availability of sources regarding land ownership and boundaries in Gallia Narbonensis are more plentiful.

We can interrogate the *Historia Augusta* in its *Life of Hadrian* and we can develop an awareness of just what a full and frantic life the emperor led and how he strove endlessly to codify the various aspects of how the empire should function. In the descriptions of Hadrian's travels across the empire, and Narbonensis in particular, it is possible to add further dimensions to our understanding both of the province, how the Romans thought about life, and the geography as it was at the time. Hadrian was a prolific builder too, and his monuments in granite and marble litter the empire and are present in various parts of Narbonensis.

It was important to Hadrian to understand the nature and breadth of the empire that he had inherited from Trajan. Hadrian's Wall was not just a strategy to keep out the Picts, but part of a much wider attempt to define the outer reaches of Roman rule and to decide on how best to defend it.

Hundreds of miles of tall, pointed wooden palisades and fortresses were also constructed along the border of Germania – another Hadrian's Wall. Some of these forts and timbers have been recently unearthed by archaeologists, while boundary markers from the time of Hadrian's reign have also been found in all parts of imperial rule, which were part of his attempt at the codification of the, just as important, internal borders. Working out exactly where one province or jurisdiction stopped and another began was a real issue for the Roman state as Roman administration came to terms with the vastness of what their armies had created. Once a territory was claimed by the Roman state, it could take decades of unrest, dispute and legal argument before a marker was finally put in place to decide where the borders were. It was not until the visit of Hadrian, for example, that the border between Narbonensis and Spain was finally decided.

In his doctoral work of 2004, Thomas Elliot of the University of North Carolina examined a wide range of evidence on boundary disputes across the Roman empire and over the lifespan of the Roman era.[140] Specific to our study of Gallia Narbonensis, we can see that internal or civic sub-divisions within the province not only existed but caused unrest and required the emperor himself to sometimes step in and take command. The example we can look at concerns the boundary between Roman Vienne (modern Vienna) and the people of the Ceutrones who were the inhabitants of Axima (modern Aime). A boundary stone marker was revealed which contained the following inscription:

Ex auctoritat[e] / imp(eratoris) Caes(aris) Vespasian(i) Aug(usti) pontifices max(imi)/ trib(unica) potest(eta) V co(n)s(ulis) V / desig(nati) VI, p(atris) p(atriae) /5 Cn(aeus) Pinarius Cornel(ius) / Clemens leg(atus) eius pro pr(aetore) / exercitus Germanici / superioris inter Viennenses et Ceutronas (sic) terminavit

By the authority of the emperor Caesar Vespasian Augustus, pontifex maximus, (holding the) tribunician power for the fifth time, consul five times, consul-designate for the sixth time, father of the country. Gnaeus Pinarrius Cornelius Clemens, his propraetorian legate (in command of) the army of Germania Superior, set the boundary between the Viennenses and the Ceutrones.

This evidence is significant on a number of levels and was evaluated by both Elliot in 2004 and Aichinger in 1982 and it was concluded that this marker indicates that, at times, even the emperor needed to appoint a very senior official to determine such matters.[141]

In this case, the commander of the army of Germania was asked to fix the boundary as perhaps he had both the authority and the gravitas to make a judgement that few could argue with. If we ponder for a moment why such matters were important, we can perhaps understand that it was not just an issue of tax revenues. Historical disputes over land did not suddenly stop because of the arrival of the Romans. Many long-standing issues between warring tribes and families just carried on and, in time, the Roman administration would tire of such disputes, especially when they crossed over in to their own needs to know what went where. An essential but often forgotten by-product of *Pax Romana* was that the Romans simply solved internal disputes of this kind by power, and the true nature of their rule was revealed in all its barbarity and callousness. A hefty group of night-time raiders could of course move a marker in one direction or another, but this is only speculation.

A second implication can be drawn from the fact that this decision on the civic boundary was not taken by the provincial governor. It might be that the governor did not feel secure enough to make a judgement that he knew would result in significant unrest – where a city, river or area was simply given to age old enemies. Far better to have an independent figure, appointed by the emperor himself to make the decision and plant the marker stones – even better if he commanded an army to enforce his ruling.[142]

Given the mass of examples of boundary disputes across the empire that Elliot is able to produce, we can reasonably assume that there were numerous such disputes in Gallia Narbonensis that needed to receive a ruling – popular or otherwise – from various governors or even emperors over time.

Hadrian's Two Visitations, 121-123

Boundary disputes certainly formed part of the workload of Emperor Hadrian when he decided to tour his newly-inherited empire from 121 CE onwards. Narbonensis is a province where we can identify and still see many of the remnants and products of the major visit of Hadrian between 121 and 123 CE.

Assuming ultimate power in 117, the first three years of Hadrian's rule were spent establishing his position in Rome. There was uncertainty bordering on rebellion at the way the transfer of power had been handled, and naturally there were always rivals ready to seize upon any weakness. By 120 CE, Hadrian felt strong enough to plan what he really wanted to do and that was to tour his empire, and between 121 and 123 CE that is exactly what he did. Before he left Rome however, there was the small matter of celebrating the 874th birthday of the founding of the city – *ab urbe condita*. Not only was 121 CE another birthday year for Rome, but it was also going to be the year of the birth of a future emperor – a certain Marcus Aurelius, who would accede to the throne of the empire in just under forty years' time.

The journey from the centre of Rome to the port of Ostia would have seen the cavalcade of pomp and colour that accompanied a God. Bright red cloaks of thousands of soldiers, interspersed with the gold and silver armour of the officers, the sun glinting and bouncing off polished copper trumpets and the carriages and wagons that spread for miles in a long line as Hadrian processed, probably on horseback, through the suburbs of Rome towards a fleet of ships waiting to embark in a huge convoy bound for Massalia. As the convoy set out into the Mediterranean, Hadrian no doubt looked back across a misty azure-coloured sea, glimpsing the hazy coastline of Italy for the last time as it was lost to sight and replaced ahead by the island of Corsica to port, and then looming out of the horizon the coastline of Gallia Narbonensis and his destination of the port of Massalia. Preparations for Hadrian's arrival would have been planned for some time, and fanfares awaited him everywhere he went, as did the clammy handshakes and adulatory bows of dignitaries' keen to impress their emperor.

Once the columns had formed up again, Hadrian headed northwards to central Gaul where Caesar had once trod and dismembered his enemies in the creation of the legacy that Hadrian had now inherited. Our sources for the details of Hadrian's famous journeys vary, but much of what we assume to be correct about his routes and timetable flow from the *Historia Augusta* (HA) – a work that was referred to by Ronald Syme as 'the most enigmatic work that Antiquity has transmitted'.

The HA is composed of a number of works that remain in a state of suspended animation as to their veracity and authorship – although more recent scholarship suggests that they were composed by the same person. Nevertheless, they have also been described as 'a mixture of fraudulent passages lifted from other works' – the challenge for the researcher is to decide which is fact and what is fiction. The HA includes *The Life of Hadrian*, which informs us that Hadrian headed north through the centre of Gallia Narbonensis and arrived and rested for a few days at Lugdunum (Lyon). Staying at this critical administrative centre would have been an integral part of any imperial visit. There would have been briefings for the emperor on the state of the province, relations with the Romanised tribes and the associated Gallic provinces, the effectiveness of tax collection, discussions on building projects, and also personal issues taken before the emperor. Not only was there time to visit the imperial mint (still in operation despite much of it having been moved back to Rome by Nero in 64 CE), but also to view the Altar of the Three Gauls with its names of the 60 subdued tribes inscribed on the base, to stand where Augustus, Drusus and Agrippa had stood and take in the magnificence of the aqueduct of the Monts d'Or – completed around 20 BCE – or that of the magnificent Aqueduct of the Gier, referred to earlier in this chapter.

Hadrian would have travelled along many roads and into numerous settlements, but at Lugdunum he would also have viewed the confluence of the great highways of the empire – it was here that the Via Agrippa split into four directions heading to all points of the compass. A Roman Piccadilly Circus of chariots, wagons, pedestrians, couriers, children and families all making their way to different parts of the provinces of Gaul – a metaphor for the beating heart of the empire, its people.

Apart from back-to-back meetings arranged by his staff, Hadrian must also have attended events at the Amphithéâtre des Trois-Gaules – especially as he is reputed to have ordered its enlargement. Completed in 19 CE and eventually able to hold 20,000 spectators, this amphithéâtre was similar to those at Nîmes and Arles. Unusually and almost uniquely, we can identify the individuals who financed this massive construction through a beautifully-preserved tablet discovered during the periodic excavations between 1956 and 1978. Similar to other great building projects of the early imperial era, the amphitheatre was joined spiritually to the cults of Rome and of Augustus. This would be the place where Christians would be brought in future years as part of the final purges by the Roman state to try to stem the spread of this monotheistic religion that posed such a threat to Rome.

Having left his mark on Lyon, *The Life of Hadrian* continues to inform that the column processed north eastwards, towards the German frontier and the territories most under threat from the tribes of the east. The imperial column moved slowly south eastwards, hundreds of miles down the southern banks of

> The Gallo-Roman Museum of Lyon holds one of the richest collections of Roman Gaul in the whole of France. The tablet of dedication by C. Julius Rufus can be seen there as can amazing views of the amphitheatre, seen through the huge glazed windows. The museum also boasts a fine collection of Gallo-Roman mosaics as well as everyday objects such as jewellery and statues salvaged from the surrounding municipality.

the Danube and then reversed north-westwards along the length of the Rhine before crossing over into Britannia. After stops at Londinium and probably Camulodunum (Colchester), Hadrian and his convoy made their way northwards up to the outposts of empire and the lands of the fearsome Picts and Celts. Here, perhaps in the large Roman *castrum* or fort in what we today know as Chester, Hadrian discussed with his surveyors, engineers and officers of the Legio II Adiutrix, who were based there to defend the frontier, how to best build a wall. Hadrian spent many days discussing the construction of the Vallum Hadriani or Hadrian's Wall. which began in the year of 122 CE.

> *'Though more desirous of peace than of war, he kept the soldiers in training just as if war were imminent, inspired them by proofs of his own powers of endurance, actually led a soldier's life among the maniples (unit of men), and, after the example of Scipio Aemilianus, Metellus and his own adoptive father Trajan, cheerfully ate out of doors such camp-fare as bacon, cheese and vinegar.'*[143]

The journey across the empire was long and, at times arduous, especially for Hadrian's wife Vibia Sabina and her own entourage. It would have been a challenge for any community of travellers to maintain the necessary probity of life, and Hadrian seems to have been tested by over-familiarity from his retinue – we may recall that it was Suetonius, historian and secretary to Hadrian, that was dismissed by the emperor for his relationship with Sabina. Falling out of favour with emperor Hadrian was not difficult. The *Historia Augusta* tells us that: '... [Hadrian] *was in all things changeable*' and describes the character of the emperor thus:

> *In poetry and in letters Hadrian was greatly interested. In arithmetic, geometry, and painting he was very expert. Of his knowledge of flute-playing and singing he even boasted openly. He ran to excess in the gratification of his desires, and wrote much verse about the subjects of his passion. He composed love-poems too.*

> *He was also a connoisseur of arms, had a thorough knowledge of warfare, and knew how to use gladiatorial weapons. He was, in the same person, austere and genial, dignified and playful, dilatory and quick to act, niggardly and generous, deceitful and straightforward, cruel and merciful...'*[144]

With such a man in whom there was ultimate power, perhaps it was wisest of all to keep away, but such is the attraction to power that men run towards it like moths to a light, and the *Historia Augusta* also reveals the following 'favourites' as casualties:

> '*... in the end he treated almost all of them as enemies, even the closest and even those whom he had raised to the highest honours, such as Attianus and Nespos and Septicus Clarus. Eudaemon, for example, who had been his accomplice in obtaining the imperial power, he reduced to poverty; Polaenus and Marcellus he drove to suicide; Helidorus he assailed in a most slanderous pamphlet; Titianus he allowed to be accused as an accomplice in an attempt to seize the empire and even to be outlawed ... and in order to prevent Servianus, his brother-in-law from surviving him, he compelled him to commit suicide, although the man was then in his ninetieth year. And he even took vengeance on freedmen and sometimes on soldiers.*'

One of the earliest rising stars of the new province was Publius Terentius Varro Atacinus (82–c.35 CE). Although not able to converse with emperors, Atacinus was born in or very near to Narbonne on the River Atax – hence his surname Atacinus. Only small fragments of his original works survive, but his name was highly regarded by many – including Ovid, who remarked: *'Of Varro too what age will not be told – And Jason's Argo and the fleece of Gold?'*[146] Just how a man was able to rise from obscurity with the help of his scribes is a question of great interest. What did it take to become noticed, and how was one's work to be recognised and recorded let alone applauded? Nevertheless, Atacinus represents the rise in the importance of Narbonensis and the very rapid acceptance into Roman culture of its most talented sons. It was Atacinus who, when reflecting on the fate of legendary men, wrote:

Marmoreo Licinius tumulo Iacet, at Cato nullo, Pompeius paruo : credimus esse deos?	In a marble tomb [the freedman] Licinius lies; yet Cato lies in none and Pompey in but a small: Do we believe there are gods?

The philosopher Favorinus (c.80-160 CE) was another celebrity from Narbonensis. Born in Arelate, Favorinus was reputed to have had Gallic ancestry, but this did not prevent him from rising to the companionship of even Hadrian himself. Displaying oratorical genius apparently on a par with Cicero, but without leaving behind the legacy to sustain a place in history, Favorinus was a fiery advocate. After being ordered to be silent in an argument with Hadrian, Favorinus sarcastically stated that it was foolish to criticise the logic of the master of thirty legions. However, perhaps because of comments like these, or possibly an over inflated sense of his own worth to the emperor, Favorinus fell out of favour with Hadrian and, just like many others was banished from Italy.

Returning to the south coast of England, by the end of 122 CE, Hadrian crossed back over the Channel and made his way due south as quickly as he could, heading down the Via Agrippa from Bononia (Boulogne) to Lugdunum, and then south into the Rhône Valley. Warmer weather and bright spring skies, together with a wonderful green landscape, must have been such a contrast to the end of the world in Northumberland and a very tempting opportunity to go hunting – one of his favourite pastimes.

Picking up the major road of the Via Domitia and passing numerous *tabernae* and arriving to stay and rest in the most opulent estates in Narbonensis, Hadrian made his way slowly westwards to Narbo Martius, where again he settled for a few days before embarking on the last stage of his journey and crossing the Pyrenees.

While the imperial caravan was on the road, numerous dispatch riders would arrive and leave daily to and from Rome to pass on information to the imperial staff and through them to Hadrian himself. His daily briefings would have reported not only on events in the senate and in Rome itself, but also personal matters, matters of intrigue, and of course matters of state, and it was during 123 CE that Hadrian received two very concerning reports and experienced a personal tragedy.

While in Britannia, or perhaps even before he arrived there, Hadrian had received news of riots that had broken out in Egypt – most particularly Alexandria. The *Apis* or Sacred Bull cult of ancient Egypt was alive and well and, under the Roman religious strategy, the cult was tolerated but not encouraged until an effigy of an ancient bull was discovered and created arguments between the cities of Egypt as to who should have the honour of displaying it. Matters became so serious that Hadrian had to deal with it from a distance, as Cassius Dio recorded:

> *'The Alexandrians had been rioting, and nothing would make them stop until they received a letter from Hadrian rebuking them. So true it is that an emperor's word will have more force than arms.'*[147]

Closer to home, Hadrian was en route southwards, travelling through Vienna, Arelate, Nemausus, and close to Vasio Vocontiorum (modern day Vaison), and no doubt local families vied with each other to attract the emperor and the empress to their estate. In the excavations of the theatre of Vasio, which was on the way to Nemausus, two statues were discovered – one of Hadrian and the other of Sabina. These could have been in a later commemoration of their joint visit to what was once the capital of the Vocontii tribe, or indeed to welcome them to the city.

Vaison-la-Romaine (Vasio)
The twin statues of Hadrian and Sabina can be seen in the Musée Theo Desplan, Vaison-la-Romaine. The town was one of those that had received the patronage of Marcus Vipsanius Agrippa, and been rebuilt with a new forum and a modest theatre, together with bath houses, and a sanctuary. The luxury of some of the town houses that have been excavated exceeds those of even Arles, Orange or Nîmes and it is here that the House of the Peacock can be viewed.

Borysthenes

A little way on from Vaison and still heading south, Hadrian probably diverted into the huge forests surrounding Apt, or perhaps had no choice but to ride through them, and it was here that a memorable event occurred which still echoes down through the ages both in the words of Cassius Dio and through the work of archaeology:

> '*Some light is thrown upon his* [Hadrian's] *passion for hunting by what he did for his steed Borysthenes, which was his favourite horse for the chase; when the animal died, he prepared a tomb for him, set up a slab and placed an inscription upon it.*'[148]

Even today, the forests around Apta Julia (Apt) are impressive, but 2,000 years ago they would have been far larger and full of wild boar, once so common in this part of France.

At the beginning of the seventeenth century, two large broken white marble fragments were uncovered in a field and transcribed at the time to indicate that this was in fact the slab that Dio had written about. Of the two, one is particularly clear and contains the line: '**[h]oc situs est in agro**' – 'buried here in the field'.

The full inscription was recorded at the time and read:

> Borysthenes Alanus, the swift horse of Caesar, [who] through the sea and the marshes and the Etruscan mounds who was accustomed to fly, while pursuing Pannonian boars, him to harm with his white tooth not one boar dared: the saliva from his mouth scattered even the meanest tail, as it is custom to happen. But in his youth, his healthy, invulnerable body, killed on its day, has been buried here in the field.'

The original fragment of marble that was discovered that day can be seen in the Lapidary Museum in Avignon.

With the tomb in the fields around Apt dedicated to Borysthenes being dated to 122 CE, we know that Hadrian was moving south. No doubt passing through Apt on his way, he would have seen a town of approaching 10,000 inhabitants, complete with a forum, temples, baths, a *Capitolium* and a theatre – all the major hallmarks of a typical Roman settlement.

After Apt, he and his column would have passed over the Pont Julien as they travelled the Via Domitia on towards Nemausus. It was here that Hadrian's adoptive mother Pompeia Plotina had been born and from here that she had, through family connections and wealth, made the ultimate step of meeting and then marrying Marcus Ulpius Traianus – Trajan. While Hadrian had been away, Plotina's health had been declining. In 121 CE, and just as Hadrian arrived in Gaul, Plotina began a regular correspondence with her 'son' over the matter of who should be the new head of the Epicurean school of philosophy in Athens – Plotina being the most influential advocate of the Epicureans, and clearly this was something of huge importance to her. Hadrian ultimately agreed with her petitions, which were the last meaningful letters between them before Plotina took ill and died in 122 CE.

The death and celebration of the life of Plotina

The news of Plotina's death arrived in time for Hadrian to be able to plan for the commemoration of his adoptive mother in the city of her birth. We do not know if the emperor diverted his convoy into Glanum as it passed by – being alongside rather than on the Via Domitia may have meant that it was simply too difficult logistically to take his huge train into the town – perhaps Hadrian rode into the settlement which, as we might recall, was situated at a dead end at the bottom of the hills.

Nîmes was, however, more than able to cope and welcomed the emperor into its open arms, no doubt with huge festivities, a blaze of colour, noise and feasting. Already a thriving Roman city of some forty-thousand citizens, with its majestic Pont du Gard aqueduct, the sanctuary of the *Augusteum* and the wonderful Maison Carrée – the Corinthian-style temple commissioned by Agrippa, Nîmes was a suitable stopping point for an emperor.

Within yet another hectic schedule of meetings and briefings, Hadrian would have taken time to discuss the best way to mark Plotina's death, and he is recorded by Dio as wearing black for nine days before either dedicating a new basilica to Plotina, according to the *Historia Augusta*, or a temple if one believes Dio. At least proof of the existence of a basilica in Nemausus can be found in the survival of an inscription discovered in Nîmes:

IOVI – E – NEMAVS.	'Titus Flavius Hermes
T – FLAVIVS – HERM.	Inspector of the works of the basilica
EXACTOR – OPER.	and the marble-workers and stonemasons
BASILICAE – MAR.	fulfil their vow to
MORARI – ET LAPI.	Jupiter and Nemausus.'
DARI – V – S.	

> Nîmes is home to the Musée de la Romanité de Nîmes in which can be found numerous traces of the basilica, as well as a superb collection of Roman statues from the later imperial period, and is well worth a visit.

Once his stay in Nîmes came to an end, Hadrian departed for what would become the final leg of his journey in Narbonensis – and before he crossed the Pyrenees into Spain. During these final few weeks, Hadrian continued along what was in fact the first and original part of the Via Domitia, constructed one hundred years before by Cnaeus Domitius Ahenobarbus. Still passing endless *tabernae* and *mansiones* with cheering families and no doubt the occasional supplicant rushing towards him entreating Hadrian for imperial mercy or judgement. The crowds would have gathered as his column passed and then it was on to Narbo Martius where our story began back in 118 BCE.

In this area of France, Mediterranean winds would have still been very warm, but strengthening as they entered the Gulf of Lion, the gentle hills of green olives interspersed with the red of estate roofs and the white washed walls of farms and barns. Small settlements, amazed at the sight of the emperor of Rome passing through their dry landscape, waited for days until the sight of marching troops, cavalry and all the wagons came into sight and then there, on a brilliant white horse, sitting with his purple robes and golden corona of leaves, rode Hadrian, emperor of the world. The emperor smiled and waved as he passed through and maybe even stopped to water his horse and talk to the overwhelmed retired veterans of his legions, or to mothers holding the hands of their children in their tiny tunics.

Passing milestones erected along the roadside and along parts of the road that needed repair, Hadrian continued to take in the scale and beauty of his empire, riding where despatch riders rode every day ferrying messages to and from the beating heart of the empire in Rome – connecting the empire together. Hadrian would now be well into the Occitanie region of Narbonensis, with the rich blue sea to his left, the inland fields rising to the foothills of the Cévennes to his right, and ahead of him, as he descended into the flat plains and marshland near the sea, was Béziers and Narbo Martius.

Before reaching them however, he would have passed through the small settlement of Saint-Thibery which sat at the confluence of the River Thongue, which flows down from the Languedoc mountains, and the River Herault, which receives the water of the Cévennes. Here a beautiful small Roman bridge still remains – mostly medieval, but with Roman bases – and spans the River Herault. Hadrian and his entire retinue of wagons, legionaries, horses, scribes, slaves no doubt in their thousands, would have passed over this tiny bridge, and through this miniature Roman town 17km east of Béziers.

When Béziers came into view, Hadrian would have seen a place that was again Greek in origin and certainly one of the oldest settlements in France. In 36-35 BCE, the town had been earmarked as a *colonia* for veterans and renamed *Colonia Julia Baeterrae Septimanorum* – or Baeterrae – which, as we might recall from an earlier chapter, was a thriving community, famous for its wine production and indeed one of the major wine producing zones in Narbonensis. This would have been a good place for Hadrian's thirsty legionaries to stop and enjoy the local produce, rest and to quench their substantial thirst. According to ORBIS, any member of this imperial caravan that had set out from the start of Hadrian's visitations would now have walked around 3,000 kilometres, so tired feet, aching limbs and constant thirst were normal companions. Without

> The bridge at Saint-Thibery is a Roman bridge on the Via Domitia crossing the River Herault. The bridge and the Roman-era mill nearby make for a wonderful, peaceful sense of time and place – with a creative imagination one can imagine the inhabitants watching the traffic crossing over the river, the wagons going to and fro and even the passage of Hadrian – which would have taken some hours.

doubt, and even for the Romans, this was an odyssey on an epic scale. Very likely a good number would not survive and die en route, to be cremated by the sides of roads and in fields in places that they did not know, their friends and colleagues sometimes placing local stone slabs and engraved stones above them to be found two thousand years later.

Off with their Heads …

By the date of Hadrian's visit, evidence of the previous Celtish presence had been erased and the centre of Baeterrae now had a thriving and vibrant Roman forum. Paradoxically and ironically, the Roman remains have, in their turn, almost disappeared, but some evidence of just how 'imperial' and grand the Roman settlement had become over the past one hundred and fifty years was discovered quite by chance.

A.L.F. Rivet reminds us that, in 1907, excavation work near the market hall of the town revealed a collection of nine marble heads and, when they had been cleaned and assessed, they were all identified as members of the imperial family.[149] They were intricately and skilfully carved to display individual features, possibly in Rome, and would have decorated either a temple – perhaps dedicated to the Augustan cult – or would have been placed around the forum on plinths or pillars. Quite why they were all found together remains a mystery, but they may have been placed there for hope of future salvation when the collapse of the Roman state overtook the city of Baeterrae – or they could have been part of some offering in the coming pagan days of the future.

But it was not just in and around Baeterrae that devotion was shown to the emperor and the imperial family. Although the find of the nine heads in the centre of the town was remarkable, and informs us more than we were aware of the lustrous nature of the forum and temples in the city, another batch of heads was discovered not so far away. The Villa at Chiragan can be found 60km south west of Toulouse, quite close to the town of Martres-Tolosane. A journey of around one-hundred-and-fifty miles west and inland of Béziers takes one to the foothills of the Pyrenees and the remains of Chiragan. The first statues were unearthed in this area in the eighteenth- and nineteenth-centuries, and Leon Joulin produced a detailed assessment of the area. This was a vast Roman estate with a complex of workshops, barns and dwellings possibly for the workers, and an exceptionally large villa which was begun in the early-Augustan period. Courtyards, large baths and a 170m long gallery made this a dramatic vision for the first owners – whoever they were.

The excavations here uncovered a series of sculptures and again, as in Baeterrae, they were buried in three pits and it was not by chance that they were divided

Chiragan is located on the banks of the Garonne and the road to Toulouse. Inhabited during the first- to fourth-century, various theories abound as to the owners. Possibly the Calagorris who were mentioned in the *Antonine Itinerary*, or perhaps the procurators of the region – hence the predilection for so many imperial statues. Devastated by an attack at some point in the fifth century, the site was plundered for hundreds of years, but still impresses today and is certainly worth a visit.

into three distinct groups – the labours of Hercules, Roman copies of Greek sculptures and, thirdly, a large group of the heads of Roman emperors. Analysis shows that, while the first and second groups had been carved from stone mined locally in the foothills of the Pyrenees, the heads were of a different quality and were of a white marble found only in Goktepe in Turkey – from which many of the greatest statues in Rome had also been manufactured.

Lots of questions arise out of these finds. If they were carved in Rome by imperial sculptors, then how did they end up in a villa near the Pyrenees? Was it that, with each new emperor, commercial orders went out for a bulk production of new busts – a way perhaps of marketing the arrival of the new reign – for wealthy families to order from the imperial workshops? Was there a Roman equivalent of Amazon to deliver these items to all parts of the empire? Or perhaps orders for new busts were received in Rome from noteworthy families across all the provinces so that they could display their wealth and loyalty, and then collected on their next visit to the senate or to their second home in Rome? Either way, this was great business for the sculptors and workshops in Rome, and the heads would have been transported along the route that our courier had taken, no doubt in one of the many wagons on the imperial highways. No doubt many more such finds still lay in the fields of southern France waiting to be discovered in the same way.

Once installed in the villa at Chirgan, we can ponder on where these busts were situated – perhaps around the courtyards or in the various rooms of the house? Such a collection as this grouping was not only very expensive to buy but also to display – after all, they were items of display and status for visitors to marvel at the marble and be overawed by the wealth and status of their hosts. The heads range from Tiberius in the first century through to the fourth, which could suggest that the villa stayed in the same family for three hundred years. An alternative suggestion has been put forward by Andrew Selkirk, that the villa was in fact an overflow point from local towns and cities – where forums and streets had become clogged with such statues and that, by the fourth century, the civic authorities wanted a clear out and they were relocated. Celebrating icons from past times who were associated with the mass slaughter of Christians may not have been popular as Christianity spread throughout the empire.[150]

> *'Fashions may have changed and the new Christian rulers (of the fourth century) may not have seen the point of having pagan images cluttering up the forum.'*[151]

Finally, why were they found buried together in a pit? Was it a similar exercise to those at Baeterrae in that they were buried for safety as the invading hordes arrived in their columns of marauding cavalry to destroy Roman settlements as Rome had once destroyed their ancestors?

> Whatever the story behind these wonderful sculptures, they can be seen up close and very personal in the Musée Saint-Raymond in Toulouse. (see also Capus, *Pascal Les sculptures de la villa Romaine de Chiragan*', Musée Saint-Raymond.[152]

Back in Baeterrae, villas of an equivalence in grandeur could be found, so that Hadrian and the empress could have either been invited to stay – or he invited himself to stay. Two sites of special interest are at Clavel, which was lived in from the first to the fourth century, and at les Pres Bas, the villa at Loupian which was also occupied over the same period. The latter villa was exquisite, the home of a cultured and educated family with a far more intricate architectural design than those built in the more angular and rustic republican period.

What created the wealth of the local families that lived at Loupian is unknown for certain but it is quite probable that they were involved in the cultivation of the rich soils for wine production or sheep farming – both of which flourished on an industrial scale and could have created the substantial wealth required for such an impressive estate complex. Whether the owners had political aspirations, whether they met the emperor on his journey through the district, and what happened to their family line as the Roman empire dissolved are all unknowns.

Once through Baeterrae, it was then on to his arrival at the seat of the provincial governor at Narbo Martius. Situated in the River Atax and central to this whole story, Narbo had been Rome's very first colony outside Italy in 118 BCE, and was now a thriving international trading port, and by the time of Hadrian's visit had expanded into what Strabo described as the 'greatest emporium'.

The fine people of this fine city saw the arrival of the emperor as the chance of a lifetime to celebrate, and the influential families both of the town and countryside would have gathered to vie for the attention of the emperor and his retinue. The governor would have had plenty of time to prepare his residence too, and a programme of religious worship, giving thanks to the Gods, would have been accompanied by the usual series of meetings and briefings. The *HA* gives a flavour of the times and the majesty of Hadrian, but again it is our ability to use our imagination that holds the key to empathising with the inhabitants of the town.

Lucius Aemilius Arcanus

We do however know of one particular event that occurred while Hadrian was in the area, through the survival and discovery of a superbly carved and ornate statue dedicated to a leading citizen of Narbo at that time – Lucius Aemilius Arcanus.

The epitaph explains that Arcanus was of equestrian rank and had served as a legionary and ultimately as a tribune across three different legions – the last of which was the *II Augusta*, based in Britannia. With service such as this completed, Arcanus had returned to his native Narbo a wealthy and influential man of proven loyalty and courage, and he went on to build a career in the provincial administration of the entire province. Arcanus knew the area well, knew the people, was trusted and probably received and guided each successive governor as they arrived for their period in office, but never becoming governor himself due to his rank.

Possibly because Hadrian knew Arcanus or perhaps due to a petition to the emperor – or even both – Hadrian used his arrival in Narbo in 122-123 CE to promote Arcanus to the senatorial order (*amplissimus us ordo).* This was no average event and would have been a grand spectacle, held perhaps in the forum or theatre of Narbo with a large crowd and his family in attendance. Perhaps Hadrian whispered to him that he looked forward to hearing his first speech in the senate and mentioned that they should reunite when they both returned to Rome.

At some point later, a statue was erected by a freedman of Arcanus whose name was Lucius Aemilius Moschus. His dedication to his former owner, and perhaps friend, led him to also ensure that this not inconsiderable token to his master, perhaps erected after Arcanus had died, was maintained in the future thanks to a donation of 4,000 sesterces to the treasury of the *augustales* (the priests and administrators of the imperial cult). Moschus himself is named as a *sevir Augustalis*, who were priests in an order created by Trajan dedicated to maintaining the cult of Augustus and the Julii.

After Hadrian had left Narbo Martius heading west and into Spain, it was to be a new era of development for the province of Narbonensis. Driven on by the need for greater financial transparency and control, Hadrian began what future emperors would impose by way of improved levels of auditing and control – trying to end financial exploitation of the provinces which lasted decades, where numerous officials and families had profited from the lack of control from Rome and the *aerarium*.

Chapter 17

Improving Financial Controls over the Province 14-235 CE

As the empire grew so did the inability of the state to comprehend and control the collection of taxes. Equally, supervision of the new multifarious budgets being created in the many new cities meant that Rome entered a period of chaotic management where the treasury or *aerarium* knew very little of the affairs of the provinces. The moral decay witnessed in the last century of the Republic was nowhere better illustrated than in the abuse of financial control and money in the provincial seats of the governors.

On his assumption of power, Augustus made reform of the financial management of the growing empire one of his top priorities. A pivotal decision was made in the requirement of a census, such as that required of Joseph and Mary in the Christian accounts of that time, in provincial lands in order to ascertain individual property ownership and therefore taxation levels for collection. However, in reality, the empire remained a mix of tax farmers and census-based tax collection, as it was really down to the governors to decide what worked best in their areas of control. We know that financial abuse was widespread and that the state itself was careless as well as powerless to intervene.

Opportunities for corruption had been everywhere prior to Augustus and remained so after his death. The personal nature of Roman government – both local and regional – created widespread nepotism and easy abuse, where client and patron depended on each other to make their way through the Roman world and up the *cursus honorum*. One of the many abuses were city officials borrowing money from the city treasury on favourable terms, perhaps never paying the loans back or dying before the loans could be paid back. Another was so called 'private' building projects funded by individuals keen to attract the glory of being a city father – when in fact it was their own companies and businesses that completed the work, so they received not only their donations back but a handsome profit too – and their family name on the construction. Slack auditing procedures mean that millions of sesterces of tax payers' money were abused and found its way in to the hands of a privileged few. G.P. Burton, in one of his many scholarly articles on this aspect of Roman rule, points out that the provincial governor could, at his own discretion, order an inspection of the finances of any city, but to do so was time consuming, perhaps embarrassing and could even lead to his own incrimination.[154]

Part of the problem with administering the financial aspects of a province was the heterogeneous nature of the sources of income. Money could flow in from all directions and, in the absence of proper audit and budget processes, could flow out just as widely and be unaccounted. General civic and state income across Narbonensis, like any other province, came principally from rents from public property and lands – land simply appropriated by the city or the emperor could equate to millions of acres across the empire. Endowments from individuals for their promotion to public office was a significant generator of income, as were customs duties on borders and in ports – such as we saw with Marcus Fontius who, as governor of Narbonensis, was accused of substantial fraud and successfully defended by Cicero in 69 BCE. Tax duties on wine, pottery, olives, timber, trading goods and food could be substantial. Market places, shops and even whore houses paid their taxes to maintain local services – and to line the pockets of corrupt officials.

As we move into the second century CE, evidence such as discussions between Pliny and Trajan clearly indicate a deep awareness of provincial fraud and a desire to do something about it. Public works were enormously expensive and not always necessary – other than to line the pockets of contractors and lenders – but gradually the ability of the state to bail out cities who overspent was running out. By the third century CE, Rome had finally reacted and it became mandatory for all cities to obtain imperial permission to fund major construction works, and state officials were appointed by the emperor or the treasury in Rome to check the projected costs and audit the final payment of bills. Aemilius Macer, in his second book on the Duties of Provincial Governors, clearly stated that:

> '*New private building is* [still] *possible without the permission of the emperor, as long as it is not of the kind done in emulation of another city nor provides the basis for rioting* [seditio] *nor is a circus, theatre or amphitheatre.*'
>
> Aemilius Macer from extracts contained in the *Digesta.*[155]

The importance of this statement is fundamental to our understanding of the psychology of power and influence in urban Roman centres. As the empire grew, so too did the fashion of the glorification of Rome and the adulation of the heroic individual. In the post-Augustan period, so too did the translation of these images into civic pride to be funded by the population. This is why whenever we follow the path of an emperor or official, or read the letters of Cicero or Pliny, or read the histories of Suetonius, Dio, Tacitus, Strabo or Livy, we see the same mental images.

Every Roman town or city worth its name needed its own functional structures of forum, public baths and temple but, in order to keep up with their municipal rivals, they also built their own theatres, or even gigantic amphitheatres, they wanted their own circus if they could afford one and they thought they needed bigger temples, more statues, two forums, larger baths, magnificent basilicas and the costs just ran away. As in today's world, the builders made huge fortunes.

The city fathers of any community liked to be associated with success and what was more successful than displays of wealth and power – especially if ways could be found to recoup investments through financial double-dealing within the city budgets – reaping the rewards of praise for generous donations to the city while making a profit at the same time.

Many buildings became white elephants in a matter of decades. When gladiatorial events became too expensive and the cost of trapping and transporting wild animals extortionate, what else would bring in 10, 20, or 30,000 people to an amphitheatre? Hence across Narbonensis, as elsewhere, we have to recognise that many Roman structures very quickly, in general terms, became derelict well before the arrival of the barbarians – local taxation simply could not afford to complete or maintain such monuments to the past. It was not much of a step after that to start to see the stone slowly plundered for new housing or smaller building projects to save costs and money on carved stone, and what we have left today are the remnants of civic pride, financial excess and over ambitious planning. This is not to suggest that this happened everywhere.

In terms of financial probity and as far as Narbonensis is concerned, A.L.F. Rivet concluded:

> *'On the whole the finances of this province were well run and only occasionally, it seems, had curators to be appointed to oversee those of individual cities – of senatorial ones L. Burbuleius Opatus Ligarianus working at Narbo in the Antonine period (probably after the serious fire there), M. Pontius Laelinus overseeing Arausio c. 130 and someone whose name is not recorded at Avennio; and of equestrians M. Cominius Aemilianus at Aquae Sextiae under Trajan and, in the second century, Q. Soillius Valerianus at Cabellio, Avennio and Forum Iulii.'*[156]

Thus, even Narbonensis, so close to Italy, was not immune from imperial investigations into fraud. The appointment of senators to lead investigations was not always the wisest course if the state really did want to rid the provinces of financial corruption. They themselves protected their peers and had no one above them to check on their own investigations. In fact, it was not until the reign of Hadrian that investigators from the imperial, rather than the state treasury, were ordered to only be selected from the equestrian order. Clearly the thinking here was that men from this rank had everything to gain and little to lose by exposing corruption amongst their superiors. But as Rivet exposes, a good number of the Narbonensian cities were investigated by imperial auditors for financial irregularities.

By the Severan period, 193-235 CE, and after the disruption and dislocation of the civil war between 193-7 CE, a series of normative processes created a more homogenous provincial administration. Each emperor either added or detracted from this evolutionary process and, with increased education and skills, coupled with the advances in technology and requirements for data, it was almost impossible to recall the chaos, corruption and mismanagement of the early years of empire – they had their own versions of corruption instead.

Epilogue

Gallia Narbonensis was not a typical Roman province – whatever that may turn out to be. In many ways, the Roman expansion and annexation of southern France was less a conquest and rather more an annexation – partly welcomed by the indigenous population, which was in itself made up of various ethnic groups who had also seen the advantages of living and trading there in previous centuries. Narbonensis was a region of cultural exchange, a series of ports and communities that had evolved from their Greek origins alongside the Celtic and Gallic tribes of the Iron Age, with little friction, living in relative harmony and recognising perhaps how fortunate they were to be living in such a place of beauty on the northern Mediterranean.

If there was a conquest, then it was might be termed a 'soft' process. After the Battle of Aquae Sextiae, which itself was a war against invading tribes rather than local ones, there was no major rebellion in the province for the rest of the Roman era. Instead, there was a gradual takeover of society, values, laws, ownership, the economic means of production and religion by a steady tidal flow of requirements and advantages from Rome. Unlike other provincial additions to the Roman empire, there was no initial invasion by conquest, no ongoing need to station troops to subdue the native populations, and no sense of insecurity – Narbonensis was an example of how Rome could indeed conquer without arms. This osmotic process separates Narbonensis in one sense, but in another it is a prime example of how, once the legions had done their job in other regions, the process of Romanisation and *Pax Romana* were established to tie the empire together. The challenge that faced generations of senators was how to treat this empire, and for the emperors, how to protect it from collapse – both from external and internal threats.

The major weakness in administering Narbonensis was finding the right people to manage what was needed and, as we have seen, it was an evolutionary process rather than something that happened straight away. Rome was critically short of good civil servants and, as the province grew, so did the need for more administrators – demonstrated so vividly by the need for even the emperor Trajan himself to lend a hand with Pliny in Bithynia. The quality of governors was another serious problem if Rome wished to be seen to treat its many new citizens fairly, and the harsh, bare-faced corruption of the last century of the Republic was slowly replaced by white collar fraud, which in turn needed to be identified and controlled – it would never be extinguished.

After the early establishment of Roman forces in the province, the future colonisation of Narbonensis was led by civilians – by traders, merchants, ship builders and warehouse owners, by engineer and surveyors, by local supportive oligarchies who saw their own takeover of Rome as a potential result of becoming a full Roman province. The Roman senate was able to concern itself with other far more troublesome parts of the empire, to acquiring new regions with real force and brutality, while being able to leave Narbonensis as perhaps the shining example of what all Roman provinces should aspire to be.

The development of and investment in the communities of Narbonensis led to the creation of some of the most beautiful Roman cities in the whole empire. Aided by municipal rivalry and economic growth, the modern world is left with an area of cultural excellence that remains even after the destruction and loss of the so-called Dark Ages. Southern France today vibrates with a stream of new archaeological finds that add to this story and continue to underline the levels to which Roman civilisation was established – perhaps even more so than many parts of Italy itself. The richness of the cultural tapestry that we can clearly see in the villas, mosaics, temples, theatres and everyday objects of Roman life display a region attractive to the Roman spirit of luxury as well as glory. If young, ambitious aristocrats needed to blood themselves in war, if generals needed to crown their life with a triumph, and if senators needed to replenish their finances exhausted by a political career then none of these could be found in Narbonensis – these could only be fulfilled by conquest elsewhere.

Finally, it was no chance decision by a series of Roman leaders holding *imperium* to settle their troops in the many new *coloniae* of Narbonensis. It was less a need to ensure a province was subdued by a regular supply of fighting manpower if needed, and more a case of settling their exhausted and loyal soldiers in one of the most peaceful and productive parts of the empire. The retired legions aided and abetted the process of Romanisation and conquest every bit as much as their active serving counterparts. It would be mistakes in other parts of the empire, and imperial rule that would lead to the ultimate collapse of Roman rule in Narbonensis.

Arriving from the south, Christianity seeped into Narbonensis late in the third century and into the fourth century – and in the days after the boundaries of this book. There were not enough amphitheatres to murder the number of converts to the new religion, and it would prosper in direct proportion to how Rome was to founder. Just as the Phoenician and Greek traders brought new ideas and wealth to Narbonensis before anywhere else in Europe, so their descendants, on faster ships, brought news of the coming of Christ in Judea, and this, like any other message arriving in the many ports of the south coast of France, was gossip and a reality that no legion could stop. Ideas are hard to erase. From the north would come the Visigoth hordes, tearing their way through the beautiful, cultured and historic centres of Roman civilisation of Narbonensis – burnt to the ground or plundered, with treasures hidden to be one day discovered again to reveal the world that was gained and then lost.

To the archaeologists and researchers of France, let us celebrate with them each new find, each new dimension that they add to our understanding, and each new museum that they open for us to see in order to live the story of the people of Gallia Narbonensis.

Notes

PART I

1. The Köppen climate classification remains the most widely used and understood system in the world for denoting different climatic regions.
2. Hobson, J.A., *Imperialism: A Study*, London, 1902. Reprinted by Routledge in 2018.
3. Champion, Craige, *Roman Imperialism – Readings and Sources*, 2004.
4. Seeley, J.R., *The Expansion of England*, 1883.
5. C.M.T. Mommsen was awarded the 1902 Nobel Prize for his historical writing and research. His most famous work however was the unfinished *History of Rome* published by Reimer & Hirzel during 1854–1856, which was in three volumes: the fourth was never completed. It is Mommsen's monumental *Corpus Inscriptionem Latinarum* that has a lasting place in the history of the study of Rome.
6. Harris, William V., *War and Imperialism in Republican Rome, 327–70 BCE*, 1979.
7. Dio, L. Cassius, *Roman History*, Book 53:19.
8. Cicero, *De Imperio*, 2:4.
9. *Ibid.*, 5:11.
10. Immanuel Wallerstein was an American sociologist and economic historian until his death in 2019. His work on capitalist economies and 'The Modern World-System' was a pivotal moment in the study of post-colonial imperialism. Instead of the Marxist views on stages of development that nations pass through, such as feudalism and capitalism, Wallerstein looked at the dichotomy between capital and labour – it was Wallerstein that magnified the concepts of core and periphery or metrocentric and pericentric.
11. Morley, N., *The Roman Empire: Roots of Imperialism*, Pluto Press, 2010. This book is a must-read for any student of Roman imperialism. A challenge to established views and a book against which to evaluate modern-day superstates.
12. Although this is one of the Latin phrases that has echoed through the centuries, there is no actual record in the work of Cato the Elder to verify that he said this. There are, however, numerous allusions that attribute these words, such as in Cicero's philosophic essay *De Senectute*. Written in 45 or 44 BCE, Cicero is one of several authors who relate Cato's desire to see Carthage destroyed – a statement he is supposed to have made many times towards the end of his life.
13. Hoyos, D., *A Companion to the Punic Wars*, Blackwell, 2015.
14. Goldsworthy, A., *The Fall of Carthage*, Orion, 2006, pp.131–2.
15. Titus Livius or Livy (59 BCE–17 CE) was a Roman historian who wrote a pivotal record of the history of Rome entitled *Ab Urbe Condita* – 'From the Founding of the City' – and contains within its pages probably the best account of the Second Punic War. A friend of Augustus and writing during his lifetime, Livy was respected for his truth and Tacitus records Livy defending his laudatory views on Cn. Pompeius and still keeping the respect of Augustus.
16. Appianus Alexandrinus was Greek but with Roman citizenship, c.95 CE–c.165 CE. Appian was popular during the reigns of the emperors Trajan, Hadrian and Antoninus

Pius. His major work was *Historia Romana*, which was written in Greek and covered 24 books, many of which survive in their entirety or in fragments.

17. L. Cassius Dio was a Roman historian and also a senator under the emperor Commodus, as well as having also been a governor of Smyrna. Dio was consul of Rome in 229 CE. Living between c.165–235 CE, Dio published an eighty-volume work on the history of ancient Rome – *Historia Romana* – and is one of only three sources that document the revolt of Boudica in 60–61 CE. His work exists mostly in collected fragments.
18. Livy, 34.
19. Plutarch is best known for his series of biographies entitled *Parallel Lives*, which covered the lives of prominent Greeks and Romans, written in the later first century CE and into the early second century (c.46–119 CE). As a magistrate and an ambassador, Plutarch travelled widely and *Parallel Lives* creates twenty-three pairs – each with a Roman and Greek life compared, using human nature, against each other. He went to great lengths to draw parallels between men and also their character and physical appearance. He was one of the earliest moral philosophers.
20. Cicero, M. Tullius, *De Officiis*, 2:27.

PART II

21. Morley, N., pp.33–4.
22. Cicero, *Catil*, 1:1.
23. *Ibid.*, 1:1.
24. White, Roderick T., *Luxury at Rome: avaritia, aemulatio and the mos maiorum*, University College London.
25. The Book of Revelation 18:11–13.
26. Howard Hayes Scullard (1903–1983) was a British historian who specialised in ancient history. A prolific and highly respected writer, his best known and most evocative work is *From the Gracchi to Nero: A History of Rome from 133 BCE to 68 CE*.
27. Gaius Sallustius Crispus (86–35 BCE) was from a plebian family and rose to fame as one of the foremost historians of the Republican period. Sallust is the earliest known Latin historian with works that survive, and these include his *Conspiracy of Catiline*, *The Jugurthine War* and *Histories* – although of the latter very little survives. A supporter of Caesar, Sallust was a legionary commander and served as a legate under Caesar so was ideally placed to observe and discuss events.
28. Sallust, *The War Against Catiline*, 7.4–6.
29. Frank, Tenny, *The Classical Journal*, Vol. V, No.3, 1910, pp.99–110.
30. Luke, Ch. 2, c.1–5.
31. William Vernon Harris was born in 1938 in Nottingham, England and became Professor of History at Columbia University in the USA. He was a ground breaker in terms of his work on the Greco-Roman world and his major work, *War and Imperialism in Republican Rome, 327–70 BCE*, attracted worldwide attention.
32. *Letters to Atticus*, 5.17.6.
33. Rivet, A.L.F., *Gallia Narbonensis – Southern France in Roman Times*, Batsford Ltd., 1988.
34. Livy, 21.18.
35. Livy, 21.19.
36. Livy, 21.19.
37. Livy, 21.20.
38. Livy, 21.20.
39. Rivet., pp.39–54.

40. The Stanford Geospatial Network Model of the Roman World is an invaluable tool of our age and simulates the movement of Romans in terms of both time and expense as well as modes of transport across different geographical regions. Taking into account seasonal variations as well, researchers can access ORBIS to more closely appreciate the travel/time horizons of people of all classes in Roman antiquity.
41. Rivet, p.20.
42. *Ibid.*, pp.162–3.
43. *Ibid.*, pp.342–3.
44. Publius Cornelius Tacitus c.56–120 CE was a Roman politician and historian – perhaps the most respected of the Roman historians. His *Histories* and *Annals* examine the reigns of the emperors Tiberius, Claudius, Nero, and those of 69 CE – The Year of the Four Emperors.
45. It was Milo that was responsible for the death of the troublesome, rebellious but popular Publius Clodius Pulcher in 52 BCE – either by accident or design after their meeting on the Appian Way. Despite being defended by Cicero, Milo was condemned – and went into exile in Massalia, where he once joked about how happy he was eating the red mullet of Marseilles.
46. Strabo was a Greek geographer, writer and historian who lived c.64 BCE–24 CE and therefore his life mirrored the transition from Roman Republic to Roman Empire. Among his works was his *Geography* or *Geographika*, which chronicled the political, economic and cultural developments of Europe: *Geographika*, 4.6.3.
47. Often shaped like small lemons, these deadly lead shots whistled through the air at tremendous speeds (up to 100mph) and could weigh 1–2oz, with a small hole to help make the fizzing noise to terrorise the enemy.
48. Diodorus, *Fragments*, XXXIV.23.
49. Gaius Marius (c.157–86 BCE) was a Roman general and statesman. A victor in numerous battles and reformer of the Roman state and the army, Marius was also consul of Rome seven times. His victory at Aquae Sextiae was not only vital to defend Rome from an early demise from a Gallic invasion but was also pivotal in launching his later career.
50. Rivet, pp.169–70.
51. Broughton, T.R.S., *The Magistrates of the Roman Republic*, Vol. 1 (1952), p.514.
52. Polybius.
53. Beard, Mary, *Roman Triumph*, Harvard University Press, 2007.
54. Rivet, p.162.
55. *Ibid.*, pp.168–9.
56. Strabo, Book IV, 6.53.
57. Gascou, J., 'Inscriptiones latines de Narbonnaise, III, Aix-en-Provence, Paris', *CNRS*, 1995, pp.24–5.
58. Rivet, pp.130–1.
59. Strabo, Book IV, 7.43
60. Bromwich, J., *The Roman Remains of Southern France – A Guidebook*, Routledge, 1996, p.84.
61. Levick, B., 'Cicero, Brutus 43. 159ff. and the Foundation of Narbo Martius', *The Classical Quarterly*, Vol. 21, No. 1 (May 1971), pp.170–9.
62. Cicero, Marcus Tullius, foremost scholar, writer, jurist and philosopher (106–43 BCE), *Pro Fonteio.*

PART III

63. Cicero, Marcus Tullius, *Epistulae ad Familiares*. Written between 62–43 BCE, the collection of letters provides an invaluable insight into everyday correspondence between Cicero and a variety of his friends. The D.R. Shackleton Bailey 2001 translation, published by Harvard University Press, remains the standard adaption.
64. Bannon, Cynthia, 'C. Sergius Orata and the Rhetoric of Fishponds', *The Classical Quarterly*, Vol. 64, No. 1 (May 2014), pp.166–82.
65. Noble, G.A., *The Development of Provence Before 1550*, Ellipsis Books, 1998.
66. Cato the Elder, *De agri Cultura*, 119.
67. Bromwich, J., p.177.
68. Favory, F., Ouriachi, M.-J., Nuninger, L., *The Transformation of Rural Structures in Southern Gaul between the 1st Century BC and the 1st Century AD: The Case of Eastern Languedoc*, September 2009, Osnabrück, Germany.
69. *Ibid.*, p.159.
70. Berdowski, P., 'Some remarks on the economic activity of women in the Roman Empire', *Studia Classica*, Poland, 2007.
71. Rivet, p.190.
72. Cicero, Marcus Tullius, *Epistulae ad Atticum*.
73. Fontaine, S., 'Marine Roman Glass Trade: An Archaeological Case Study of Arles Harbour', *Journal of Glass Studies*, Vol. 56 (2014), pp.357–64.
74. Plutarch, *Life of Marius*, 11.1.3.
75. *Ibid.*, 27.1.3.
76. Cicero, Marcus Tullius, *Pro Fonteio*, 5.12–13.
77. Rogan, John, p.34.
78. Beard, Mary, *The Fires of Vesuvius*, pp.295–8.
79. Bromwich, J., pp.93–4.
80. Fishwick, D., 'The Imperial Cult of the Latin West', *Studies in the Ruler Cult of the Western Provinces of the Roman Empire*, Vol. III, Part 4, Brill, 2005.
81. Bromwich, J., p.205.
82. Della Casa, P. and Deschler-Erb, E., 'Rome's Internal Frontiers: Proceedings of the 2016 RAC Session in Rome', *Zurich Studies in Archaeology*, 2016.
83. Anneus Florus remains something of an enigma amongst the ranks of Roman poets. Born around 74 CE in Africa, he lived during the reigns of both Trajan and Hadrian but could have been any one of a number of Romans identified as Florus. Very little of his work remains extant. Florus, 1.33.8.
84. See Lavan, M., 'Florus and Dio on the Enslavement of the Provinces', *Cambridge Classical Journal*, Vol. 59 (2013), pp.125–51.
85. Taken from Sallust, with an English translation by J.C. Rolfe, Loeb Classical Library, G.P. Putnam's & Sons, New York, 1920, pp.414–19.
86. Cic., *Pro Fonteio*, 7.16.
87. *Ibid.*, 5.11.
88. Ward, Allen M., 'Cicero's Support of Pompey in the Trials of M. Pompeius', *Latomus*, T.27, Fasc.4 (October–December 1968), pp.802-809.
89. Rivet, p.305.
90. Dio, *Roman History*, 53.
91. Augoustakis, A., 'Cutting Down the Grove in Lucan', *The Classical Quarterly New Series*, Vol. 56, No. 2, December 2006, pp.634–8.
92. Rivet, p.75.

93. Gaius Plinius Caecilius Secundus (61–c.113 CE) – or Pliny the Younger – is one of the Roman authors that dominate the post-Augustan period. As with Cicero, we are fortunate to have many of his works preserved. As a lawyer, author, friend to Emperor Trajan and magistrate, Pliny was well connected in every aspect of the establishment of Rome. 247 of his hundreds of letters still survive – *Epistulae* – including two which describe the eruption of Vesuvius and the destruction of Pompeii, where Pliny the Elder, his uncle, perished on the beach near Herculaneum.
94. Dio, Book 53.12.
95. Gaius Plinius Secundus (23–79 CE) – or Pliny the Elder – was an author, naturalist, philosopher and army and naval commander, as well as being a friend of Emperor Vespasian. He is renowned for his *Naturalis Historia* – Natural History – which was an early model for an encyclopaedia. He wrote a history of the German Wars and was present in a senior position at numerous battles and in parts of the empire. He was uncle to Pliny the Younger and was killed at Stabiae, a small town near Pompeii, trying to rescue a friend from the ash clouds during the eruption of Mount Vesuvius.
96. Cic., *Letters to Atticus*.
97. Pliny, *Letters*, Book X, 15.
98. Pliny, *Letters*, Book X, 18.
99. Brunt, P.A., 'Charges of Provincial Maladministration under the Early Principate', *Historia Zeitscrift fur Alte Geschicte*, April 1961.
100. *Ibid.*, pp.191–2.
101. Hough, J.N., 'A Few Inefficiencies in Roman Provincial Administration', *The Classical Journal*, Vol. 35, No. 1, October 1939, pp.17–26.
102. Fransworth, R. 'Contextualising the Pliny/Trajan letters. A case of critiquing the myth of deliberative discourse in Roman Society', *Rhetoric Society Quarterly*, Vol. 26 No. 1, Winter 1996, 29–46.
103. Pliny, *Letters*, Book XI, 87.
104. Hartmann, B., *The Scribes of Rome – A Cultural and Social History of the Scribae*, Cambridge University Press, 2020.
105. Cicero, *Fam,* 10.3.
106. For any student of the great men of the republic, they could do no better than to study the life of Lucius Munatius Plancus. A true survivor amongst the turmoil of the collapse of the republic, political manipulator, shapeshifter and correspondent with Cicero. One of the few Romans for whom we can definitely identify a burial tomb, and worthy of study.
107. Burgers, P., 'The Narbonensian Colonial Elite 1958–1995.' *Ancient Society*, Vol. 28, 1997, pp.89–106.
108. Pflaum, H.-G., *Les Fastes de la Province de Narbonnaise*, 1978.
109. Gaius Suetonius Tranquillus is a respected Roman historian of the first and early-second century CE. His book *De Vita Caesarum – The Twelve Caesars* – remains his only extant work, although fragments of other writings do exist. Suetonius probably wrote *The Twelve Caesars* during the reign of Hadrian and he was a friend of Pliny the Younger. He became part of the court surrounding Hadrian, although was exiled from the court for an alleged affair with the empress Vibia Sabina.

PART IV

110. Pliny, *Naturalis Historia*, Book III, 31.
111. Gaius Plinius Secundus – The Elder (23–79 CE).

112. Anderson, J.C., *Roman Architecture in Provence*, Cambridge University Press, 2013.
113. Robertson, A., *The Crossroads of Civilisation: A History of Vienna*, Pegasus Books, 2022.
114. Rivet, pp.230–1.
115. Greene, K., 'Technological Innovation & Economic Progress in the Ancient World', *The Economic History Review*, New Series, Vol. 53, No. 1 (February 2000), pp.29–59.
116. Silva-Sanchez., N. and Armada, X.-L., 'Environmental Impact of Roman Mining and Metallurgy and its correlation with the archaeological evidence', *Environmental Archaeology*, 2023.
117. Preunkert, S. 'Lead and Antimony in Basal Ice from Col du Dome. Dated with Radiocarbon: A Record of Pollution During Antiquity', *Geophysical Research Letters*, 2019.
118. *Ibid.*
119. *Ibid.*
120. Jackson, M.D. et alia, 'The Judicious Selection and Preservation of Tuff and Travertine Building Stone in Ancient Rome', Archaeometry, Vol. 47, Issue 3, pp.485–510.
121. Rochette., P. et al 'Systematic sourcing of granite shafts from Gallia Narbonensis and comparison with other Western Mediterranean areas', *Journal of Archaeological Science Reports*, 42, 2022.
122. Pliny the Elder, *Naturalis Historia*, Book III.
123. Pliny the Younger, *Letters*, 90.
124. *Ibid.*, 91.
125. Frontinus, *On the water-management of the city of Rome*, translated by R.H. Rogers, Cambridge University Press, 2003.
126. Montauzon, G. de, *Les aqauducs antiques de Lyon*, 1909.
127. Dunning, D., 'The Aqueducts and Water Supply of Ancient Rome', *Groundwater Journal.*
128. Rogan, p.95.
129. Faure, Patrice, 'Les provinciaux de Gaule Narbonnaise et la garde pretorienne', *Revue Archaelogique de Narbonnaise*, 2016, Vol. 49, pp.85-111.
130. Bowman, A., *Life and Letters on the Roman Frontier: Vindolanda and its people*, Psychology Press, 1998, p.89.
131. Beard, M., *Emperor of Rome: Ruling the Ancient World*, Cambridge University Press, 2023.
132. Dio, *Roman History*, 54.19.
133. Burns, Mary Ann T., 'Pliny's Ideal Roman', *The Classical Journal*, Vol. 59, No. 6, March 1964.
134. Boatwright, Mary, 'Agrippa's Building Inscriptions', *Zeitschrift fur Papyrologie und Epigraphik*, Bd. 189 (2014), pp.255–64.
135. Powell, L., *Marcus Agrippa: Right-Hand Man of Caesar Augustus*, Pen & Sword, 2015.
136. John Murray III, *A Handbook for Travellers in France*, 1843.
137. Pliny the Elder, *Historia Naturalis*, Book XXIX, translation by John Bostock.
138. *Princeton Encyclopaedia of Classical Sites*, Princeton University Press, 1976.
139. Strabo, *Geographika*, Book IV, 3.7.
140. Elliot, T., 'Epigraphic Evidence for Boundary Disputes in the Roman Empire', PhD Thesis, University of North Carolina, 2004.
141. Aichinger, A., 'Grenzziehung durch kaiserliche Sonderbeauftragte in den romischen provinzen', *ZPE* 48, 1982.
142. Elliot, T., pp.217–18.
143. *Historia Augusta*, 'Life of Hadrian', Ch. 10, 10.1.
144. *Ibid.*, Part II, 14.8.

145. *Ibid.*
146. Ovid, *The Love Poems*, OUP, 2008, p.27 and p.188.
147. Dio, *Roman History*, 69.8–1a.
148. *Ibid.*, 69, 10.2.
149. Rivet, p.152.
150. Selkirk, A., *Minerva Magazine*, 2002.
151. *Ibid.*
152. Capas, Pascal, 'Les sculptures de la villa Romaine de Chiragan', Musée Saint-Raymond.
153. For an exhaustive examination of the *HA* one could not do better than to read *The Sources of the Historia Augusta Re-examined* by David Rohrbacher of the New College of Florida.
154. Burton, G.P., pp.311–42.
155. Aemilius Macer was a jurist in the third century CE, and the author of at least five legal works. Sixty-five extracts of his work exist in the Justinian Digest of fifty books, which was a codification of all Roman laws between 530–533 – later to be known as *The Corpus Juris Civilis and the Codex.*
156. Rivet, 89.

Bibliography

BOOKS

Beard, M., *Emperor of Rome: Ruling the Ancient World*, Cambridge University Press, 2023.

Beard, M., *The Roman Triumph*, Harvard University Press, 2007.

Bowman, A., *Life and Letter on the Roman Frontier*, Psychology Press, 1998.

Bromwich, James, *The Roman Remains of Southern France*, Routledge, 1996.

Broughton, T.R.S., *The Magistrates of the Roman Republic*, Vol. I, 1952.

Brunt., P.A. *Roman Imperial Themes*, Oxford University Press, 1990.

Burton, G.P., *The Resolution of Territorial Disputes in the Provinces of the Roman Empire*, Chinon, 2000.

Champion, C., *Roman Imperialism – Readings and Sources*, Wiley-Backwell, 2004.

Della Casa, P. and Deschler-Erb, E., *Rome's Internal Frontiers: Proceedings of the 2016 RAC Session in Rome*, Zurich Studies in Archaeology, 2016.

Elliot, T., *Epigraphic Evidence of Boundary Disputes in the Roman Empire*, Doctoral Thesis, University of North Carolina, 2004.

Favory, F., Ouriachi, M.-J. and Nuninger, L., *The Transformation of Rural Structures in Southern Gaul between the 1st Century* BC *and the 1st Century* AD. *The Case of Eastern Languedoc*, Osnabrück, Germany, 2009.

Goldsworthy, A., *The Fall of Carthage*, Orion, 2006.

Harris, W.V., *War and Imperialism in Republican Rome, 327–70* BC, Oxford University Press, 1985.

Hartmann, B., *The Scribes of Rome – A Cultural and Social History of the Scribae*, Cambridge University Press, 2020.

Hobson, J.A., *Imperialism: A Study*, London, 1902.

Hoyos, Dexter, *A Companion to the Punic Wars*, Blackwell, 2015.

Mattingly, Harold, *Tacitus – Agricola and Germania*, Penguin Classics, 2009.

Morley, Neville, *The Roman Empire: Roots of Imperialism*, Pluto Press, 2010.

Noble, G.A., *The Development of Provence Before 1550*, Ellipsis Books, 1998.

Pflaum, H.-G., *Les Fastes de la Province de Narbonnaise*, 1978.

Powell, L., *Marcus Agrippa: Right-Hand Man of Caesar Augustus*, Pen & Sword, 2015.

Radice, Betty, *The Letters of the Younger Pliny*, Penguin Classics, 1969.

Rogan, John, *Roman Provincial Administration*, Amberley, 2011.

Stephenson, G.H., *Roman Provincial Administration*, Blackwell, 1949.

Rivet, A.L.F., *Gallia Narbonensis*, Batsford, 1988.

Scullard, H.H., *From the Gracchi to Nero: A History of Rome from 133* BC *to* AD *68*, Routledge, 2010.

Seeley, J.R., *The Expansion of England*, London, 1883.

Stephenson, G.H., *Roman Provincial Administration*, Blackwell, 1949.

Williams, Wynne, *Pliny: Correspondence with Trajan from Bithynia*, Aris & Phillips, 2007.

ANCIENT SOURCES

Alexandrinus, Appianus, *Historia Romana*, second century CE.
Cato, M. Porcius, *De agri Cultura.*
Cicero, M. Tullius, *Pro Fonteio.*
Cicero, M. Tullius, *Epistulae ad Familiares.*
Cicero, M. Tullius, *De Officiis.*
Cicero, M. Tullius, *Epistulae ad Atticum.*
Diodorus, Siculus, *Fragments.*
Dio, L. Cassius, *Historia Romana.*
Frontinus, J. Sextus, *De Aquaeductu Urbis Romae.*
Livius, Titus, *Ab Urbe Condita.*
Ovid, *The Love Poems.*
Polybius, *The Histories*
Crispus, G. Sallustius, *Histories..*
Crispus, G. Sallustius, *The War Against Catiline.*
Strabo, *Geographika.*
Tacitus, P. Cornelius, *Histories.*

ARTICLES

Aichinger, A., 'Grenzziehung durch kaiserliche Sonderbeauftragte in den romische provinzen', *ZPE* 48, 1982.

Augoustakis, A., 'Cutting Down the Grove in Lucan', *The Classical Quarterly New Series*, Vol. 56, No. 2, December 2006, pp.634–8.

Bannon, Cynthia, 'C. Sergius Orata and the Rhetoric of Fishponds', *The Classical Quarterly*, Vol. 64, No. 1, May 2014), pp.166–82.

Berdowski, P., 'Some remarks on the economic activity of women in the Roman Empire', *Studia Classica*, Poland, 2007.

Boatwright, Mary, 'Agrippa's Building Inscriptions', *Zeitschrift fur Papyrologie und Epigraphik*, Bd. 189, 2014, pp.255–64.

Brunt, P.A., 'Charges of Provincial Maladministration under the Early Principate', *Historia Zeitscrift fur Alte Geschicte*, April 1961.

Burns, Mary Ann T., 'Pliny's Ideal Roman', *The Classical Journal*, Vol. 59, No. 6, March 1964.

Burton, G.P., 'The Roman Imperial State, Provincial Governors and the Public Finances of Provincial Cities 27 BCE–235 CE', *Historia Zeitschrift fur Alte Geschicte*, Bd. 53, 2004, pp.311–42.

Faure, Patrice, 'Les provinciaux de Gaule Narbonnaise et la garde prétorienne', Revue archaelogique de Narbonnaise, 2016, Vol. 49, pp.85-111.

Fishwick, D., 'The Imperial Cult of The Latin West', *Studies in the Ruler Cult of the Western Provinces of the Roman Empire*, Vol. III, Part 4, Brill, 2005.

Fontaine, S., 'Marine Roman Glass Trade: An Archaeological Case Study of Arles Harbour.' *Journal of Glass Studies*, Vol. 56, 2014, pp.357–64.

Frank, Tenny, 'Roman Imperialism' *The Classical Journal*, Vol. V, No. 3, 1910, pp.99–110.

Fransworth, R., 'Contextualising the Pliny/Trajan letters. A case for critiquing the myth of deliberative discourse in Roman society', *Rhetoric Society Quarterly*, Vol. 26, No. 1, Winter 1996, pp.29–46.

Gascou, J., 'Inscriptions Latines de Narbonnaise', III, Aix-en-Provence, Paris, *CNRS*, 1995, pp.24–5.

Greene., K., 'Technological Innovation and Economic Progress in the Ancient World', *The Economic History Review*, New Series, Vol. 53, No.1, February 2000, pp.29–59.

Hough, J.N., 'A Few Inefficiencies in Roman Provincial Administration', *The Classical Journal*, Vol. 35, No. 1, October 1939), pp.17–26.

Jackson, M.D. et alia, 'The Judicious Selection and Preservation of Tuff and Travertine Building Stone in Ancient Rome', *Archaeometry*, Vol. 47, Issue 3, pp.485–510.

Lavan, M., 'Florus and Dio on the Enslavement of the Provinces', *Cambridge Classical Journal*, Vol. 59, 2013, pp.125–51.

Levick, B., 'Cicero, Brutus 43. 159ff. and the Foundation of Narbo Martius', *The Classical Quarterly* 2, Vol. 21, No. 1, May 1971, pp.170–9.

Hough, J.N., 'A Few Inefficiencies in Roman Provincial Administration', *The Classical Journal*, Vol. 35, No. 1, October 1939, pp.17–26.

Silva-Sanchez., N. and Armada, X.-L., 'Environmental Impact of Roman Mining and Metallurgy and its Correlation with the Archaeological Evidence', *Environmental Archaeology*, 2023.

Preunkert, S., 'Lead and Antimony in Basal Ice from Col du Dome. Dated with Radiocarbon: A Record of Pollution During Antiquity', *Geophysical Research Letters*, 2019.

Ward, Allen M., 'Cicero's Support of Pompey in the Trials of M. Pompeius', *Latomus* T.27, Fasc.4, October–December 1968, pp.802-809.

White, Roderick T., 'Luxury at Rome: *avaritia*, *aemulatio* and the *mos maiorum*', University College London: humanities.exeter.ac.uk›Luxury_at_Rome

Index